J. M. SYNGE AND TRAVEL WRITING OF THE IRISH REVIVAL

Irish Studies

James MacKillop, *Series Editor*

# J. M. Synge

## and Travel Writing
## of the Irish Revival

GIULIA BRUNA

Syracuse University Press

∞ The paper used in this publication meets the minimum requirements of the American National Standard for Information Sciences—Permanence of Paper for Printed Library Materials, ANSI Z39.48-1992.

For a listing of books published and distributed by Syracuse University Press, visit www.SyracuseUniversityPress.syr.edu.

ISBN: 978-0-8156-3545-1 (hardcover)      978-0-8156-3533-8 (paperback)
978-0-8156-5411-7 (e-book)

**Library of Congress Cataloging-in-Publication Data**

Names: Bruna, Giulia, author.

Title: J. M. Synge and travel writing of the Irish revival / Giulia Bruna.

Description: First edition. | Syracuse, New York : Syracuse University Press, 2017. | Series: Irish studies | Includes bibliographical references and index.

Identifiers: LCCN 2017034884 (print) | LCCN 2017043630 (ebook) | ISBN 9780815654117 (e-book) | ISBN 9780815635451 (hardcover : alk. paper) | ISBN 9780815635338 (pbk. : alk. paper)

Subjects: LCSH: Synge, J. M. (John Millington), 1871–1909—Criticism and interpretation. | Travelers' writings, Irish—History and criticism. | Travel writing—Ireland—History. | Ireland—In literature.

Classification: LCC PR5534 (ebook) | LCC PR5534 .B78 2017 (print) | DDC 822/.912—dc23

LC record available at https://lccn.loc.gov/2017034884

*Manufactured in the United States of America*

*To Will and to my families in
Cuneo, Dublin, and Boston,
with deepest gratitude*

# Contents

# Illustrations

# Acknowledgments

$\mathcal{T}$his book has been a life-changing experience that took me on a journey to Ireland, where I found the support of colleagues, family, and numerous friends. First of all, I thank P. J. Mathews at the School of English, Drama, and Film at University College Dublin. He has been a fantastic mentor, and I am grateful beyond words for his intellectual guidance, expertise, and constant support throughout my career.

At University College Dublin (UCD), I found a supportive and thriving academic community that helped me and sustained me from the first moments I set foot in Belfield. I acknowledge most sincerely the UCD Humanities Institute and its directors over the years, in particular Gerardine Meaney. The institute has been a comfortable academic home to me. Its research support, the stimulating intellectual environment, as well as the other researchers' company and camaraderie were crucial to me in many phases of this project. John Brannigan in the UCD School of English also deserves a special mention for his mentorship in 2015, when I worked there and for the Humanities Institute as a research assistant. In the School of English, I am also indebted to the numerous staff, fellow lecturers, and tutors with whom I worked. Among them, I thank in particular Fionnuala Dillane for her help and guidance in teaching matters and for her ongoing support.

I thank Professor Melita Cataldi for the passion and intellectual acumen she demonstrated for Irish literature at the onset of my Irish journey (in Italy!). She inspired my travels to Ireland and in the academic world and always encouraged me during my studies in Italy and Ireland during her numerous visits. At the beginning of my Irish journey in Ireland,

Professor Declan Kiberd was a wonderful teacher while I was pursuing an MA in Anglo-Irish literature at UCD. I thank him for his encouragement that I undertake doctoral studies and for his ongoing support over the years.

For this book, I had the fortune to carry out research in a number of libraries, archives, and special collections in Ireland and the United States. I am thankful to various institutions for granting permission to publish various manuscript materials and illustrations. The Board of Trinity College Dublin generously gave me permission to quote from Synge's manuscripts and to reproduce his Aran photographs. Sincerest thanks to the National Gallery of Ireland for also granting me license to reproduce important material held in the Jack B. Yeats Archive: two photographs by Synge, Jack Yeats's sketch from his trip to the Congested Districts with Synge in 1905, and the postcard with a photograph of a jaunting car that graces the cover of this book. At the National Gallery, I am thankful to Barry McLoughlin and in particular Sean Mooney for their help in retrieving these important materials. All of Jack Yeats's material used here is published with permission from the Estate of Jack B. Yeats, Design and Artists Copyright Society (DACS) London/Irish Visual Artists Rights Association (IVARO) Dublin. I thank Adrian Colwell at IVARO for his assistance. The Henry W. and Albert A. Berg Collection of English and American Literature in the New York Public Library, Astor, Lenox and Tilden Foundations, granted permission to reproduce three of Jack Yeats's sketches in chapter 3. I am indebted to the Berg curator Isaac Gewirtz and in particular to Berg librarians Joshua McKeon and Mary Catherine Kinniburgh for their assistance. My friend Irene Bulla, teaching fellow in Italian and comparative literature at Columbia University, also provided invaluable help in retrieving the reproductions. The images from Mary Banim's book *Here and There through Ireland* in chapters 1 and 2 have been published courtesy of the National Library of Ireland, Dublin. J. M. Synge's poem "Abroad" in the epilogue is printed by permission of Oxford University Press.

I am also most indebted to Ondřej Pilný at Charles University in Prague for providing important Czech sources used in chapter 4. I also thank him for permission to reproduce material in chapter 3 that had previously appeared in my article "'I Like Not Lifting the Rags from My Mother Country for to Tickle the Sentiments of Manchester': Synge's Subversive Practice in 'In the Congested Districts,'" in *The Politics of Irish Writings*, edited by Kateřina Jenčová, Michaela Marková, Radvan Markus, and Hana Pavelková (Prague: Centre for Irish Studies, Charles Univ., 2010), 46–56. Dr. Pilný's Centre for Irish Studies hosted an unforgettable postgraduate conference in 2009 that proved crucial for me to rehearse some of the ideas contained in this book. Some material in chapter 3 also appeared in my article "On the Road in the Congested Districts with John Synge and Jack Yeats: Visual and Textual Shaping of Irishness," in *Founder to Shore: Cross-Currents in Irish and Scottish Studies*, edited by Shane Alcobia-Murphy, Lindsay Milligan, and Dan Wall (Aberdeen: Arts and Humanities Research Council Centre for Irish and Scottish Studies, University of Aberdeen, 2010), 43–54. I am grateful to Shane Alcobia-Murphy for granting me permission to republish that material. The conference he organized in 2009 at the University of Aberdeen Centre for Irish and Scottish Studies provided another useful forum for discussion.

In 2009 on Inis Meáin, I attended the launch of an exhibition of J. M. Synge's photographs arranged by Siamsa Tíre (National Folk Theater of Ireland) that I discuss in chapter 1. I thank its curator, Ciarán Walsh, for facilitating my visit to the island for the exhibition launch.

A special mention must also be made of the staff at Syracuse University Press. This book would have never seen the light of day without the unstinting support of acquisitions editor Deborah Manion, whose enthusiasm, professionalism, and always helpful guidance have sustained me throughout the publishing process. I am grateful to her for passionately believing in this project and for seeing it through completion. I would also like to acknowledge the two anonymous readers who reviewed my manuscript and offered precious advice.

Warmest thanks go to my friend and colleague at UCD Catherine Wilsdon for her friendship, collegiality, and support in this and other projects. With Catherine, I share a passion for J. M. Synge and many academic adventures: from Irish Revival conferences to the Irish Revival Network and more.

My gratitude also goes to a number of friends I have made in Ireland since 2006—Carlos Castro, Leo Close, Tom Cronin, Ritchie Jorge Fernandez, Ciaran McCabe, Anna Molinari, Anne Mulhall, Robert Murphy, David Ryan, and others. They have sustained me with their laughter, innumerable coffees, dinners, pints, and unforgettable literary chats in front of the library and football matches. Very special thanks go to Elena Boychenko, Gabriella Caminotto, Paola Cortese, Chih-Hsien Hsieh, Sonka Ihnen, my "Irish sister" Monica Insinga, Michiko Okazow, Antonio Pieri, Silvia Pischedda, Maurizio Pittau, Corinna Ricasoli, Viviana Spagnuolo, Chiara Tedaldi, Ben Tsutomu, Kumiko Yamada, and Ciarán Young as well as to all the Radio Dublino crew. Grazie to Marguerite Duggan for her kindness and support. Thanks also to Barry Curran, Lorraine Forde, and the Curran families in Headford.

I am indebted to all my friends in Cuneo, Italy, for remaking home for me every time I traveled back there and for visiting in Dublin. Thanks to Luca Barbero and the rest of the Sisimizi ska band, Anna Bottero, Elisa Candela, Luciano Cavallero, Ottavia Emmolo, Sara Garis, Paolo Ghibaudo, Enrico Gerardo Giorda, Luisella Mellino and Carmen Musilli at Radio Piemonte Sound, Alessandro Oreglia, Federica Ramella-Bon, Alessandra Rostagno and the Champions volleyball team, and Valentina Tortone, along with everybody else whom I forgot to include. In Verona, where I completed this book, I thank my friends Lorenzo Agostinis, Elinor Anderson, and Patrick O'Connor, who have provided much needed destressing moments and support.

Finally, this book is dedicated to my families in Cuneo, Dublin, and Boston. I am indebted to my family in Ireland—Manuela Costamagna, Mark Guildea, and Sophia Guildea—for providing necessary distractions from research, for feeding me, and for entertaining me with familial warmth and the deepest affection. In Boston, Paul and Mary Hutchinson and the Hutchinson household always made me feel welcome, providing hospitality, unforgettable Christmas parties, and summer days at the beach. My family in Italy—my father, Sergio; my mother, Valeria; my brother, Michele—deserve all my gratitude for their untiring love and unobtrusive support and for always accepting and encouraging my choices. They have also followed me on a couple of memorable wind-swept journeys in Ireland, and I thank them for that, too. To William Hutchinson go all my love and gratitude for always being there as well as for his never-ending support and understanding, his generous advice, and his loving care.

# Abbreviations

| | |
|---|---|
| *AI* | *The Aran Islands* |
| CDB | Congested Districts Board |
| *CL1* | *The Collected Letters of John Millington Synge*, vol. 1: *1871–1907* |
| *CW1* | *Collected Works*, vol. 1: *Poems* |
| *CW2* | *Collected Works*, vol. 2: *Prose* |
| IAOS | Irish Agricultural Organization Society |
| *LM* | *Letters to Molly: John Millington Synge to Maire O'Neill, 1906–1909* |
| *TI* | *J. M. Synge: Travelling Ireland, Essays 1898–1908* |

J. M. SYNGE AND TRAVEL WRITING OF THE IRISH REVIVAL

# Introduction

*Traveling Ireland and Writing Travel
with J. M. Synge during the Revival*

John Millington Synge (1871–1909) was a gifted travel writer. He saw travel as engrained in his academic and artistic aspirations and wrote some of the most poignant travel writing of the early twentieth century. In the lines he jotted down to his fiancée, Abbey Theatre actress Molly Allgood, while he was heading to England to visit Jack Yeats on May 30, 1907, a vivid snapshot of Synge as a travel writer comes into focus: "It seems funny to me to be on the road again I have been so long shut up. Certainly there is nothing like traveling. I feel better already. It is one of the wettest nights I have ever come across, it is coming down in bucketfulls so I cant [sic] walk about anywhere. This is like writing when you are hypnotised because I'm scribbling away as hard as I can and all the time I'm listening to the talk at the table behind me. I dont [sic] know how much this trip will cost, I like this route it has something out of the common."[1] In the passage, Synge's journey is forced into a temporary rest owing to a heavy rainfall. During this break from traveling, Synge's physical dynamism—his delight to be "on the road again" and his renewed energy after a relapse of the disease (Hodgkin's) that would be fatal to him in 1909—is channeled into writing. In these rushed lines, the ideas of mobility and creativity seem to be almost interchangeable, to the point that one could almost substitute the word *traveling* with *writing* (and vice versa), and the sense would remain unaltered. Broadly speaking, this book ponders the interlocking of traveling and writing in Synge's nonfiction about

Irish places. Travel, in James Clifford's inclusive definition, encompasses "a range of more or less voluntarist practices of leaving 'home' to go to some 'other' place." Clifford further notes how this displacement "takes place for the purpose of gain—material, spiritual, scientific. It involves obtaining knowledge and/or having an 'experience' (exciting, edifying, pleasurable, estranging, broadening)."[2] Synge left home both to return and to "re-turn" to it physically and imaginatively—his gain from travel being undoubtedly artistic and inspirational for his playwriting and, significantly, for his experience as a travel writer. This book offers a comprehensive reappraisal of Synge's travel nonfiction and of his role as a travel writer in Ireland during the early-twentieth-century Irish Revival.

Synge traditionally sits among the pantheon of Ireland's greatest playwrights and founding figures of the Irish national theater. His plays, from *Riders to the Sea* to the controversial *The Playboy of the Western World*, have been praised by critics for their unflinching portrayal of rural Ireland and for their bravura in the use of Hiberno-English. Alongside his dramatic production, Synge also wrote poetry and nonfiction—ranging from book reviews to journalism and travel writing about Ireland[3]—but they are generally considered writings of minor impact. Among the artists of the Irish literary Revival, he was one of the most widely traveled. In his early twenties, he visited Germany, France, and Italy, spending a few months in each place and becoming well acquainted with each language, literature, and culture.[4] Although he did not publish travel writing about his journeys on the Continent, he did bring his European experience and his keenness for languages to bear on his approach to home travel, and in his late twenties he started traveling around Ireland and writing about it. Out of more or less ten years of home travel (1898–1908), which complemented his career at the Abbey Theatre, Synge produced a travel book, *The Aran Islands* (1907) and a series of travel essays about Wicklow, West Kerry, Connemara, and Mayo that appeared in newspapers and periodicals while he was still alive and that were anthologized in posthumous editions of the *Collected Works* under the all-encompassing title *In Wicklow, West Kerry, and Connemara*.[5]

This study historicizes Synge's travel texts within the context of contemporaneous travel literature and journalism about Ireland written by

Irish artists and activists during a crucial time for Ireland's national self-determination. It argues that Synge's travel texts, far from being solely source material for his plays, are ground-breaking narratives that privilege plural and dialogic constructions and that challenge inherited modes of place portrayal associated with imperial and nationalist discourses. In this book, Synge's travel narratives are studied not as a minor accomplishment but rather as the output of an original ethnographic and journalistic imagination. As noted, in general Synge's nonfiction about Ireland has been analyzed primarily as a kind of rough work for his plays.[6] Although this approach is certainly necessary for a fuller understanding of his dramatic aesthetic, along with being amply sanctioned by his own manuscripts and letters, this book takes that reading as a given and does not look at Synge's plays or dramaturgy: it instead focuses on his travel narratives in their own right. To highlight Synge's achievement in nonfiction writing, it provides new interpretative frameworks in which his nonfiction can be read and analyzes critically neglected sources: Irish travel writing of the Revival period.

Recent criticism has added original contexts to the study of Synge's topographical nonfiction. His travel writing, especially his travel book *The Aran Islands*, has been widely examined within the framework of anthropological discourse and compared with ethnographic writing.[7] However, although this approach has drawn interesting parallels between Synge's nonfiction and heterogeneous scientific writings by others (e.g., the work of Claude Lévi-Strauss and contemporaneous Aran Islands ethnographies such as the one by Alfred Cort Haddon and Charles R. Browne), it has generally overlooked more popular travel writing. Mary Louise Pratt notes the indebtedness of ethnographic writing to genres such as travel writing and journalism, adding that at times "ethnography blinds itself to the fact that its own discursive practices were often inherited from . . . other genres (travelogues, memoirs, journalism and official institutional and colonial reports)."[8] In light of this remark, this book examines Synge's travel nonfiction in connection with critically neglected contemporaneous travel writing and journalism. In addition to correlating Synge's work to official ethnographic writing, some critics have also traced his indebtedness to an old-Irish tradition of travel texts. For instance, Tony

Roche persuasively identifies textual connections between *The Aran Islands* and the eighth-century tale *The Voyage of Bran*, arguing that "Synge composed the account of his journey to the Aran Islands with growing awareness of the literary and mythic antecedents of such voyages."[9] In a similar way, John Wilson Foster parallels *The Aran Islands* with the medieval *immrama* and *echtrae*, tales about sea voyages to the Otherworld and about adventures to the Otherworld, respectively.[10] Furthermore, Synge is also directly influenced by Breton writers such as Pierre Loti; for instance, Synge brought Loti's novel *Le pêcheur d'Islande* (1886) with him to the Aran Islands during his first trip there[11] and mentioned it in a typescript draft of his introduction to *The Aran Islands*.[12] This monograph, however, is not a study of the literary influences on Synge's travel texts because the critical works I referred to earlier, along with others,[13] have already traced that subject in detail.

This book takes a different approach. It provides a new context in which Synge's travel writing can be read and sheds light on a critically overlooked genre: travel writing compiled by Irish artists and activists affiliated with Revival networks. Following Synge's travels to the Aran Islands, Connemara, Mayo, West Kerry, and Wicklow, this study explores both Synge's and the broader Revival movement's poetics and politics of place and travel. Synge's travel book *The Aran Islands*, his journalistic series about poverty in the so-called Congested Districts of Connemara and Mayo written in 1905 for the *Manchester Guardian*, his travel essays about West Kerry and Wicklow are compared with a selection of travelogues and journalism dealing with the same areas. This comparison contributes to a fuller understanding of Synge's innovative achievement as a nonfiction writer. Shawn Gillen has suggested that *The Aran Islands* can be considered an "early masterpiece" of literary nonfiction in that it contains many different genres in a hybrid "pastiche of lyricism, reportage, precise description, and dramatic vignettes rendered in journalistic detail."[14] It is this ability to draw from such a multifaceted heritage that makes Synge's travel narratives a great accomplishment in the genre and a vehicle to assert a precise local identity, transcending rigid taxonomies of empire and nation.

In particular, Synge's topographical journalism—his series about distress in the Congested Districts of Connemara and Mayo as well as his articles about West Kerry and Wicklow—has always been overlooked and considered a minor attainment in comparison with both his theatrical oeuvre and *The Aran Islands*. There are several reasons for this underestimation. According to Nicholas Grene, the first person who contributed to a misjudgment of Synge's travel articles was the same person who participated in the myth making of Synge as playwright of genius and artist par excellence, W. B. Yeats. Grene recalls how, despite Yeats's opposition to collecting and publishing Synge's journalism (especially the *Manchester Guardian* articles) after Synge's premature death in 1909, the executors finally won the battle.[15] In 1910, the prose volume of *Works* was issued and contained Synge's travel journalism along with a juvenile piece entitled *Under Ether*.[16] The following year another edition of the travel essays left out *Under Ether* and published the topographical essays under the new, all-encompassing title *In Wicklow, West Kerry, and Connemara*, trying somehow to assemble for posterity a sequel to the fully shaped travel book *The Aran Islands*. Synge had actually intended to collect his travel essays in book form, but death prevented him from doing so. Subsequent editions that appeared in the early 1960s followed the pattern of the prose volume of the *Works* in 1910, integrating the travel pieces with excerpts from Synge's unpublished material from the manuscripts, such as his early prose and miscellaneous articles about literature, all accompanied by scholarly notes that contributed to a more accurate understanding of his aesthetics. However, in part because of these inevitable anthologizations, in critical analysis the travel articles have been read as an integrated text rather than referred to as individual and separate pieces worthy of a more specific investigation. In this sense, the recent edition of the travel essays edited by Nicholas Grene and collated from the periodicals in which they were first published, *J. M. Synge: Travelling Ireland, Essays 1898–1908*, redirects the focus toward each single piece, therefore restoring the historical contingency in which Synge's journalistic artifacts were produced.

The emphasis on reading Synge's topographical writings as part of a travel literature tradition is due in part to the fact that *The Aran Islands* and Synge's essays were marketed as travel narratives at the time of their publication. For example, in some of the ads that appeared in an issue of *The Shanachie* in 1907, an enthusiastic reviewer noted how *The Aran Islands* superseded the expectations of the genre: "Worth any hundred ordinary travel books. It is full of strange suggestions to the eye and to the imagination."[17] Thus, this study also illuminates a wider tradition of revivalist nonfiction and the Revival milieu in which Synge's oeuvre took shape. As P. J. Mathews contends, the Revival was far from being an elitist movement preoccupied "with a backward-looking Celtic spirituality, a nostalgia for Gaelic Ireland and an obsessive anti-modern traditionalism." The Revival instead needs to be understood, he argues, as "a progressive period that witnessed the co-operation of the self-help revivalists to encourage local modes of material and cultural development."[18] These revivalist modes and ideas were showcased and publicized through low-brow periodicals that were often packaged to appeal to a general audience. Recent scholarship on the Revival has increasingly given critical attention to popular and low-brow cultural and literary forms that had an impact on the transmission of revivalist ideas. For example, Kevin Rafter has worked on preindependence journalism;[19] Karen Steele has looked at Irish women activists in the nationalist press and at the influence of the nineteenth-century New Journalism on Irish periodical culture;[20] in her critical biography of the Revival writer and activist Alice Milligan, Catherine Morris has emphasized Milligan's clever use of dramatic *tableaux vivants* and journalism to further the nationalist cause.[21] Alongside more widely explored Revival genres such as poetry and drama, prose also flourished with innovations and experimentalism evident not only in fiction but also in Irish-language journalism.[22] All these studies, however, do not pay specific attention to the genre of Irish travel writing, which was nonetheless thriving in both periodical and book form.

During the nationalist ferment of the turn of the twentieth century, Irish localities and the Irish language became powerful signifiers of nationality as well as pivotal elements in the construction of an Irish identity in opposition to an English one. As a consequence, the rural and most westward spots in the West of Ireland, where Irish was still more widely spoken, became a pilgrimage site for Revival artists and activists. Many literary figures glorified these western shores in their writings as a means to reconnect with a more "authentic" Irishness. Although the appeal of the Irish West is a well-studied trope of the revivalist aesthetic,[23] it is normally analyzed within fictional prose and poetry. Yet a large number of authors ranging from literary figures to political and Irish-language activists also wrote travel accounts to rediscover Irish localities from a nationalist standpoint. As such, much travel literature that appeared during the Irish Revival was intertwined with radical Irish politics and cultural-nationalist activism. In the same way that English imperial travelogues from the eighteenth century on sought to "engage metropolitan reading publics with (or to) expansionist enterprises,"[24] making those readers sympathetic to imperialist projects, travel writing about Ireland, written by Irish authors and activists at the turn of the twentieth century, often aimed at fashioning an Irish nationalist subject and at actively "engag[ing] [its] audience with (and to)" nationalist projects.

Despite the proliferation of the genre in a variety of print outlets and its partaking in the formation of an Irish national identity, the Irish travel writing of the late nineteenth and early twentieth century is generally understudied. Within the field of Irish travel-writing studies, whereas travel writing about Ireland written by English or foreign tourists (thus from the outsider's perspective) has been the subject of several critical works and anthologies,[25] less critical attention has been paid to Irish writers traveling Ireland (from the insider's perspective). Even the latest study on Irish travel writing by Raphaël Ingelbien has focused on Irish people traveling abroad.[26] Moreover, criticism of Irish travel literature has generally granted a great deal of attention to earlier periods and specific social issues, notably the Great Famine of the mid–nineteenth century.[27]

However, as I contend in this book, the turn of the twentieth century is equally a very interesting period for Irish travel writing about Ireland owing to the entanglement between the genre and various forms of nationalist activism. Contributors to the genre include a range of well-known and less-known authors. For instance, in addition to Synge, Anglo-Irish novelists Edith Somerville and Martin Ross were very prolific travel writers; nationalist member of Parliament Stephen Gwynn wrote a guide book about Ireland and an account of his cycling rambles in Donegal and Antrim;[28] Alice Milligan started her writing career by coauthoring a travelogue about Ireland with her father;[29] Belfast revivalist Joseph Campbell wrote about and sketched a trip in Donegal;[30] in 1912, James Joyce wrote articles in Italian about the Aran Islands and the West of Ireland for the Trieste newspaper *Il Piccolo*.[31] In this book, however, the sample of texts examined comprises travel writing written or published mostly during Synge's lifespan (1871–1909) and dealing specifically with the same areas he visited. Thus, texts compared with Synge's work in chapters 1, 2, and 4 include, among others, Mary Banim's *Here and There through Ireland* (1891–92), William Bulfin's *Rambles in Éirinn* (1907), Emily Lawless's essay about Kerry (1882), Robert Lynd's *Rambles in Ireland* ([1909] 1912), Agnes O'Farrelly's *Smaointe ar Árainn* (*Thoughts on Aran*) (1901), Edith Somerville and Martin Ross's Aran piece in *Some Irish Yesterdays* (1906), Katharine Tynan's Irish guide (1909) and journalism about Wicklow (1890), and Arthur Symons's Aran essay in *Cities and Sea-coasts and Islands* (1896), based on a visit to the islands he undertook with W. B. Yeats. Chapter 3, on Synge's investigative journalism in the *Manchester Guardian*, uses as comparisons a number of journalistic pieces written for various periodicals and documenting the distress in the West of Ireland. This selection has been made to foreground Synge's travel writing as the main case study and in an effort to contextualize as much as possible his nonfiction both historically and geographically. Considering also that a number of political events that influenced the course of the nationalist struggle in Ireland took place after Synge's death (e.g., the Home Rule Bill of 1912, the Lockout of 1913, the Easter Rising of 1916), Irish travel writing after 1909 has been generally left out of this book because it is perhaps best understood in light of a partially altered political and social landscape.[32]

In literary history, the turn of the twentieth century is also a crucial time for the emergence of modernist movements across Europe, America, and the British Isles. Carl Thompson links modernism with a series of technological improvements in transportation and communication that increased global interconnectedness: the "disorientating kinesis that is seemingly characteristic of modernity" and the new sensory experiences produced by the advent of faster technologies of travel were part of the material conditions that spearheaded experimentation and new modes of expression.[33] These aspects of modern life were also negotiated in interesting ways in travel accounts of the time. In Ireland during the nineteenth century, ameliorations in transportation and infrastructure for

land travel benefited both local communities and tourists. For instance, in 1851 the inauguration of the Great Western Railway, which connected Dublin to Galway, further enhanced land connections between the East and the West of Ireland.[34] Even more isolated outposts such as the Aran Islands were inscribed into tourist itineraries with "the introduction of 'a pleasure-boat service' from Galway" in 1863,[35] followed by a steamer service in 1891, which also assisted the work of the Congested Districts Board in modernizing the local fishing industry.[36] By the 1850s, "most of Ireland's railway network was . . . in place," connecting urban centers with rural peripheries and enhancing circulation of both people and commodities; the extensiveness of the railway system and its affordability directly affected a number of phenomena, such as "the standardization of time, the spread of national daily newspapers, and the growth of seaside resorts."[37] At the same time, tourists and travelers also continued to utilize a number of horse-drawn transports. Particularly popular were the so-called Bianconi cars, roofless cars that could carry up to twenty passengers in their largest versions. Even if the heyday of the Bianconi coach system is linked to the early decades of the nineteenth century, by the turn of the twentieth century long cars were still deployed, as both Mary Banim's travelogue and Synge's *Guardian* series testify.[38]

The Irish tourist industry by the end of the nineteenth century could also avail itself of the bicycle, alongside trains and horse-drawn transports. After its first appearance in Ireland in 1819 in its earliest guise, the "*Draisienne* or dandy-horse or hobby-horse," and after its subsequent midcentury transformations (the "ordinary," the "penny-farthing," the tricycle, and the safety bicycle with pneumatic tires), the bicycle took over the Emerald Isle and spread among the higher and middle classes.[39] Cyclists in the British Isles congregated in cycling associations, read specialist periodicals (in Ireland, *The Irish Cyclist*), and consulted tailor-made tourist guides for their rambles. Moreover, Irish nationalist organizations such as Sinn Féin and the Gaelic League also boasted their own cycling groups, which embraced and constructed cycling as a dignified nationalist pastime.[40] Alice Milligan wrote the poem "The Man on the Wheel" to eulogize the League's Irish-language teacher cycling to reach his or her students in remote localities.[41]

Throughout the nineteenth century, both electric- and steam-pow-ered motor cars were introduced in Europe, but it was not until Karl Benz developed the internal-combustion engine in the mid-1880s that automo-biles could be manufactured more efficiently.[42] Their circulation on the streets became more frequent, and they were also legalized in 1896 with the Locomotives on Highways Act, which allowed "'horseless carriages' on British roads."[43] Though substantially remaining a luxury commod-ity until the First World War, the automobile was publicized in travel-ogues and specialist periodicals, such as *The Autocar* (founded in 1895).[44] In the first decade of the twentieth century, wealthy tourists also started to visit Ireland using motor cars, such as the American Michael Myers Shoemaker, who traveled using a Panhard model.[45]

Last, in the 1890s an electric tram service was introduced in Dublin, sparking literary interest most famously in James Joyce, who would write about it in the "Wandering Rocks" episode of *Ulysses*, but also in Synge, who compared the introduction of electric tramways in Rome and Dublin in an article for the *Irish Times* in 1896.[46] Increasing interconnectedness in Ireland was also brought about by new communication technologies: for instance, Guglielmo Marconi's wireless telegraphy was tested and pat-ented in the mid-1890s after experiments were conducted on the western coasts of County Kerry.[47]

These various ameliorations affected Irish society at various levels, making travel increasingly more accessible and affordable for the middle classes and also, among other categories, for women, who fully exploited tourist infrastructures and various modes of transportation for business and leisure. As the substantial sample of women travel writers surveyed in this book testifies, Irish women made the most of this enhanced democ-ratization of travel to partake in Revival cultural activism. These women travel writers often traveled with the company of men or other women, presumably for safety and respectability reasons, but in some cases they also traveled alone. To an extent, some precautions were in place to pre-vent dangers to women travelers—for instance, in the allocation of car-riages and seats especially for women. In a document titled *By-laws and Regulations* issued by the Sligo, Leitrim, and Northern Counties Railway, the company forbid any person of the male sex older than eight years of

age to "travel or attempt to travel or remain in any compartment of a carriage marked or notified as being reserved or appropriated for the exclu-
sive use of the female sex," with the penalties for not complying including
a fine of forty shillings and removal from the train.[48] Social issues that
could potentially affect tourists may have included vagrancy, which was
widespread in post-Famine Ireland. Historical research has highlighted
that national and local newspapers did not seem to voice too many com-
plaints about disruptions seemingly caused by vagrants because homelessness and vagrancy were kept at bay in towns through institutions
such as workhouses, asylums, and youth reformatories and were often tol-
erated in rural areas.[49] Moreover, vagrancy was not very often denounced
in tourist literature as a potential danger for visitors, nor was it flagged
as potentially affecting female travelers. Brian Griffin has recently noted
that cycling travelogues aimed at women cyclists tended to construct Ireland as a "crime-free" and perfectly safe place for cycling holidays, reporting only very few instances of criminal incidents. Griffin had to dig into
the archives of the provincial press to spot a few cases of women cyclists
who were assaulted by vagrants; he also mentions a woman who carried
a revolver as a precaution during her rambles, but he concludes that "the
threat that [tramps] posed was exaggerated" in part because of the social
stigma associated with vagrancy.[50]

Partaking in the creation of a quaint and safe space for the tourist is
Mary Banim's travelogue. Banim, traveling under the commission of the
*Freeman's Journal* for pleasurable business, was accompanied by her sister,
Matilda, who sketched the illustrations for the travelogue. They used a
wide range of transports such as trains, ferries, and long cars, and they
often walked. Many of the areas they visited (e.g., Wicklow, Connemara,
and even Aran) were listed in a number of fairly well-known tourist itineraries. In her travelogue, however, Banim does not seem to be too concerned with issues of safety for female travelers; rather, she is devoted
primarily to the rediscovery of Ireland's cultural and physical heritage.

According to Susan Bassnett, the impulse to leave the comfort zone
of urban dwellings to travel was for women a way of gaining access to
a male-dominated public sphere.[51] For example, studies on women who
took part in colonial enterprises, such as Mary Kingsley, read their work

and experience as being ways for them to enter contemporaneous debates about colonialism. According to Pratt, Kingsley's *Travels in West Africa* sought to recover "European innocence. Politically she argued for the possibility of expansion without domination and exploitation."[52] In a similar way, all the women travel writers analyzed in this book, despite divergent political opinions and different class extraction, were equally motivated to seize new possibilities of expression through travel and travel writing. For instance, it is plausible to read Banim's travelogue of the early 1890s as a way to participate in Irish cultural nationalism. This commitment to Ireland would become more militant in the travel writing of Gaelic Leaguer Agnes O'Farrelly at the turn of the twentieth century.

The Anglo-Irish cousins Edith Somerville and Martin Ross also traveled as a duo, following in part the beaten track and often lodging in tourist hotels. In the 1890s, they visited and published on Connemara (*Through Connemara in a Governess Cart*, 1890), Bordeaux (*In the Vine Country*, 1891), Wales (*Beggars on Horseback*, 1893), Denmark ("In the State of Denmark," 1893), and Aran (1895). Their experience and the fact that they sometimes followed tourist itineraries may have worked as a deterrent against possible dangers to be found on the road. For Somerville and Ross, traveling and travel writing certainly had an emancipatory function, albeit not directly in terms of militant nationalist activism, as in O'Farrelly's case. According to Andrew Garavel, travel writing was for them a way "to help subsidize their more ambitious efforts as novelists, as well as to contribute to the upkeep of their families' estates (while simultaneously trying to establish a measure of independence from those same families)."[53]

Unaccompanied female travelers, however, were not impossible to find. In one of his essays about West Kerry, Synge recalls that he was asked to chaperone a young woman about twenty years old traveling alone from Kerry to a hospital in Dublin. The young woman, visibly distressed because of the journey, was then left by her mother in the company of Synge and another respectable lone traveler, a young woman returning from America (*TI*, 163–64). Another lone traveler of the Revival was the playwright, folklorist, and Abbey Theatre cofounder Lady Augusta Gregory, who spent a week on Inisheer, Aran Islands, in 1893 to collect folklore.[54] According to James Pethica, this journey was a lonely and remarkable endeavor for a woman at that time.[55] Gregory unfortunately did not publish any travel writing: in her diaries she only comments in passing about drafting a magazine article,[56] which appears not to have survived. Her subsequent visit to Aran took place May 5–19, 1898, around the same time Synge also visited the islands for the first time.[57] As is well known, they caught a glimpse of each other on the islands but did not interact directly; their first official meeting took place on June 27, 1898, at Coole Park with W. B. Yeats, who acted as the intermediary. During her second visit to the islands, Gregory wrote scattered diary entries and sketched the Aran landscape and architecture: stone-built churches, wells, funeral monuments, *cloghauns* (beehive dwellings built with dry masonry), and the hearth of one particular cottage[58]—perhaps the Mac-Donnchadha's cottage, affectionately called "an Ollscoil," the University,[59] by numerous Gaelic Leaguers who lodged there. In sketching the human-built heritage of Aran, Gregory, like many nineteenth-century visitors, demonstrated her antiquarian interests in the islands. She also partook in a widespread tourist activity for educated women at the time: sketching—the same interest cultivated by Somerville and Ross as well as by the Banim sisters.

It was during this period of an increasingly democratized tourism across class and gender, of new transport and communication technologies, and of nationalist cultural ferment that Synge did his travel writing. He availed himself of various types of transport and technology, such as typewriters and portable cameras, and in his immersive travel writing he looked at the way the larger societal changes affected the everyday life of local and often marginalized rural communities. The comparison this book makes between Synge's travel narratives and significant revivalist contemporaneous productions shows that Synge ultimately eschewed dominant discourses such as empire and nation but rather problematized them in order to express a more complex idea of Irishness grounded in his empathetic observation of the local rural communities he traveled among.

The chapter progression in this book attempts to follow Synge's travels regionally and, to an extent, chronologically. Chapter 1 details his first travel experience to the Aran Islands. Synge's annual visits on Aran started in 1898 and ended in 1902. He did not publish *The Aran Islands*

until 1907, however. From 1903 to 1907, he devoted his attention and summer holidays to West Kerry, so chapter 2 follows his travels in West Kerry
and the resulting series published in the periodical *The Shanachie* in 1906–
7. Chapter 3 discusses how in the summer of 1905 Synge undertook the
trip to Connemara and Mayo sponsored by the *Manchester Guardian*. He
had already visited North Mayo and Sligo from September 17 to October
1, 1904, on a cycling trip he planned at the last minute because an outbreak
of typhus had prevented him from going to the Aran Islands.[60] Chapter
4 explores the literary products of Synge's frequent rambles in Wicklow,
where he had spent innumerable summer holidays since his early child-
hood. Although the Wicklow articles were written intermittently beginning in 1903, they are the subject of the final chapter because of Synge's
more prolonged investment in that locality.

With the purpose of highlighting Synge's potential as a nonfiction
writer, each chapter in this book borrows from various theoretical frameworks. Chapter 1 about Aran and chapter 2 about West Kerry draw on
seminal work in the overlapping fields of postcolonialism and travel-
writing studies to ponder Synge's novel narrative strategies and his negotiation of tradition and modernity.[61] In particular, adapting Mary Louise
Pratt's notion of "contact perspective" to Synge's narrative tactics, chapter 1 analyzes the way *The Aran Islands* negotiates the coeval existence
of opposite cultural formations—tradition and modernity, Irish and English, orality and literacy. Chapter 2, about the West Kerry series, highlights
how Synge draws attention to relations of travel and displacement in the
area, challenging one-dimensional representation of the anthropological
field as characterized primarily by dwelling communities.

Chapter 3 draws on current debates in literary journalism studies by
Norman Sims, Richard Keeble, and others[62] and on recent developments
in the study of Irish journalism and the press[63] to shed light on Synge's
journalistic commission for the *Manchester Guardian*. This chapter also
retrieves additional journalistic sources from magazines and periodicals
of the time that deal specifically with the Congested Districts, those pov-
erty-stricken areas of the western seaboard that were in the process of
being revitalized by the governmental agency called the Congested Districts Board. These writings possess a more sociological slant and, unlike

the travelogues mentioned earlier, were often compiled by journalists and officials traveling in those areas on a specific mission—that is, not for leisure. The comparison with previous journalism about the distressed areas of Connemara and Mayo highlights Synge's unpatronizing and empathetic stylistics as well as his willingness to frame from below—that is from the point of view of the disenfranchised—his critique of the work of colonial structures such as the Congested Districts Board.

Cartographer and environmental writer Tim Robinson is one of the first to point to a re-reading of Synge's nonfiction in light of an altered planetary and global consciousness. In his seminal introduction to *The Aran Islands*, he comments, "Now that our planet has shrunk to an island in space (if not a Congested District, and with no fatherly Board set over it!) all past efforts to unriddle our being-on-the-earth have to be re-read; perhaps Synge's book will reach another maturity in this age of secular eschatologies."[64] Chapter 4 follows Robinson's lead in order to examine Synge's complex representation of Wicklow's physical and human-built environment. Drawing on theories of postcolonialism and ecocriticism,[65] the work of Michel Foucault,[66] and the historiography of Irish mental institutions in the nineteenth century,[67] the chapter analyzes Synge's interest in the landscape of the coercive institutions that populated the region as well as in the cultural and environmental disconnect experienced by communities inhabiting the Wicklow margins, where place had been redefined in hegemonic terms.

Finally, in addition to a sustained analysis of Synge's travel texts, chapters 1 and 3 also examine relevant visual material, therefore providing an interrelated study of visual and textual travel documents. In his journeys in Europe and Ireland, Synge brought along a camera and took various photographs, including snapshots of Paris, Dublin, and rural Ireland. Chapter 1 looks at his Aran Islands photographs, which have been traditionally examined within the discourse of anthropological photography or in the context of the technological innovations and increasing democratization of the medium at the turn of the twentieth century.[68] This chapter adds an important context for the analysis of Synge's photo taking: the use of photography in cultural-nationalist revivalist activities. Another important visual source for understanding Synge's experience of travel is the work of Jack B. Yeats, who traveled with Synge in 1905 to the Congested Districts of Connemara and Mayo. In addition to the pen-and-ink illustrations that were published alongside the articles, Jack Yeats also drew sketches of the trip and of Synge as the journey was progressing. These sketches are examined in chapter 3 as important travel documents that shed light on Synge's journey and on the journalistic commission of two artists of the Irish Revival.

# 1

## "The Cuckoo with Its Pipit"

*Travel and Modernity in* The Aran Islands

In 1968, inspired by John Millington Synge's travel book *The Aran Islands*, the Welsh poet Andrew McNeillie spent a year on Inishmore, subsequently writing a memoir entitled *An Aran Keening*. McNeillie describes his landing upon Aran after a turbulent sea voyage and the crowd that gathered on the quay: "The boat and its arrival constituted an event of some curiosity and interest, to be observed at first hand should you be remotely in the vicinity. If you had a package ordered you could speed its progress home by coming down to meet the boat yourself, and in the process you might hear the news, how things had been, who was it stranded now from Inishmaan, things to connect together, food for talk."[1] The arrival of the boat on Aran is a moment that brings into play and connects two seemingly separate realities, remote islands and the outer world. This moment, as McNeillie has it, can spark connections, verbal intercourse, communication, "things to connect together, food for talk."

It is in passages such as this one that the legacy of Synge in McNeillie becomes most apparent. In this chapter, I show how Synge's main interest in *The Aran Islands* is to make the dialogic correspondence between the islands and the rest of the world a specific concern of his text and a narrative strategy that enables him to transcend essentialist formations such as empire and nation. In *The Aran Islands*, many snapshots of life on Aran at the turn of the twentieth century take place in close proximity to piers and shores, liminal spaces where Synge gathers his "food for talk." In these spaces, the reader is offered a picture of the Aran Islands not as an isolated microcosm of picturesque distinctiveness recalcitrant to modernity, but rather as part of a wider and transnational network of economic, social, cultural, and political relations, *connected* to modern formations.

For example, in part 1 Synge goes down to the pier to watch the cattle being shipped for a fair in Galway. He documents the islanders' complicated and laborious task at the pier, which was "crowded with bullocks and a great number of people."[2] A year later he goes down to the same pier, this time to see the horses coming back from their summer's grazing in Connemara. There he meets a man who asks him for news about the war in the Transvaal and observes the process of stacking and delivering turf from the pier to the cottages (*AI*, 65–66). In another episode in part 3, Synge describes a foreign *ceannaí* (peddler) just landed on Aran selling his wares and bargaining with the local women in a sort of improvised pidgin because the women "professed to know no English [but] could make themselves understood without difficulty when it pleased them" (*AI*, 90). These episodes are examples of Synge's commitment to representing Aran as embedded in specific local and global processes affecting rural Ireland at the turn of the twentieth century.

Synge's transnational and European outlook in his dramatic work has been powerfully asserted in recent studies: from Ben Levitas's essay on Synge's European influences to many essays about his drama in Patrick Lonergan's collection *Synge and His Influences*.[3] In the collected volume *Synge and Edwardian Ireland*, edited by Brian Cliff and Nicholas Grene, the historian David Fitzpatrick has pointed out that "Synge's peculiar achievement [in *The Aran Islands*] was not his portrayal of a primitive culture at the point of collapse, a theme for many previous observers, but his revelation of the cultural ambivalence of people living simultaneously in two worlds."[4] In the same collection, Nicholas Allen utilizes the useful framework of archipelago to ponder the "transnational imprint [that] runs through Synge's work," addressing his plays as well as *The Aran Islands* and the articles about the Congested Districts. Allen argues that "Synge's work in Ireland, relates materially to a global archipelago of text that runs in chain internationally through the distribution networks of empire and its cultural diasporas." According to Allen, for Synge Aran becomes "a place between, not an end . . . a hub through which several worlds pass."[5] Therefore, Aran is not the uncorrupted pristine environment shut out from modern society and its socioeconomic dynamics. From the beginning, Synge points clearly to the economic dependency of the islands on immigration to America and the commercial relations between the two countries (*AI*, 15). Eruptions of modernity are evident also in Synge's attention to the islanders' knowledge of modern mechanisms, such as global travel and tourism. The islanders are not simply farmers communally working in the fields during the day and narrating stories beside the fireplace at night. In one of his first encounters with the locals, Synge is reminded about the mechanisms of tourism that have affected the inhabitants' seasonal activities as some girls he meets explain "how they guide 'ladies and gintlemins' in the summer to all that is worth seeing in their neighbourhood, and sell them pampooties and maidenhair ferns, which are common among the rocks" (*AI*, 9). Synge's remark shows how the islanders had internalized mechanisms pertaining to modern tourism and how they were acclimated to intercultural and interlinguistic exchanges with America and Europe.

The co-option of the Aran islanders into mechanisms of tourism can roughly be traced back at least to the so-called Antiquarian Revival of the early nineteenth century and connected with the studies and travels of George Petrie, who visited Aran in 1822.[6] In the mid-1850s, a significant contribution was made by Martin Haverty's study of the Aran Islands for the British Association.[7] His report of the excursion to the association, "The Aran Isles," according to Nicola Gordon Bowe, "provided the sort of structured search for the vernacular which artists, archaeologists and historians would increasingly favor."[8] In the report, before transcribing the speeches of the luminaries, Haverty describes their "banquet" in Dun Aengus, "washed down with some excellent sherry" and "terminated with an Irish jig, in which the French Consul joined *con amore*." He concludes by quoting Paddy Mullin, the academics' island guide, who "made a short speech in Irish, very much to the purpose. He reminded his fellow-islanders that for the sake of their honor as well as their interest, they should endeavor to preserve their ruins."[9] This anecdote documents how the inhabitants, at least since 1857, had a clear idea of the role that they could play and of the islands' antiquarian heritage as an exploitable resource, "their interest," within an emerging antiquarian tourism. Moreover, as Breandán Ó hEithir and Ruairí Ó hEithir contend, "the amazing banquet ... held in 1857, attended by many of Ireland's leading scholars, might be seen as marking Aran's 'coming out' into the modern academic world."[10] Significantly, in July 1900 another picnic took place at Dún Chonchubhair on Inis Meáin. This time it was attended by Gaelic League language activists, including Agnes O'Farrelly, who would author the Irish-language travelogue *Smaointe ar Árainn* (*Thoughts on Aran*, 1901).[11] The banquet featured "excellent roast mutton, ham and a giant fruit tart."[12] Ríona Nic Congáil observes how "such images of leading Gaelic Leaguers eating well and happily together, forging lifelong friendships, reveals how these visitors could look favorably upon Inis Meáin as a holiday destination when they had brought with them all they needed to live comfortably rather than opting to embrace the frugal lifestyle of the islanders." Nic Congáil further records that O'Farrelly brought along two unprocurable items for her Aran stay: "her French percolator and coffee."[13] Thus, visitors kept repeatedly exposing the islanders to products of modernity. Synge, notably, brought an alarm clock and was one of the first to bring a camera.

As mentioned in the introduction, the Aran Islands at the turn of the twentieth century became a *locus amoenus* to be visited and written about by a wide range of Irish writers and activists because of their remoteness, the presence of archaeological antiquities, and the general use of Irish there. The islands thus functioned as a kind of internal "contact zone,"[14] a site where different encounters were taking place not only in a colonial sense but also in a nationalist and revivalist sense. As will become apparent in this chapter, travel writing compiled by Irish writers and activists affiliated with these networks, in addition to documenting these revivalist "contacts," also exposed some of the contradictions and conflicts inherent in many of these revivalist projects.

In the first section of this chapter, I analyze how Irish travel writing of the Revival period engaged with a number of representational strategies recurrent within the genre. I show how Synge deconstructs tropes such as "transvaluation" and "textual attitude" as well as strategies of "othering" in favor of a transformative dialogic practice that takes into account and further problematizes his own position within the community and the environment he travels through. I call Synge's transformative textual practice "contact perspective," borrowing again from Mary Louise Pratt, and in the second section of the chapter I argue that this strategy makes Synge's travelogue move toward a modernist sensibility. In subverting tropes common in many typologies of travel writing, Synge displays a keen understanding of the essentialisms evident in much travel literature of both colonial and revivalist origin. The final section of the chapter concentrates on Synge's Aran Islands photographs and analyzes his engagement with photography in the context of the photography practiced by a number of Revival activists and intellectuals.

### Robinson Crusoes, Indians, and Irish Peasants

In the essay "Postcolonial Synge," C. L. Innes defines Synge as "an 'anticolonial' writer, since his drama and essays address the situation of a colonized Ireland seeking to free itself from physical and cultural domination by England." She also praises *The Aran Islands* for its ability to "capture the voices of the islanders" without sentimentalizing them.[15] Applying the framework of David Lloyd's theoretical categorizations "transvaluation" and "transformation,"[16] it can be said that Synge's appraisal of life on Aran in anticolonial terms does not advance merely a "transvaluation"—a reversal of negative values into positive ones typical of a certain strand of nationalist travel literature. In this literature, transvaluated models of Irishness are essentially constructed in opposition to ideas of Englishness and are therefore still dependent on and connected to those ideas. The transformative potential in Synge's narrative strategy instead hints at an independent path to be sought for constructing these models, a path unleashed, in part, by dominant discourses. Synge's text problematizes the transvaluation of aesthetic formations by presenting a dialogic confrontation between the Aran culture and the culture embodied in his persona on the island. His narrative strategy, which I refer to as "contact perspective," alternatively enables a "transformation" in *The Aran Islands*. The book, with its discontinuities and hybrid aesthetic formations, shies away from the entrapments of holistic and stereotypical representations that appear in previous travel writing about Ireland, of both an imperialist slant and a nationalist slant, and that are the inevitable consequence of the transvaluation process, following Lloyd's theorizing. As a consequence, *The Aran Islands* does not conform to previous specimens of travel literature, which still fall under an essentialist dynamic; rather, the book subverts these inherited modes, expressing an alternative anticolonial potential.

Examples of Lloyd's idea of transvaluation can be found in *Here and There through Ireland* (1891–92), Mary Banim's cultural-nationalist travelogue in two series published before the constitution of the Gaelic League in 1893 and of the Irish Agricultural Organization Society (IAOS) in 1894.[17] Banim was the daughter of the Irish novelist Michael Banim.[18] Her articles of Irish interest also appeared in American periodicals such as *The Catholic World* and the *Providence Sunday Journal* from approximately 1885 to 1893.[19] Banim's friendship with *Providence Sunday Journal* editor Alfred Williams probably laid the foundations for subsequent contributions to the paper by Irish writers such as Katharine Tynan (also an acquaintance of Banim), W. B. Yeats, and Douglas Hyde.[20] In *Here and There through Ireland*, evidence of the author's compliance to a cultural-nationalist ethos resides in the overt attempts to portray the Irish peasant in a good light. In particular, Banim makes an effort to demythologize stereotypical characteristics traditionally associated with stage Irishness and to appraise locally made Irish objects in opposition to English mass-produced goods. She describes Irish clothes, for instance, as "far warmer and more durable, and also healthier than any others." During one of her tours of Connemara, when hearing negative remarks made by two English ladies about the supposed "Irish uncleanliness" of a hotel, Banim is ready to deconstruct the stereotype through another strategic transvaluation: "I could not help earnestly hoping that the superior English cleanliness (if it existed) would go down in the bill next morning."[21] In the account, she carefully provides a dignified description of the accommodation that the two English ladies so much feared and praises the kindness of the Irish chambermaid:

> We sat down to a cosy tea and toast and salmon—the latter fresh and curdy, as it is never eaten in London. Neither did I see any of the obnoxious commodity in a very plainly furnished but tidy bed-room, attended

by a young chambermaid who certainly lacked proper hotel manners, for she had the audacity to feel very anxious that I should be comfortable, to come very often to make sure that I was so, and so far to forget the fitness of things as to address me once or twice as "asthore." But somehow—I suppose I have no proper dignity—I thought it very pleasant and felt very grateful for the young girl's attentions.[22]

In particular, Banim's positive description of the young chambermaid directly counteracts unkind portrayals of Irish rural women widespread in English travelogues. An earlier travelogue by the Quaker philanthropist William Reed describes a Kerry girl working in an inn as possessing "a roguish kind of sparkle in her dark eyes." He further comments on her physical appearance, noting "the complete absence of all those fine traits (flowing lines and graceful curves) which, according to the laws of taste constitute the principle of beauty. In brief, it was like one of those rude unfashioned figures which a common hedge-carpenter, half blind and half foolish, might have chipped with his hatchet from the timber of the blackthorn or crab-tree, to place as a characteristic statue on the tomb of departed symmetry."[23] This description of the girl seems an embodiment of Ireland under the colonial gaze, wherein she is debased both as a grotesque creature and as a servant. In judging her supposed lack of candor in undressing in the dark in front of him, Reed does not see as problematic the fact that it is actually he that peeped through the darkness to describe the female body. His final patronizing remarks about how the servant is "very civil and obliging" seem to be there only to reinforce his position as the male colonial authority.[24] Hence, whereas English travel writing had often depicted Irish peasant women in negative and racialized terms, Mary Banim's transvaluation achieves a positive, dignified, and humane depiction of them.

Banim's eulogistic treatment of Irish women presiding over domestic spaces clearly partakes in cultural nationalist discourses. In *Revival: The Abbey Theatre, Sinn Féin, the Gaelic League, and the Co-operative Movement*, P. J. Mathews notes how periodicals such as *The Irish Homestead* (the organ of Horace Plunkett's cooperative association, the IAOS) were putting emphasis on the external care of the houses that had to meet aesthetic requirements of cleanliness and tidiness in order to live up to English standards and to defeat English stereotypical assumptions about the filthiness of the Irish peasant.[25] To achieve this standard, a strong division of gender roles was advocated, resulting in the relegation of the woman to the domestic space.[26] Describing Sinn Féin party founder and Irish Free State president Arthur Griffith's outlook on female roles in the struggle for Irish independence, Susan Cannon Harris aptly calls it "home-and-hearth nationalism."[27] In context, a few years before the foundation of the Gaelic League and the IAOS, Mary Banim's transvaluated account admirably debunks colonial stereotypes, praises women's mastery of the house, and celebrates Irish artifacts over the English ones. Yet it must be noted that her transvaluated representations also contribute to reinforce and essentialize certain cultural formations such as the nationalist construction of women as primarily homemakers and child bearers, a trope that saw its apex after the Revival in Éamon de Valera's constitution.

For his own travel book, Synge would adopt a similar kind of transvaluation strategy, albeit with less patriotic and patronizing tones. For instance, *The Aran Islands* portrays the local farmers as industrious while working in the fields, shipping animals to the mainland, and thatching. He praises the islanders' everyday artifacts as unique and "artistic," and he magnifies their qualities in a hyperbolic way in lines such as the following: "The simplicity and unity of the dress increases in another way the local air of beauty" (*AI*, 14). Synge's descriptions of the people, however, are also tempered at times by a harsh realism, as in part 4 when he remarks, "Although these people are kindly towards each other and to their children, they have no feeling for the suffering of animals and little sympathy for pain when the person who feels it is not in danger. I have sometimes seen a girl writhing and howling with toothache while her mother sat at the other side of the fireplace pointing at her as if amused by the sight" (*AI*, 115). According to Oona Frawley, Synge's counterbalancing of celebrative views of Aran with a sharp, unadorned realism is the way in which he "displays a canny understanding of his own idealizations, and offers a commanding critique of not only his own text, but of the Revival itself and its nostalgias."[28] Unlike Banim's travelogue, Synge's Aran book does not merely antagonize English formations with

Irish cultural constructs and exempla; it complicates this transvaluation of aesthetic formations with a critical attitude.

This critical outlook is also evident in Synge's approach to another common trope in travel writing, which Edward Said registers in his seminal work *Orientalism* as "textual attitude": "to apply what one learns out of a book literally to reality."[29] Banim's articles about Aran offer, again, a useful starting point to look at this particular trope in an Irish context. In the second series of *Here and There through Ireland*, Banim immediately reads the Aran Islands as a quintessential embodiment of Robinson Crusoe's desert island and fantasizes parallels with Daniel Defoe's book: "From the day when I first read that book of books, 'Robinson Crusoe,' I had longed to taste life on an almost desert island—to taste a mitigated Robinson Crusoe life. . . . That is my idea of a genuine island, and that is what I know I could have in Arran, with besides, complete isolation and loneliness if I wanted them (i.e., was in bad temper), or again, plenty of human beings to associate with when in good humour."[30] Banim's personal fascination with Defoe's book has interesting thematic and theoretical underpinnings. According to Ian Watt, Crusoe has always embodied "a kind of culture-hero representing . . . the Rousseauistic creed of 'back to nature[,]' . . . the notion of the 'dignity of labor' . . . and the embodiment of economic individualism, . . . Weber's 'capitalist spirit.'"[31] For the same reasons, Defoe's novel has been traditionally associated also with discourses that legitimized imperial conquest and has been read as an apologia for colonialist enterprises such as slavery.[32] In Mary Banim's impressions of "an almost desert island" and her willingness to taste a "mitigated Robinson Crusoe's life," Aran, like Crusoe's island, seems to be there for the enjoyment (and exploitation) of the visitor and ready to accommodate her needs, expectations, and even her very moods. According to David Spurr, "if the news establishes a consumer's relation to events, travel writing may be said to establish a consumer's relation to entire cultures."[33] In Banim's account, this consumer's relation is further heightened by her rhetorical strategies, and the paralleling of herself with Robinson Crusoe suggests a hegemonic relationship between the gazer and the gazed upon.

Banim's mention of such a popular best seller as a substantial reason for her traveling to Aran can be read as an emblem of that "textual attitude" Said describes. According to Said, "textual attitude," or applying what one learns in a book to reality, generates a sense of familiarity and reassurance in the traveler, particularly when dealing with new, unknown, and perhaps frightening experiences; it also provides the traveler with a sense of success or, better, the "appearance of success," brought about when statements and descriptions read in texts find a real and physical occurrence that confirms the "truth" of what we had read. Ultimately, Said concludes, "such texts can create not only the knowledge but also the very reality they appear to describe."[34] Banim's "textual attitude," manifested in her recurring mentions of Defoe's book, *creates* her view of a supposedly desert island and a kind of paradise to be exploited by the tourist. Thus, her fascination with Robinson Crusoe and her presence on Aran remain a tokenistic strategy that reads Aran and its community from her one-dimensional vantage point, which ends up being an encounter with herself and her own bourgeois culture.

Another example of this "textual attitude" is evident in Arthur Symons's essay "The Isles of Aran," first published in the December 1896 issue of Symons's own periodical *The Savoy* and later collected in his book *Cities and Sea-coasts and Islands*. Symons traveled on the Aran Islands in 1895 with W. B. Yeats and Edward Martyn and lodged at the Atlantic Hotel. On their way to the islands, the artists read Emily Lawless's popular novel *Grania: The Story of an Island*, which had come out in 1893. Symons admits to reading only "what was needed" of *Grania* but to preferring an older seventeenth-century ethnographic account entitled *A Choreographical Description of West or H-Iar Connaught* (1684) by Roderick O'Flaherty, which combines geography with legends and lore. "Its quaint minute seventeenth-century prose," Symons writes, "told me more about what I was going to see than everything else that I read then or after on the subject of these islands."[35] Just like Banim, Symons finds exactly what O'Flaherty's accounts instructed him to find: barren landscapes, venerable antiquities, and curious folklore. Symons's account accordingly covers these topics in plenty of detail but does contain a significant change: as opposed to the more linear structure of O'Flaherty's scientific account, Symons opens his narrative with a scene that chronologically recalls the end of his trip— his return to Tyllira Castle, the home of his traveling companion Edward

Martyn. The same homecoming scene also concludes the article, therefore conferring to the account a kind of cyclical structure. This framing allows for the creation of his Aran experience as an oneiric one: "I seem to have stepped out of some strange, half magical, almost real dream."[36] Symons's Aran article can be categorized as what Carl Thompson terms the "more self-consciously 'literary' mode of travel writing," which emerged in the nineteenth century and often "claimed to capture impressionistically or poetically the 'spirit' of a place or culture, rather than offer a comprehensive, factual account of it."[37] The cyclical structure and the reference to a dreamlike experience are devices that enhance this self-conscious literariness. In Symons's account, the islands' characteristics of being "so far from civilization" and almost frozen in an undefined time heighten the artist's perception of a spiritual reawakening. Here is Symons after contemplating a liminal spot on the Aran coast:

> I have never realized less the slipping of sand through the hour-glass; I have never seemed to see with so remote an impartiality, as in the presence of brief and yet eternal things, the troubling and insignificant accidents of life. I have never believed less in the reality of the visible world, in the importance of all we are most serious about. One seems to wash off the dust of cities, the dust of beliefs, the dust of incredulities.[38]

Such passages clearly showcase Symons's symbolist depiction of the Aran Islands as a gateway for his spiritual illumination. In sum, in constructing these symbols mostly from textual models, his travelogue reveals more about his own culture and aesthetic aspirations than about the Aran culture per se. Even Symons's limited interactions with the locals, who tell him eerie stories, appear to be rather tokenistic and included in the article only to emphasize his own personal quest for a spiritual experience.

Synge's account is certainly not immune to the influence of previous models, nor is it exempt from a certain degree of "textual attitude." However, in *The Aran Islands* there is a more creative negotiation of influences and models, along with an awareness of the textual attitude's limiting effects. Several commentators have traced Synge's influences and inspirational templates for *The Aran Islands*—for instance, in the Breton ethnographies. Drawing on his diaries and notebooks, scholars have also documented what he was reading and all the books he brought to Aran.[39] Synge also read and notably dismissed Lawless's novel *Grania* owing to its supposed unfaithfulness to the real life of the islands (*CW*2, 102 n.). According to Tony Roche, moreover, another influential reading for Synge was the Irish mythic voyage tale *The Voyage of Bran*, to which *The Aran Islands* owes "a specific verbal indebtedness."[40] All these influences notwithstanding, Synge's travel book more subtly absorbs these textual models by negotiating his own experience and personal narrative in a dialogic fashion. Compared to Symons and Banim, Synge interacted with a larger number of people. Banim, for instance, admits that her planned rendezvous with a local Aran woman for a "lesson in the good old art of spinning"—an episode specifically immortalized in an illustration of the travelogue (figure 1)—was her only "opportunity of learning something of the island people."[41] In short, even if these models taught Synge what to see and how to see it to an extent, his account in several parts displays more forcefully the author's search for an alternative way of expressing the often conflictual "encounter between self and other" at the core of all travel writing,[42] as will become evident later in this chapter.

In the attempt to express this encounter, travel writers often implement strategies of othering, whereby cultural differences between the traveler and the local community are considerably heightened, often to the latter's disadvantage. In an Irish context, as Catherine Nash points out, the West of Ireland "functioned as a primitive other against which the superiority of the colonial power could be measured. Yet the West continued to function as internal 'other' through which to articulate differences, a difference valued in a national context."[43] In several accounts of the islands, a degree of fetishism, exoticism, and primitivism in the representation of the Aran culture is not uncommon. For example, in Symons's account the people of Aran are fetishized and represented as a sort of estranged monstrosity with zoomorphic features. In narrating his first encounter with a local beggar upon landing on Aran, Symons defines him as "a strange being . . . with a curiously beast-like stealthiness and animation; it was a crazy man, bare-footed and blear-eyed." This depiction seems to reinforce Symons's subsequent description of the Aran Islanders as "sturdily primitive."[44] Arguably, this bestialization of the islanders

1. Matilda E. Banim, *A Lesson in Spinning*, illustration in Mary Banim, *Here and There through Ireland*, series 2 (Dublin: Freeman's Journal, 1892). Image courtesy of the National Library of Ireland, Dublin.

is present even in a curious folk story that Symons gathers from a local inhabitant and that narrates the reversible metamorphosis of men into seals ("roons"), thus adding to the islands' mystical and surreal aura.[45] In contrast, Synge, when discussing his arrival scene and his first encounters with the local people, is struck in the first instance by the language they use and by the vitality of a group of youngsters. He concisely records his brief encounter with "an old half-blind man" who "spoke to me in Gaelic" (*AI*, 6). The portrayal of the old man is given a few paragraphs later, with empathy and without zoomorphic allusions: "As we talked he sat huddled together over the fire, shaking and blind, yet his face was indescribably pliant, lighting up with an ecstasy of humor when he told me anything that had a point of wit or malice, and growing sombre and desolate again when he spoke of religion or the fairies" (*AI*, 6).

The exoticization of the Aran inhabitants is a recurrent trope in other Revival travelogues, such as the essay "An Outpost of Ireland" by the

Anglo-Irish cousins Edith Somerville and Martin Ross, first published in the periodical press in 1895 and later included in their collection *Some Irish Yesterdays* (1906) with a number of watercolor illustrations. In the essay, the islanders are described as having "'a way of their own' . . . 'like the Indians'" and "an air of a foreign race and of an earlier century."[46] The comparison with the Indians, in particular, is a narrative detail that sets the scene for the authors' journey to Aran because the remark is reportedly made by the cousins' host in Galway. This repeated comment works as a refrain that allures the authors to travel to the islands and arguably contributes to the final impression of Aran as a place where a "foreign and tingling air" can be breathed.[47] Even if similar allusions can also be found in *The Aran Islands*—for example, "The red dresses of the women who cluster round the fire on their stools give a glow of almost Eastern richness" (*AI*, 6)—Synge's exoticization of the local inhabitants is counterbalanced by moments in which he attempts to voice the islanders' perception of him as "exotic" to them, "a waif among the people": "I can feel more with them than they can feel with me, and while I wander among them, they like me sometimes, and laugh at me sometimes, yet never know what I am doing" (*AI*, 66).

Synge's preoccupation with the indigenous culture of Aran has sometimes been dismissed because of his use of Orientalist and primitivist imagery. However, critics have also highlighted how his primitivism is a problematizing "discursive practice,"[48] critical of its own language and internal structures. Sinéad Garrigan Mattar, for instance, traces the features that inform Synge's primitivism back to his experience within the milieu of the Parisian academy and his studies of comparativist science. She argues that his academic and scientific knowledge contributed to the construction of a "dynamic primitivism" informed by naturalist Charles Darwin, Herbert Spencer, sociocultural evolutionists James Frazer and Alfred Nutt, and French celtologists Anatole Le Braz and Henri D'Arbois De Jubainville. This knowledge, moreover, enabled him to discover "the paradox of modernist primitivism," embodied in *The Aran Islands* by the tensions between his perception of himself in relation to the community and the community's perception of him. As Garrigan Mattar has it, "The narrative of *The Aran Islands* itself enacts a shift in attitude towards the islanders from a relationship based on a measure of sameness—of shared artistic and aristocratic values—to a relationship based on difference."[49] Synge's primitivist élan in *The Aran Islands*, therefore, is rationalized through a dialogic awareness of his position as an outsider of the community.

Another way in which Synge's account rationalizes his sympathy for the premodern is through pondering the coeval existence of both modern and seemingly outdated formations. One of the most famous episodes about the eruption of modernity in the supposedly unspoiled Aran territory happens in part 3, while Synge is observing a flock of sea birds fighting over an unidentified object. The writer suddenly realizes that the object in question in the playful pursuit is a shabby golf ball (*AI*, 126). The golf ball, a remnant of a typical late-nineteenth-century upper-class recreation,[50] uncannily draws attention to the fact that the Aran Islands were inscribed in a specific sociopolitical order with its related networks of tourism and leisure. In his reading of the episode, James F. Knapp also remarks that Synge's text displays an interest in relativizing dichotomies such as modernity and primitiveness, creating a sense of "dissonance that tends to undermine the absolute dominance of either."[51] Synge's critical primitivism can be understood further as an example of the "dissident potential" of *The Aran Islands*. Alan Sinfield, drawing from Louis Althusser's concept of ideology, elaborates a notion of "dissident potential" that "derives . . . from conflict and contradiction that the social order inevitably produces within itself, even if it attempts to sustain itself." He explains that literary texts "address controversial aspects of our ideological formations" and that the "dissident" text "may derive its leverage, its purchase, precisely from its partial implication with the dominant[,] . . . embarrass[ing] the dominant by appropriating its concepts and imagery."[52] In an analogous way, *The Aran Islands* borrows from a primitivist discourse in order to point out the inconsistencies and limitations of that representational model. Synge challenges certain primitivist attitudes by querying his position as an interloper among the local community and by constantly highlighting the coeval existence of the outside world along with the interconnection between Aran and external places such as America, England, Europe, and the mainland.

## "Vagaries of Fashion" on the Aran Islands: Contact Perspective

As mentioned at the beginning of this chapter, during the nationalist ferment of fin-de-siècle Ireland, the Aran Islands had become a Revival "contact zone," a site visited by numerous writers and activists affiliated with revivalist networks. These Revival travel writers often expressed in their accounts conflicting notions of Irishness and revivalism. Synge's travel book *The Aran Islands*, though fully enmeshed in these revivalist dynamics, is an innovative travelogue that also queries some of the absolute revivalist stances evident in previous Irish travelogues. As this section sets out to demonstrate, Synge adopts a "contact perspective" that reflects on his own position as a participant-observer in a dialogic way. Pratt's coinage of the expression *contact zone* borrows the term *contact* from its use within linguistics, wherein contact languages are defined as "improvised languages that develop among speakers of different native languages who need to communicate with each other consistently, usually in the context of trade." She applies this notion of contact language to places, "contact zones," which essentially represent the colonial frontier. In seeking to retrieve the complexity and to problematize the representation of places of colonial encounters as well as to destabilize the hegemonic/Eurocentric twist implied in the expression "colonial frontier," whereby "the frontier is a frontier only in respect to Europe," Pratt talks about the need to develop a "contact perspective"—that is, a representational strategy "emphasizing how subjects are constituted in and by their relations to each other." This perspective, Pratt continues, "treats the relations among colonizers and colonized, or travelers and travelees not in terms of separateness and apartheid, but in terms of co-presence, interaction, interlocking understandings and practices, often within radically asymmetrical relations of power."[53]

Pratt's theorizing is particularly useful to a reading of Synge's Aran prose and *The Aran Islands'* transnational and dialogic trajectories. Unlike much travel literature about the islands that appeared during the Revival, Synge's travel text stresses the clashing and colliding nature of different social, economic, and cultural formations that were at stake on Aran at the turn of the twentieth century, therefore adopting a representational strategy very similar to Pratt's idea of a "contact perspective." Synge's contact perspective accounts for the dissonant "critical primitivism" of *The Aran Islands* and for his attempts not simply to transvaluate cultural constructs but to ponder their essentialism.

Through this contact perspective, Synge provides a glimpse of the Aran Islands as a site where different encounters were also taking place in a nationalist and revivalist sense, where modernizing and conservationist forces underpinning various revivalist projects interacted. In addition to the episode about an eviction,[54] whose emphasis on hostile and unequal contacts is made clear, Synge's text highlights also other cultural interactions between the local community and numerous visitors to the islands, including nationalist activists, modern urban tourists, antiquarians and academics from the Continent, diasporic subjects returning from America, and migrant workers. One of the contact moments par excellence in *The Aran Islands* is described in part 3 when a foreign peddler lands on Aran to sell modern, mass-produced artifacts:

> When the curaghs [canvas canoes] came back—one of them towing a large kitchen table that stood itself up on the waves and then turned somersaults in an extraordinary manner—word went round that the ceannaí (pedlar) was arriving. He opened his wares on the slip as soon as he landed, and sold a quantity of cheap knives and jewellery to the girls and the younger women. He spoke no Irish, and the bargaining gave immense amusement to the crowd that collected round him. I was surprised to notice that several women who professed to know no English could make themselves understood without difficulty when it pleased them. "The rings is too dear at you, sir," said one girl using the Gaelic construction; "let you put less money on them and all the girls will be buying." After the jewellery he displayed some cheap religious pictures—abominable olcographs—but I did not see many buyers. I am told that most of the pedlars who come here are Germans or Poles, but I did not have occasion to speak with this man by himself. (*AI*, 91)

Here, Synge is keen on emphasizing how language barriers and rooted linguistic identities are far from immovable but rather soon to crumble and transform themselves by contingent necessity. In this emblematic episode, not only do we have an exchange—which is linguistic in parts—between two different cultural formations, but we also see a "speaking through" of these formations, a sublimation of differences exemplified in the moment when the women "could make themselves understood." This is indeed a rich passage that problematizes notions of a pristine Irishness by implying a bilateral correspondence between supposedly separate cultural realities. In their linguistic interaction, albeit momentarily, these differences result in a new hybrid formation. This attention to cultural and linguistic contacts is an instance of Synge's contact perspective, which enables a dialogic way of representation profoundly transformative of previous modes of representation.

Synge's attention to contact moments and the ensuing tensions are best understood if analyzed comparatively with other Irish travelogues of the time. Although some of these Irish writers were arguably motivated by a common impetus to revive a distinct Irish culture, their travel writing often mirrors some of the conflicts inherent in revivalist organizations. Moreover, some of these texts often have contrasting ways of dealing with disruptive elements and formations that are dissonant with a singular notion of Irishness. In her popular travelogue *Here and There through Ireland*, Mary Banim comments on the Aran women's costumes by providing a curious anecdote about a "dress-improver" (bustle), or, as she describes it, "a fashionable item of my travelling suit." At first, she remarks about the unsuitability of dress-improvers on Aran because during her rambles she has to squeeze through small loopholes in the stone walls. Banim further explains that as she "was going amongst simple, innocent, uncorrupted young island maidens," she asked herself, "Was I to bring to their shores such a horrible corrupter of grace and simplicity into the midst of such pastoral innocence of all the vagaries of fashion? Never." To her incredulity and shock because she thought the Aran women did not use dress-improvers, while she is staying "in the primitive (very primitive) hotel in Aran," she discovers that a female costume left there had "the unmistakable bulge out" in the skirt and "the well-known rows that marked the bars of steel!" The anecdote climaxes when Banim performs a symbolic gesture of rebellion: she pulls from the folds of her dress the bars of steel in her dress-improver and locks them into a trunk, experiencing a sense of renewed freedom.[55] From a documentary perspective, like the golf-ball episode in Synge, this contact moment testifies to the existence of tradition ("primitiveness" in Banim's acceptation) and modernity as coeval and provides a glimpse of a more historicized Aran, a place incorporated in a specific historical and economic system of commodity production and circulation that reaches globally.[56] Yet this portrayal of Aran as inserted in and connected to a transnational modernity is not Banim's main concern in *Here and There through Ireland*: she reacts to the intrusion of the dress-improver she finds in her room with an idealistic rejection of this object that epitomizes modernity, adding indignantly that she thought about "using my return ticket and going straight back to Galway."[57] Although Banim constructs the episode with a tone of ironic self-mockery that may suggest a sort of disenchantment and relativizing attitude toward rigid taxonomies, and even though she is elsewhere a sympathetic observer of rural life, this attitude of denial toward modern intrusions into her idea of Aran as "charming Robinson Crusoe's unsophisticatedness"[58] nonetheless asserts her positioning of herself as consumer and of Aran as tourist commodity.

Remarks on the local Aran clothing appear also in "An Outpost of Ireland" by Somerville and Ross. With regard to the traditional pampooties worn by men, they observe how the "effeminacy" of the pampooties is tempered by the men's "singularly emphatic tread." They subsequently describe one of the women's homespun skirts as "excessively short," further remarking how the woman's "stride showed to admiration the grey woolen ankles under her short skirt."[59] The remark on the effeminacy of the men's pampooties and the repeated emphasis on the shortness of the women's skirts in part reflect a cultural bias on the authors' part, who adopt a traditional view on gender and a standard of fashion informed by their higher social class. Synge, in contrast, remarks on the different length of the women's skirt more factually by simply pointing out how "their skirts do not come much below the knee, and show their powerful legs in their heavy indigo stockings" (*AI*, 14). Even if he indulges in Orientalist descriptions of the women's colorful outfits, his text strikes a better balance between celebratory pictorial hyperboles and a more empirical style of reporting that aims at contextualizing and explaining details more thoroughly. For example, when Synge describes the islanders' clothing in part 1, he makes clear from the beginning that their picturesque costumes are linked to their material conditions of production—for example, he notes that "as flannel is cheap—the women spin the yarn from the wool of their own sheep, and it is then woven by a weaver in Kilronan for fourpence a yard—the men seem to wear an indefinite number of waistcoats and woolen drawers one over the other. They are usually surprised at the lightness of my own dress, and one old man I spoke to for a minute on the pier, when I came ashore, asked me if I was not cold with 'my little clothes'" (*AI*, 14). Here, unlike Somerville and Ross, who reinforce their own class bias in their description of the women's skirts, Synge deals with the issue of different clothing by speculating on the possible reasons behind such difference and by incorporating the perspectives of both the observer and the observed.

Ten years after Mary Banim, with the advent of the Gaelic League the scenario on Aran seems somehow to have been altered. In 1902, Gaelic League activist and first Irish-language female novelist Agnes O'Farrelly (Úna Ní Fhaircheallaigh) published *Smaointe ar Árainn* (*Thoughts on Aran*) in several installments in *An Claidheamh Soluis* (The Sword of Light), the Gaelic League periodical. Her travelogue was inspired by another Irish-language series about the islands compiled by Reverend Eugene O'Growney for the periodical *Irisleabhar na Gaeilge* (Gaelic Journal) in 1889.[60] O'Farrelly had earned a "master's degree in the Irish language from the Royal University," and her writings participated in the league's efforts to create Irish-language reading material.[61] In *Smaointe ar Árainn*, O'Farrelly provides a different perspective on the local women's costumes. She describes a scene with a group of girls heading to the *feis* (Irish cultural festival); their eyes "are as blue as the summer sky, and their cheeks are the color of health, the 'color of berries' according to the poet." After this bucolic image, O'Farrelly strategically digresses to point out that one of these girls had just got back from America, bringing "a big box of clothes with her." However, O'Farrelly notes that on the day of the traditional *feis*, in an Aran co-opted by the Revival, the girl "is now wearing a red coat, just like the other girls are wearing and she speaks Irish as well as any of them."[62] She also adds an ethnographic note, which further highlights the incorruptibility of Inis Meáin traditions:

> Ní mheasann muintir Inis Meáin gur oiriúnach an rud é éadaí a bhaineas le háiteanna eile a bheith á gcaitheamh acu. "Ní ceart ná feiliúnach an rud é hata a bheith ar aon chailín san oileán seo," a deirtí liom go minic; agus chualas fear óg ag rá aon uair amháin nach bpósfadh sé cailín as Inis Meáin dá bhfeicfeadh sé hata uirthi ar nós na gcoimhthíoch, "agus í ag cur maige uirthi féin."

> The people of Inis Meáin do not believe that it is proper for people to wear clothes from other places. "It is neither right nor suitable for any girl of the island to wear a hat," I was often told; and I heard a young man say once that he would not marry a girl from Inis Meáin if he saw her wearing a hat after the manner of foreigners "and swaggering around."[63]

Thus, O'Farrelly's juxtaposition of the American clothes and the local ones aims strategically at highlighting the rootedness of local traditions, the "foreign" influences notwithstanding. It reinforces the construction of Aran as a bulwark of a self-conscious Irishness, defended with pride and loyalty by its own "indigenous" people. This tactic participates in O'Farrelly's Gaelic League propagandist mission. Notably, this fashioning of Aran as distinctively Irish is shared also by Gaelic Leaguer and revolutionary Patrick (Pádraic) Pearse. In comparing Synge's and Pearse's contrasting approach to folklore, Anne Markey has observed that, unlike Synge's "increasingly sympathetic, impartial, and comprehensive" approach to Irish folklore, "Pearse's accounts of Gaeltacht life reveal a selective interest in Irish folklore that reflects a reluctance to acknowledge those aspects of popular tradition that did not sit well with his idealized image of Ireland as a divinely sanctioned ancient nation capable of living up to the past glory in the modern world."[64] In highlighting the selection of the local clothes over the imported foreign ones, O'Farrelly's account shares a similar "selective" attitude in dealing with folklore—privileging cultural formations that align with the Gaelic League's more conservationist priorities.

In *The Aran Islands*, a well-known episode in part 3 depicts Synge's exchange with a boy who is substituting for Michael, Synge's local Irish teacher on the island. Synge recounts how they "nearly quarreled because he wanted me to take his photograph in his Sunday clothes from Galway, instead of his native homespuns that become him far better, though he does not like them as they seem to connect him with the primitive life of the island" (*AI*, 85). The boy's reaction suggests the opposite sentiment to that demonstrated in O'Farrelly's description of the islanders' pride in wearing their traditional clothes. Justin Carville has read this episode as Synge's deployment of photography to reinforce his ethnographic authority. He argues that "in [Synge's] social relations with the indigenous population, photography is deployed as a coercive device, a means of engaging with the Aran islanders on his own terms."[65] However, this reading downplays some aspects of the whole passage. For instance, Carville concentrates only on the exchange about photographic representation but does not comment on the broader context in which this exchange takes place. This exchange about photography comes at the end of a more complex scheme of interaction and cultural exchange between Synge and the boy dealing not only with photography but also with language and local culture. This interaction epitomizes Synge's contact perspective in *The Aran Islands* as it highlights the simultaneous existence of tradition and modernity as well as the clashes deriving from them.

Through this episode, Synge questions essentialist ideas about culture and the constructedness of notions such as tradition and modernity. In the text, the boy, who has been summoned to substitute for Michael in "schooling" Synge, reads Irish to him every afternoon. This contact gives Synge the occasion to reflect on how oral practices have been substituted by a kind of literacy that has not developed at a local level but whose methods (and the same books the boy reads to Synge) are imported from Dublin by the Gaelic League educational activists: "A few years ago this predisposition for intellectual things [the boy enjoys reading to Synge] would have made him sit with old people and learn their stories, but now boys like him turn to books and to papers in Irish that are sent them from Dublin" (*AI*, 84). Such passages ponder how the sense of tradition and culture are not immanent phenomena but are rather inscribed in a specific temporality and subject to historical change; in the case of the Aran Islands, moreover, they are partly of recent genesis. The pride of the islanders for their own language and culture, as Synge suggests, has been instilled by the recent activism of organizations such as the Gaelic League. In the passage, Synge consciously embodies two roles: an agent of change and modernization—with his camera, tricks, social status—and at the same time a salvaging agent, photographing the boy in his traditional homespun and documenting the local naming traditions later on in the passage. At the beginning of the passage, Synge acts like a sort of trickster and challenges the boy's sense of tradition, provoking in him a reaction of indignation "if I say that he knows English better than Irish" (*AI*, 84). In opposition to that, at the end of their exchange (the incident about photographic representation) it becomes clear that the same sense of tradition the boy clings to with such pride is questioned by the boy's own refusal to be photographed in his traditional homespun in favor of imported modern clothes. Hence, I contend that in Synge's interaction with the boy, his priority is not simply to prove and impose his own sense of modernity,[66] but rather to expose, in a dialogic mode, the way tradition and modernity both feed into each other and clash with one another. This is indeed a significant example of Synge's contact strategy in *The Aran Islands*, whereby the controversial and contradictory cultural collisions are played out not as a footnote but as a specific interest of his text.

Previous typescript drafts of this particular passage further highlight Synge's interest in investigating contacts between opposing mindsets and formations. In MS 4344, folio 517, after mentioning the quarrel, Synge writes: "The intellect [*sic*] activity seems to be always attuned with an effort to free themselves [from] what they think primitive in their island."[67] In a subsequent draft, Synge changes the sentence again: "He is self-consciously ambitious to free himself from the local distinction of the islands, as well as from its weakness."[68] These omitted sentences testify to Synge's awareness that the distinctive culture of the Aran Islands is a complex phenomenon that is often bound up with dire material conditions such as lack of opportunity and poverty. Far from the one-dimensional representations of Irish traditions typically aggrandized in Revival travel writing, Synge's prose subtly attempts a more complex interpretation not only from the part of the observer but also from the part of the observed. As

Gregory Castle concludes at the end of his investigation of *The Aran Islands* and ethnography,

> By assimilating his own subjective responses to the Aran Islands and their inhabitants into the discursive space of ethnography, by allowing the contradictions and tensions of ethnographic discourse to unfold in a dialogic play of voices and cultural authorities, Synge calls into question the most basic assumption of cultural representation: that there is a singular and essential "culture" and that it can be represented and preserved—in a word redeemed—by a discourse essentially foreign to its participants.[69]

Thus, despite the power imbalance between the ethnographer and the ethnographically observed, Synge's inclusion of the cultural clashes deriving from his fieldwork is part of his contact strategy. Differently from the other travel writing discussed in this chapter, Synge's text does not simply reject formations that do not conform to his specific idea of Irishness but rather initiates a more subtle negotiation. His own position as participant-observer problematizes the collocation of modernity and primitiveness as separate and isolated temporal spheres, and his immersion in the Aran culture highlights convergences between the two spheres in a dialogic way—in conversation. As Veerendra Lele argues in an article that focuses on the linguistic issue on Aran, Synge "develops a novel ethnographic disposition, a dialogic disposition" whereby "self [becomes] a dialogic practice."[70]

Synge's contact perspective is evident also in his treatment of other linguistic issues on the Aran Islands. His text displays more forcefully than other contemporaneous travel writing a canny awareness of the contradictions inherent in the Irish-language movement. Synge, it must be noted, shared with Gaelic Leaguers a genuine love for the language, such as when he was moved to tears upon hearing his guide's "exquisite purity of intonation" when reciting Gaelic poetry, even though he "understood but little of the meaning" (*AI*, 10). More importantly, on Inis Meáin he stayed at the same cottage where many other revivalists and scholars had lodged and practiced their Irish.[71] The cottage was a perfect example of what Michael Cronin calls "rambling houses, . . . where neighbors would come together and swap stories or retail the latest news. Traveling storytellers were also welcomed . . . [as] the travelers' tales were their passport to hospitality."[72] Despite this common ground, Synge's work does not share hyperbolic and rhetorical endorsements that are common in many leaguers' writing. For example, in an address at the inauguration of the first League branch on Inishmore in 1898, Pearse advocated for bilingualism as an empowering tool for the islanders, but he also tried to instill a shared sense of pride in making Irish the language of the hearth.[73] Pearse's strategic bilingualism, as Mary Burke has observed, is informed, to an extent, by evolutionary theory, which also illuminates Synge's attitude toward the Irish language: "Pearse . . . utilizes botanical vocabulary in the manner of Synge when conceding that English and Irish would eventually have to co-exist peacefully."[74] Yet Pearse and Synge would take different perspectives on the issue, despite sharing this common ground. Elsewhere in the periodical *Fáinne an Lae*, Pearse constructs the Irish language as associated with a sort of childlike innocence: "I often spoke to little boys and girls who hadn't a word of English. They only had Irish. I think there is no sound to be heard on the face of the earth as sweet as the Irish language coming from a child's mouth. Aren't they lovely, those children, God bless them?"[75]

Similarly, in her travelogue O'Farrelly constructs the Aran Islands as a place that sparks her nationalist naturalization into an Irish speaker. Upon hearing Gaelic for the first time from native speakers in Galway and despite not understanding it properly, she describes its sound as soothing as wine or water. Subsequently, in her hosts' cottage kitchen, she has a kind of linguistic revelation:

> Bíodh nár thuigeas a raibh á rá acu, b'amhlaidh gur airíos gurbh í an Ghaeilge an teanga ba dhual dom. D'airíos, mar a déarfá, macalla dá fuaimeanna binne i mo chroí cheana, agus níl Éireannach beo faoi láthair nach mbeadh an scéal céanna aige.

> Even though I did not understand all that they said, I actually felt that Irish was my natural language. I felt, as they say, the echo of its sweet sounds in my heart already, and there is not a living Irish person now who would not feel the same.[76]

O'Farrelly's epiphanic naturalization into an Irish speaker engages in the broader Gaelic League project of naturalization of other precolonial traditions, such as its recuperation of older forms of entertainment such as the *feis*. This ultimately artificial "staging of tradition," as Nic Congáil maintains, was undertaken in order to "assert the authenticity of the ancient Gaelic culture" and possessed a "blatantly propagandist function."[77]

In contrast, Synge does not refer to Irish as his native tongue, despite his love and knowledge of Gaelic and his growing mastery of it through immersion on Aran. He spotted the contradictions of the language movement in Ireland but was also aware of its potential to instill a sense of pride and national self-determination in the people.[78] In *The Aran Islands*, he records the islanders' own opinions about the Irish language and their reactions to the language revival on the islands. In part 3, he reports an old man's remarks about his faith in the survival of Irish by virtue of the connections between Irish, the natural environment, and the local community: "[Irish] can never die out, because there's no family in the place can live without a bit of a field for potatoes, and they have only the Irish words for all they do in the fields! They sail their new boats—their hookers—in English, but they sail a curagh oftener in Irish, and in the fields they have the Irish alone" (*AI*, 101). On this specific argument, Alan Titley remarks that although it is interesting, it is "hardly one that sociolinguists would easily accede to."[79] However, the fact that Synge reports the argument is noteworthy because it is made not by an academic but by a local seafaring man. This example shows the way in which Synge constructs his account in a polyphonic way—letting the Irish-speaking islanders voice their own concerns and beliefs about their own native tongue. In the same exchange, Synge voices also the old man's theories about Archbishop John MacHale's translation into Irish of Thomas Moore's collection of airs *Irish Melodies*. The old man also provided his own versions of the melodies. Synge is struck by the lucidity of the old man's criticism grounded in linguistic evidence and is impressed by the vigor of the "poor sailor and night-watchman" in criticizing "an eminent dignitary and scholar" (*AI*, 101). The remark about the different social classes of the seafarer and the scholar draws attention to the subversive quality of this islander's temperament in delegitimizing received notions about his own culture superimposed by specific power structures such as the church and the academy. Thus, Synge's reporting of the old man's remarks also suggests that alternative literacy practices of learning and argumentation are striving to assert their legitimacy. In the same excerpt, Synge also interrogates the islanders about the work of the Gaelic League and reports two contrasting opinions about it—one criticizing "their organizers and their secretaries, and their meetings and their speechifyings, and start a branch of it, and teach a power of Irish for five weeks and a half!"; the other in favor of the League's work as a defense against the growing presence of English (*AI*, 102). In *The Aran Islands*, Synge's contact angle and his polyphonic record of local linguistic phenomena and literacy practices contribute to shaping a different sense of naturalization of the Irish language that stands in opposition to the romanticized, artificial, and epiphanic effect sought after, for instance, by O'Farrelly. Synge's concern for the precarious future of the Irish language is shared with the speakers' own concerns and views about it and about the changes brought along by the Gaelic League activity. These dialogic and polyphonic features of the text transform *The Aran Islands* into a "narrative of cultural remembrance,"[80] making the Irish-speaking peasants participants in telling their story.

In *The Aran Islands*, Synge is very much concerned about reporting moments when the marginal culture and the dominant culture—in David Lloyd's terms—collide. This collision embraces in a self-reflexive way the framework of cultural production, as is evident in the example of Synge's Irish lessons discussed earlier. Throughout *The Aran Islands*, Synge shows awareness of the processes that underpin cultural formations. Another emblematic scene occurs in part 1, when Synge meets his first storyteller and on his last day on Inishmore visits "the antiquities that abound in the west or north-west of the island" (*AI*, 10). Synge is with Old Máirtín, his blind guide who has accompanied him on many other tours around the island and who has told him stories of the fairies. From the very beginning, Synge is made aware of his own intruding presence by a group of girls "who smiled at our fellowship" (*AI*, 10). His host describes the same fellowship in this way: "Old Máirtín says we are like the cuckoo with its pipit" (*AI*, 10). The expression probably refers to the close dependence between two things or persons—in this case, presumably the blind man's dependence on Synge to walk around the island. However, we can also read the relationship of dependence in opposite terms—that is, Synge's own dependence on the blind man to learn about the island. Old Máirtín's comment to Synge is not expanded or further developed. However, this uncanny ambiguity resonates and can be taken to signify not only the "contemporaneity of marginal and dominant forms," as Lloyd puts it,[81] but also the parasitical relationship between Synge and his storytellers, which hints at the seizure of the Aran culture by antiquarians, ethnographers, revivalists, and tourists. As Declan Kiberd observes, "All culture is parasitic: what lives feeds off what dies and feeds without scruple. Synge's was in truth a carrion vision, but he was always critically aware of its costs."[82] If we embrace Diarmuid Ó Giolláin's reading of Antonio Gramsci's remarks about folklore as "part of the culture of subaltern groups,"[83] in *The Aran Islands* we are immediately confronted with the problem of the representation and the rewriting of folk culture as subaltern to the mainstream. In part 1, when Old Máirtín tells Synge about all the antiquarians and historians he had interacted with, he narrates with fondness the case of "Mr Curtin of America . . . who had brought out a volume of his Aran stories in America, and made five hundred pounds by the sale of them" (*AI*, 6). Mr. Curtin's reappropriation without official recognition and the emphasis on the material gain seem to stand at the beginning of Synge's book as a warning against parasitical practices. As Kiberd maintains, "If Synge's art were simply an analysis of the relation between barbarism and culture in Ireland, it would merit our respect: but it gains an added depth by serving also as an example of that relation."[84] Accordingly, *The Aran Islands* not only tackles the relation between tradition and modernity, reflecting a contact perspective, but also, in a way that can be defined as metacultural, is constructed to be an instance of the parasitic nature of cultural processes. In discussing Synge's relationship with authenticity and the regional, Patrick Lonergan notes how Synge and islander Pat Dirane in *The Aran Islands* construct their authenticity as storytellers in similar ways, even though "Synge is also keen on drawing attention to the artificiality of his [own] work."[85]

As is well known, despite Synge's dialogism and empathetic approach to the writing of culture, the process of assembling material for

the book did not happen without controversy. One of the first commentators on Synge's work, Maurice Bourgeois, states that initially "'Michael'
had a grudge against Synge for having quoted *in extenso* the letters
which he had addressed to him," but that he forgave Synge afterward.[86]
Kiberd further points out that "Synge was anxious to patch up his quarrel with Martin McDonagh (the real name of "Michael," Synge's Irish
teacher on the islands) and felt genuinely humiliated by his own insensi-
tivity."[87] Despite these inevitable clashes, in some respects Synge's travel
writing is committed to implementing a number of empathic strategies,
such as the dialogic and polyphonic approach discussed in this chapter.[88] Moreover, in *The Aran Islands* we may read Synge's precision in the
transcription of folktales as an additional empathic gesture toward the
people who shared their knowledge and art with him. On his skills as
folklorist, Eilís Ní Dhuibhne remarks that Synge was an excellent field-
worker who transcribed Pat Dirane's story of the unfaithful wife (*AI*,
26) very accurately and possessed an "exceptional sensitivity to folklore
and an understanding of its character and functions."[89] Despite the problematic nature of Synge's ethnographic work on the Aran Islands and
the tensions ensuing from the writing and rewriting of culture, Synge's
book, unlike previous travel writing compiled by Revival travel writers,
displays a more cogent awareness of the processes underpinning these
cultural translations.

Castle's assessment of *The Aran Islands* posits that the book occupies
a sort of middle ground between "revisionist anthropology . . . and . . .
anthropological modernism that exploits the constitutive tension between
tradition and modernity."[90] Like Synge's plays, which have often been
defined as protomodernist for their iconoclasm and critique of modernization,[91] his travel book can be considered an instance of early modernist
travel writing along the lines of seminal work by English writers such as
D. H. Lawrence (*The Sea and Sardinia*, 1921) and W. H. Auden and Louis
MacNeice (*Letters from Iceland*, 1936). Tim Youngs notes that

> much modernist travel writing is self-conscious about its own conven-
> tions. It experiments with point of view, invites critical attention to its
> narrator, examines the relationship between observer and observed,

questions the location and use of power, parodies its progenitors, and wonders about its own function. All of these features have the potential to undermine the authority of the traveler and of the travel book. The potential is not always realized, but it is present, and by being present goes some way to fulfilling it.[92]

All of these characteristics are equally defining features of *The Aran Islands*, as I have shown in this chapter.

The modernist sensibility of *The Aran Islands* is also evident through the way its contact perspective makes the text transcend the often closed boundaries of regionalist writing, reaching to global trajectories and networks of commerce and cultural production. This characteristic aligns with many of the concerns of "regional modernisms" theorized recently by Neal Alexander and James Moran, among others. Alexander and Moran contest the grand narrative of modernism's internationalist supraspace by drawing attention to "regional and local attachments that provide contexts for modernist experimentation"; they argue that regional modernisms are "rarely bound to any one place exclusively" but rather "shuttle restlessly between multiple and overlapping spatial frames: local, regional, national, and international."[93] By showing through a contact perspective how the local culture of the Aran Islands is woven into complex national and international relations of travel and material production, and by chronicling his own position and displacement in relation to these local and international attachments, Synge created a text that can be read as an instance of that "regional modernism," simultaneously drawing on a specific locale and transcending it.

## J. M. Synge and Revivalist Photography

Synge's annual visits to the Aran Islands began in 1898 and lasted until 1902. His travelogue *The Aran Islands* had a long gestation, with Synge struggling to find a publisher for several years until Maunsel and Elkin Mathews finally printed it in 1907. In the interim, as numerous drafts and typescripts testify,[94] he was constantly reworking sections and published a few excerpts in periodicals. For example, in November 1898 "A Story from Inishmaan" was published in the *New Ireland Review*; "The Last

Fortress of the Celt" appeared in the Irish American monthly *The Gael* in April 1901; "A Dream on Inishmaan" featured in the little magazine *The Green Sheaf* in 1903 and in *The Gael* in 1904; and "An Impression of Aran" was printed in the *Manchester Guardian* on January 24, 1905. As is well documented, Synge's experience of the Aran Islands is also recorded visually in photographs he took with a handheld Klito camera during his stay. However, in 1907, when *The Aran Islands* was finally published, the photographs were not included. Drawings by Jack B. Yeats inspired by Synge's snapshots were chosen instead. Synge took care to personally send his photographs to the painter in 1906, even writing captions on the back of some of them so that Yeats could make the drawings.[95] Yeats's pen-and-ink illustrations for Synge's travel book contributed to the creation of a distinctive and aesthetically pleasing Irish book artifact, certainly in line with Maunsel's commitment "to support the revivalist impulse"[96] and to emulate models of quality printing and design such as those embodied by the Arts and Crafts movement. Hence, most of Synge's Aran photographs never appeared in print during Synge's lifetime,[97] with the exception of four photographs that accompanied the article "The Last Fortress of the Celt" in the April 1901 issue of *The Gael*.

The publication context of these four snapshots deserves some attention. As Nicholas Grene notes, *The Gael* was a periodical of clear nationalist sympathies.[98] In the article "The Last Fortress of the Celt," Synge takes an ethnographic approach, recording local customs and attempting participatory techniques of fieldwork observation that will become one of the landmarks of *The Aran Islands*. He highlights the contemporaneous existence of the world outside the islands and the islands' connections with it, such as the impact of America on the Aran economy as well as the islanders' own idea of America (*TI*, 12). However, in the article Synge displays primarily an academic interest—a reflection of what he had assimilated in Paris while studying comparativist folklore and mythology at the Sorbonne—and some of his remarks (subsequently omitted in *The Aran Islands*) overtly borrow from comparativist and anthropological discourses about race types: "The faces of the men were somewhat unlike the Irish type, and showed traces of the Pre-Celtic blood, which has lingered in the west of Europe, while among the women were some curiously Mongolian features rather resembling the Bigoudennes of the south coast of Brittany" (*TI*, 12).

If compared to other topographical articles published in *The Gael*, "The Last Fortress of the Celt" arguably lacks a more overt cultural-nationalist agenda. The photographs published with the article are captioned "photo by Synge, Paris" (*TI*, 13, 14, 16, 18) and work well as a visual compendium to his scientific observations for their portrayal of island occupations and objects. In the article, because of the documentary approach in illustrating the Aran customs and the lack of a stronger autobiographic impulse, the Synge from Paris could have been mistaken for a foreign academic. Despite the text's more scientific approach, Synge's photographs are not directly or methodologically linked with late-nineteenth-century and early-twentieth-century scientific photography, unlike the anthropometric photography of racial types featured in Alfred Cort Haddon and Charles Browne's ethnographic survey of the Aran Islands in 1893.[99] Rather, despite the article's ethnographic tone and subject matter, Synge's amateur photographs align more with *The Gael*'s interest in popularizing images of rural Ireland. Photographic series were published quite often in the periodical: in the December 1903 issue, an article by John J. Burke featured two photographs of the Claddagh—its title, "A Stronghold of the Gael," echoing Synge's title, "The Last Fortress of the Celt." The opening of Burke's piece identifies the Claddagh as a place of interest "to the folklore seeker and to those who desire to become acquainted with a remaining remnant of our people who cling to the traditions of the past."[100] This remark is reminiscent of the ending in Synge's piece, where he extends the same idea of "remaining remnants" from a merely Irish context to a global context: "It is vain to seek for a people like this in civilization; the type is disappearing from Ireland and not from Ireland only but from the world" (*TI*, 21).

As mentioned earlier, Synge's Irish identity seems to be subsumed by the captions signed "Photos by Synge, Paris." In addition to indicating Synge's possible location when later handling the photographs, the Parisian location also resonates as a kind of self-fashioning of Synge as a foreign scholar. In the Jack B. Yeats Archive at the National Gallery of Ireland in Dublin, among the photographs of Aran that Synge gave Yeats

2. J. M. Synge, photograph of people waiting for the steamer on Kilronan Pier, Aran Islands, c. 1900. Y1/JY/14/4, Parcel 38, Jack B. Yeats Archive, National Gallery of Ireland. Image courtesy of the Board of Trinity College Dublin.

to complete the pen-and-ink drawings for the book, there are two copies of the same snapshot representing a group of women waiting for the steamer at Kilronan pier (figure 2).

On the back of one of these two photographs, Synge has handwritten the caption "On the Pier—Kilronan . . . Synge Paris." This could be one of the copies of the photograph that Synge had intended to send to *The Gael* but that ultimately did not make it into print (or to the editorial board at *The Gael*). *The Gael* published four other snapshots, one depicting women around a spinning wheel ("Spinning Girls"), two capturing men with *curraghs* ("Launching the Curraghs" and "The Fishermen's Return"), and the last showing a man and a boy posing beside a stone wall with a horse and captioned "Going for Turf." It seems clear from looking at similar articles in the periodical that these photographs were perhaps accepted for publication in part because they could be easily framed in the cultural-nationalist slant of the periodical in their visualization of everyday moments of peasant life praised as the core of an Irish national identity during the Revival. To an extent, such images and the nostalgic headline fit in better with the periodical's philosophy. If we also consider the article mentioned earlier on the vanishing Claddagh in Galway, Synge's photographs can be labeled a kind of "salvage photography,"[101] a specific use of photography in ethnographic study aimed at visually preserving ethnographic knowledge that is on the verge of extinction.[102] Despite Synge's scholarly tone in the piece, the photographs endorse, in their ethnographic subject and in their complicity with discourses of "salvage photography," *The Gael*'s reviving mission very effectively.

These reflections on Synge's article and the photographs that accompany it draw attention to the importance of reading the context for Synge's photographs and photographic practice in Ireland at the turn of the twentieth century. As Edward Chandler explores in *Photography in Ireland*, in the second half of the nineteenth century photography took over the British Isles and was then widely practiced by the "gentlemen amateurs" coming from the upper classes.[103] In the 1880s, after the invention of dry plates, portable cameras, and various technical simplifications, many amateur photographers started to emerge also from the middle classes.[104] Carville further notes that toward the end of the nineteenth century "the cultural hegemony of amateur photography began to shift towards the urban middle class."[105] Irish playwright and critic George Bernard Shaw is perhaps the quintessential amateur photographer who also wrote about photography in various outlets. He did not own a Kodak camera until 1898, when he was forty-two, but had been interested in the medium from the late 1870s.[106] An omnivorous photographer, he took, among others, pictures of Irish landscapes and of people and fellow intellectuals he knew; he also made a few photographic self-portraits.[107] Chris Morash has recently pointed out that Synge lived during the "technological sublime" of the Edwardian era, a time when improvements in a vast range of communication technologies (e.g., transatlantic cables, wireless telegraphy, typewriters, cinema, photography) not only increased the speed of transmission of the word but also encouraged an aesthetic engagement with speed.[108] In relation to the Blickensderfer typewriter Synge bought in 1900 and used for composing many of his works, Morash contends that "for the writer . . . composing directly on the typewriter, the new accelerated writing was a way of keeping pace with the spontaneous fluency that Synge so admired in the people of the Aran Islands, West Kerry, and Wicklow." Regarding Synge's camera, Morash says that Synge used it as a "form of time machine" to capture images from an older world,[109] in contrast to faster visual technologies such as the moving pictures that were gathering momentum during Synge's time.

Synge was a "hoarder by nature [who] kept old notebooks, diaries, scraps of manuscripts."[110] In the diary entry for Tuesday, May 17, 1898, from Aranmor, he even noted, "Camera [came],"[111] alongside his frequent annotation "écrit" (the past participle of the French verb écrire, "to write," referring to his moments of writing productivity) and mentions of authors he was reading. Synge's Aran photographs played a part in his interaction with the locals but also helped him in his writing process because with them and his diaries he could recollect his Aran experience later, while he was in Paris. As W. J. McCormack maintains, photography "provided Synge with means of focusing his impressions of Aran, obliging him to select images, and to interpret the 'negatives' as a stage towards understanding."[112] During his life and especially in his travels, Synge took pictures while wandering in the West of Ireland or in County Wicklow. He also took some photographs of Paris and always used to bring along his "wallet of photographs," showing his plates to the islanders of Aran and the Great Blasket. Synge owned first a Lancaster hand camera purchased by a fellow visitor to Aranmor in May 1898, with "twelve quarter-plates which were developed by his nephew, Francis Edmund Stephens" (*CL1*, 48 n.), and then a Klito. Photography had always been part of his everyday familial and social background, as his personal letters show.[113] Synge was part of that class that joined photography clubs, and, according to McCormack, he even used his pictures to impress his first love interest, Cherrie Matheson, on some occasions, given that her family also pursued that hobby.[114]

Recent criticism on Synge's photography has focused on reading it within a number of contexts: the "visual hegemony" of fin-de-siècle scientific anthropology;[115] the increasing commoditization of photographic technology and its spread across social classes in the late Victorian and Edwardian era; and the emergence of genres such as the urban practice of street photography.[116] Within these politics of the visual, another important milieu needs to be added for a fuller understanding of Synge's approach to amateur photography: the use of photography in the cultural-nationalist movement. As I show in the remainder of this chapter, none of these contexts seems to fully encapsulate Synge's photography. It is perhaps this characteristic of not fully fitting that makes his photographs a less-stereotypical representation of the Aran community: they are in part unleashed from the grand narratives of race and nation evident in other Revival collections and photographs. Rather, they attempt to represent the community in a more localized and empathetic way.

When Synge used photography as an important part of his peculiar fieldwork on Aran and West Kerry, photography was a well-established and popular practice both within the scientific academy and amateur field clubs as well as in Edwardian everyday life. However, Synge's way of employing photography as a channel for mutual interaction on the islands was an anthropological practice quite ahead of its time.[117] Justin Carville, drawing from the visual anthropologists John Collier and Malcolm Collier, notes how "showing photographs to the community being observed allows for a better rapport with the subjects" and an easier integration into the local community. As mentioned earlier, He also maintains that Synge's photography reinforces his ethnographic authority over the islanders.[118] The reading of Synge's photographs within an anthropological framework is certainly relevant, even if, so far, it only juxtaposes Synge's photo taking against the colonial surveillance by the anthropologists who were archiving images of racial types. McCormack notes how Synge's pictures "sometimes look like attempts to 'deconstruct' the rigidly formal record keeping of the ethnographers."[119] In fact, his pictures are not anthropometric shots collected to build an archive of racial types, which was instead Haddon and Browne's aim in their expedition to the Aran Islands in 1893. That trip was organized to gather material for the Anthropometric Laboratory in Trinity College Dublin (established in 1891). As Carville explains, "In their 'pursuit' of photography as anthropological method, Haddon and Browne . . . reproduce 'photographic types,' a series of photographs that attempt to duplicate the codes and conventions of the anthropological 'type' photograph."[120] Elizabeth Edwards observes in her study on photography and anthropology how "the photograph totalizes culture through the massing of fragments within one frame, both body and object held up for inspection."[121] In the case of Synge's Aran photographs, it might be worth asking what kind of totalization they reflect. If they are not anthropometric pictures and did not serve the purpose of governmental anthropological surveys, race cannot be considered what they are totalizing.[122] Edwards further explains how the field of anthropological photography was complicated by scientific collections' absorption of ethnographically flavored photos popularized in the press.[123] Although the ethnographic flavor of Synge's snapshots seems to be the main perspective from which they are read, it is hard to gauge the impact they had in Irish popular culture. In fact, Synge's photographs, with the exception of their fleeting appearance in *The Gael*, remained largely unpublished during his lifetime and seem to have circulated only privately among his fellow artists in the theater movement.

Carville's recent study of Synge's photography has framed Synge's photographic practice within the visual politics of street photography, a practice that emerged out of the increasing industrialization of photographic processes and the mass production of cameras during the Edwardian era. Carville discusses Synge's snapshots alongside J. J. Clarke's urban street photographs of Dublin at the turn of the twentieth century, arguing that although they were taken in different settings, both engage with increasing "anxieties about the technological modernity of photography . . . [and] its incorporation into mediating social relations across class and gender divides." Carville observes that Synge "textualizes his visual experiences" in *The Aran Islands* as a way to cope with his own apprehension about modernity and technology and his own "anxieties about his inability to discipline his ocular exchanges between himself and the Aran Islanders."[124] Similarly, referring to some of the snapshots portraying an eviction on Aran, Luke Gibbons states that "Synge's images also invoke the shadows thrown by the dark side of modernization."[125] Clarke's Dublin photographs capture people of various walks of life in "fugitive poses" while walking on the streets or going about their business.[126] Clarke's subjects are not always aware that they are being photographed and at times are taken by surprise. This representation of random encounters between the photographer and his often startled subjects may be regarded as voy-euristic and invasive. Although the same unstudied poses are evident in a few snapshots taken by Synge in Dublin and in Aran (e.g., the photo-graphs about the eviction and the one representing a group of women standing on Kilronan pier waiting for the steamer), Synge negotiated other photographs and poses in agreement with their subjects, as a few exchanges in his travelogue testify. For this reason, his Aran album pro-vides both a combination of street snaps and more staged scenes and portraits. Commentators such as Declan Kiberd have described Synge's pictures as possessing a noninvasive quality and Synge as a photographer aware of "the dangers posed by the camera."[127] Hence, if on the one hand Synge's photographs partly participate in the practice and discourse of street photography, on the other hand his collection of Aran photographs cannot be confined to that genre only.

In addition to these discourses and praxes of ethnographic and street photography, the use of photography and its technologies within nation-alist activism constitutes an additional and partly neglected context in which to situate Synge's Aran pictures. Castle defines the Irish Revival as being enabled by a "sophisticated media environment,"[128] in particular the print media exploited by revivalists in multifarious ways. Photogra-phy was another crucial medium that revivalists used for their activism, and Synge was not the only Revival enthusiast who took pictures of the West of Ireland. As Catherine Morris's work on Alice Milligan has shown, Milligan used photography and visual culture as an integral part of her activism. For instance, when she was appointed "traveling teacher" for the Gaelic League, she traveled "with her own portable magic lantern and a camera that she used to collect pictures for slides,"[129] and she lectured communities in Ireland and abroad, showing images of fellow Gaelic Leaguers at work in the West. Morris explains that Milligan had learned about early photography and magic lanterns during field trips and con-ferences with the Belfast Naturalist Field Club in the 1880s. From 1905 on, "Milligan also worked then with local communities to re-embody the pic-tures as theater and devise new pictures for the stage from local folklore, the cultural life of the community, and from Irish songs and legends." Milligan was certainly a pioneer in her deployment of visual technologies as teaching tools "for the advancement of the Revival's educational and nationalist agenda" and was also extremely clever and modern in understanding "the necessity of entertaining in order to instruct audiences." Photography and magic lanterns had been deployed for politicized initiatives since the 1880s, when, for example, as Morris points out, "the Land League . . . photographed scenes of Irish distress and evictions," restaging them *en plein air* or projecting them at rallies and fund-raising initiatives. Similarly, Morris also states that "during the 1897 royal visit to Dublin, James Connolly and Maud Gonne used a magic lantern to project onto Dublin's city walls photographs of famine that they had witnessed in the West of Ireland."[130]

Photography was also practiced by another Gaelic League activist, Agnes O'Farrelly, and features in her travelogue *Smaointe ar Árainn*. Her photographs, taken with a "hand-held camera,"[131] were published in the League's periodical *An Claidheamh Soluis* on December 21, 1901, and portray religious and historical monuments and people, including the Women's Branch of the Gaelic League that she founded. O'Farrelly, like Alice Milligan, could be considered a sort of Irish "Kodak girl"—the gendered stereotype of the amateur photographer popularized by Kodak advertising in 1893. O'Farrelly and Milligan somehow embodied a new generation of Irish educated women who partook in urban nationalist movements and who seized the potential and power of modern technology and media for their activism. Despite a nostalgia for a precolonial past, the Revival was thus a product of modernity and modernization. Far from being only backward looking, Revival activists and movements embraced modernity and technological advancements for the benefit of their work of cultural recovery. Nic Congáil parallels O'Farrelly's snapshots with Synge's, claiming that they constitute images "closer to cultural performance than [to] an objective view of Aran life." O'Farrelly's photographs, Nic Congáil points out, combine images of the physical landscape and built heritage with "group shots [that] emphasize the presence of women" and the work of the Gaelic League.[132] It is this combination of topics that enhances the propagandist effect of her reportage—some photographs, for example, illustrate recreational activities promoted by the League on the islands, such as *an aeraíocht*, the open-air entertainment.

Certainly, Synge's photographs conform to this idea of "cultural performance" in their visualization of peasant culture broadly. However, they do not reflect purely a cultural-nationalist ideology. McCormack, for instance, proposes a reading of Synge's photography as a stepping stone toward the visual art of the theater: "As a photographer who also developed his pictures from plates, and as one with a keen interest in painting, Synge chose deliberately when he found himself through literature, the visible literature of the stage-drama."[133] McCormack's observation is interesting in that it establishes a nexus between photography and Synge's artistic achievements, just as Alice Milligan used photography in preparation for her *tableaux vivants*. In a letter to Lady Gregory dated July 1, 1898, Synge enthusiastically talks about his Aran pictures: "My Aran photos seem a success[.] I will send you some when I can print them" (CL1, 48). This comment shows that Synge's snapshots circulated privately among his fellow revivalists, helping them visualize the West of Ireland. Arguably, they could have served as a visual aid in preparation for staging the plays produced by the Irish Literary Theatre—in the same way that, for example, they were passed on to Jack Yeats to make pen-and-ink illustrations for Synge's book. In the Jack B. Yeats Archive at the National Gallery of Ireland, a collection of twenty-eight photographs of the Aran Islands that the playwright sent to Yeats around 1900 may shed some light on Synge's photographic intentions. Some of the captions written on the back of the photographs draw attention to the artifacts (spinning wheel, *sugawn* rope) included in his frames and therefore reinforce McCormack's reading of the photographs as connected with the visual art of the theater in that some of those objects will become central props in some of his plays. Synge's attention to the material culture of the Aran Islands in staging his plays and his wish to have the props sent directly from Aran are well known.[134] In the photographs and captions he sent to Jack Yeats, this attention is clearly visible. For instance, at the back of a photograph portraying a man walking alongside his pony, which is carrying straw, Synge wrote, "Bringing home straw for thatching, Ball of sugawn on [view] left. M[iddle] Island."[135] In the introduction to *My Wallet of Photographs*, a collection of Synge's photographs, compiler Lilo Stephens also suggests that "the camera was used to produce a visual record of the types of people he brought to life in his literary and dramatic works."[136] In this sense, Synge's photographs can be identified as akin to a "cultural performance,"[137] the visual foundation for the cultural performance of the Irish Literary Theatre.

Among these Aran photographs, there is one in particular where scene construction and the photographer's intent are most striking. The photograph showing a man and boy rolling up a rope on Inis Óirr (figure 3) is an example of how "the longer exposure encouraged subjects to 'grow into' the frame."[138] This prolonged exposure shows that Synge was accepted not just as a mere interloper but "as a recorder for those involved in the events photographed."[139] The photograph in question shows a man twisting a rope with the help of a boy dressed in a petticoat, which boys traditionally wore in the West to ward off the fairies. Synge minutely describes the activity in his book:

> Two men usually sit together at this work, one of them hammering the straw with a heavy block of wood, the other forming the rope, the main body of which is twisted by a boy or a girl with a bent stick especially formed for this employment. In wet weather, when the work must be done indoors, the person who is twisting recedes gradually out of the door, across the lane, and sometimes across a field or two beyond it. . . . When this work is in progress in half the cottages of the village, the road has a curious look, and one has to pick one's steps through a maze of twisting ropes that pass from a dark doorways on either side into the fields. (*AI*, 83).

The back of the copy of the photograph given to Jack Yeats contains a handwritten comment jotted by Synge (figure 4): "Storyteller twists sugawn or rather rolling it after the twisting of it. South Island."

Synge's handwritten caption has fascinating implications. First of all, what is striking is that Synge identified as the central subject of his photograph a "storyteller," not simply a common islander, farmer, or peasant, and that he signaled this fact to his fellow artist, Yeats. What is also crucial is that Synge chose to depict a storyteller working at the practical task of rope making. Arguably, the photograph illuminated by this caption visually sums up the link between craftsmanship and storytelling recurrent in

3. J. M. Synge, photograph showing a man and boy rolling up a rope on Innis Óirr, c. 1900. Y1/JY/14/6, Parcel 38, Jack B. Yeats Archive, National Gallery of Ireland Collection. Photograph courtesy of the National Gallery of Ireland, Dublin.

parts of *The Aran Island*: the islanders are craftsmen in their several métiers, which they perform communally, but they are also artisans of the word, for their bilingualism, for their storytelling, for the way they name their own environment and their own people. The photograph and its caption identifying a storyteller at work may also be reminiscent of a famous scene in the first Irish-language play staged by the Irish Literary Theatre in 1901, *Casadh an tSúgáin* (*The Twisting of the Rope*) by Douglas Hyde. In the play, the wandering poet Hanrahan is tricked by his rival into twisting a long rope of *sugawn*, therefore interrupting Hanrahan's courtship of Oona during a dance. When Hanrahan exits the cottage while twisting the rope, he is locked out by his rival, irremediably separated from his love interest and ostracized by the community. Synge, who visited Aran for the fourth time that year between September 21 and October 19, managed to attend the performance of Hyde's play at the Gaiety Theater when he returned to Dublin on October 21. In the illustration to the book, Jack Yeats would not

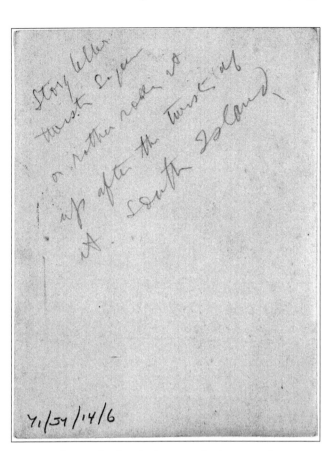

4. J. M. Synge, back of photograph documenting rope-
making activity on Aran, c. 1900, with Synge's handwritten
caption: "Storyteller twists sugawn or rather rolling it after
the twisting of it. South Island." Parcel 38, Sheet 4 (back),
Jack B. Yeats Archive, National Gallery of Ireland Collection. Photograph courtesy of the National Gallery of Ireland, Dublin.

follow the composition of Synge's snapshot but rather would depict "the
man who told the stories" leaning on his stick on the threshold of a cottage, about to walk in. In the same picture, Yeats draws a little child who is
chasing a hen with a twig in the stone-paved yard in front of the cottage,
therefore assembling in one drawing two of the photographs that Synge
gave him. Synge had captioned the second photograph on the back "My

5. J. M. Synge, photograph of the MacDonagh cottage on Inis Meáin, Aran Islands, c. 1900, with Synge's handwritten caption on the back: "My Cottage Micheaeleen Beug." Y1/JY/14/2 (back), Parcel 38, Jack B. Yeats Archive, National Gallery of Ireland, Dublin. Image courtesy of the Board of Trinity College Dublin.

Cottage Micheaeleen Beug," and it shows a little boy dressed in a petticoat in front of a cottage and a woman who is about to enter the house (figure 5).

Following Edwards's idea of the photographic image's totalization of culture, Synge's photographs can be said to reflect, to an extent, Irish national life in a way similar to that of the photographs by Gaelic Leaguers O'Farrelly and Milligan. However, Synge's Aran photographs take a slightly different approach in visualizing this idea of national life. Despite showcasing the local people and traditional customs of Aran, they never represent architectural buildings, cultural landmarks, or scenic views alone. These features appear extensively in the photographs in O'Farrelly's travelogue *Smaointe ar Árainn* (which includes also a pen-and-ink sketch of the Dun Aengus fort[140]) and in Alice Milligan's collection of landscape views for her educational magic-lantern slides. In their use of photography for their activism, both Milligan and O'Farrelly participated in the creation of a public Irish visual identity and therefore collected a larger variety of Irish themes for their "cultural performance," from landscapes to people to Revival activities. In contrast, Synge's photographs, by avoiding majestic landscape and architectural features, lack a more staunch propagandism and deviate from the general type of illustrations of popular travel writing often aimed at English tourists, which showcased landscape views of Aran in a variety of formats, both photographic and pictorial.[141] Synge's celebration of craft focuses more on the people at work. His photographs, in part unleashed from narratives of racial stereotyping, even if involved in the narratives of national performance, prioritize the community he interacted with on the islands. Elaine Sisson argues that Synge's photographs, "like Yeats's drawings, are neither sentimental nor condescending to the life of the peasant; instead they both offer realistic and humane portraits of their subjects."[142] Ciarán Walsh, the curator of the commemorative exhibition *John Millington Synge, Photographer* in 2009, speaks about Synge's "empathy" in taking pictures, an empathy that other visitors and photographers lacked.[143] If, on the one hand, this community of people, according to some readings, is arguably objectified and abstracted into a revivalist idea of peasant Irishness, it is, on the other hand, also exalted and empathetically portrayed by Synge through his choice of subjects and his photographic negotiations with the locals on the islands.

The emphasis on the local community at the core of Synge's collection of Aran photographs has been effectively captured in the exhibition *John Millington Synge, Photographer*, which toured Ireland and Paris in 2009 as part of a number of initiatives that commemorated the centenary of Synge's death. Set up by Siamsa Tíre (National Folk Theater of Ireland), the exhibition was mounted in crucial places connected with Synge's photography and travels: Inis Meáin; the Blasket Centre in Dunquin, County Kerry; and the Irish Cultural Centre in Paris. For the importance of those places and communities in which the photographs were relocated, the exhibition did more than just salvage Synge's photography from dusty archives. Albeit temporarily, it returned the images to those places where they had initially belonged and symbolically reconnected places and communities with their representation, thus sparking an interesting process of remembrance. On Sunday, May 16, 2009, the exhibition was launched with an introduction by Tim Robinson on the premises of the Cniotáil Inis Meáin (Inis Meáin's Knitting Centre) among woolen sweaters and scarves. At the launch, which I was privileged to attend, some of the descendants of the families that Synge had met during his stay on the Aran Islands admired the snapshots, pointing at old familiar faces. This scene was striking because it recalled similar scenes that had happened more than a century earlier, which Synge describes in *The Aran Islands,* such as at the beginning of part 2: "When my photographs of this island had been examined with immense delight, and every person in them had been identified—even those who only showed a hand or a leg—I brought out some I had taken in County Wicklow" (*AI*, 61). The scene at the launch struck me not just because of the sense of déjà vu it generated and the parallels with Synge's text but also because it reenacted a performance of mutual recognition that had started more than a hundred years earlier. As such, this exhibition seemed to unleash the potential for a collective act of remembering: at the turn of the twentieth century, when the photographs were deployed as tools of interaction with the islanders, they served as a sort of mirror in which the community gathered together could see itself reflected; in the twenty-first century as well, they validated similar moments of communal cohesion.

Between October 2010 and February 2011, Synge's Aran photographs were exhibited again in Dublin in an eclectic exhibition at the Irish Museum of Modern Art entitled *The Moderns,* which showcased Ireland's engagement with the visual arts between 1900 and 1975. In this broad-sweeping exhibition, Synge's photography was presented alongside that of two other Irish amateur photographers, George Bernard Shaw and Roger Casement. The selection of Shaw's photos in *The Moderns* testified to his diverse approach to his hobby and his attempts at experimenting with perspective, light, and subject. The selection was also thematically wide ranging: views of children in County Kerry,[144] a breathtaking shot on the Skelligs depicting a photographer with a tripod in the mist,[145] views of Paris and France,[146] portraits and self-portraits, including nudes.[147] The photographs by Casement in *The Moderns* came from his travels in the

Putumayo region of Peru in 1910 as part of an inspection he conducted on behalf of the British government to investigate humanitarian abuses against local tribes working for rubber traders. The snapshots complemented his reports, which provided evidence of the abuses. Despite the publicity that these reports received, according to Michael Laffan, the Putumayo tribes "were saved not by the intervention of foreign consuls and governments but by the collapse of the market for wild rubber."[148] In addition to some photographs documenting indigenous workers with their overseers, Casement also took some ethnographic pictures, such as "Group of Putumayo Girls, Facing Away from the Camera,"[149] in which eight girls with traditional body painting and decorations are photographed from the back, lined up against a wall. Luke Gibbons highlights that Roger Casement's diaries describe the locals' reactions to the camera. When summoned to be photographed, the Putumayo workers were terrified of the objective, and even if they were armed with weapons, according to Gibbons, the rifles were without cartridges and had only an ornamental purpose for their traditional dances.[150]

The exhibition *John Millington Synge, Photographer* captured Synge's localized interest in the cohesion and daily work of Irish rural communities living on the fringes of Ireland. It also reignited a process of interaction between the image and its subjects that had been performed one hundred years earlier, when the photographs were taken. *The Moderns* situated Synge's photography both within a transnational and modernist milieu embedded in global networks of imperialist and colonial exploitation as well as within new trends in the visual arts that developed at the turn of the twentieth century. However, *The Moderns*, in its limited photographic selection, largely ignored other revivalist groups' engagement with photography, which also photographed the Aran Islands through spectacular and self-celebratory group snapshots and which were equally up to date in their use of modern photographic technologies for propaganda purposes. Nonetheless, both exhibitions framed two central aspects of Synge's Aran photography: his empathetic and interactive attention to local rural communities and his distinctive and critical engagement with modernity, of which his travel writing is also a fine example. Often discussed as anthropological records despite not qualifying as anthropometric, even if seizing the possibilities of the faster technology of handheld cameras and betraying the anxiety of the gaze typical of street-photography discourse and even if closer to the nationalist "cultural performance" of Revival activism and propaganda, Synge's photographs also transcend all these categories. As I have shown, his pictures advance a totalization of Irishness, which adds the idea of community to the idea of "cultural performance" and which involves a negotiation and a dual relationship between the gazer and the gazed upon. Synge's photographs participate in Revival activism in a more oblique way. They are of the Revival in that they share the engagement with modern technology that many revivalists and revivalist groups embraced, but they are not purely propagandistic and instead, arguably, salvage a sense of cohesion in the marginalized rural communities they depict.

# 2

# Reimagining Travel and Popular Entertainment

*The West Kerry Essays*

The Kerry region had long been celebrated in travel writing and tourist publications since at least the eighteenth century, when some of its areas, in particular the Killarney area, were increasingly landscaped and packaged for the tourist as a romantic retreat along the lines of the Lake District area. In the second half of the century, as Glenn Hooper notes, "the traditionally harsher, more austere West of Ireland received the greatest attention, . . . as travelers went first in search of scenery on a grander scale, and then on increasingly anthropological forays."[1] In Kerry, places such as the Dingle Peninsula and the Blasket Islands provided breathtaking scenery and, for some, an alternative to more commodified attractions such as the Killarney lake and mountain areas. Despite his anthropological interests in the culture of the more marginalized West of Ireland, Synge was not completely immune to the romantic fascination of Dingle's majestic natural landscape. His articles about West Kerry, first published in the little magazine *The Shanachie*, contain some scattered contemplative impressions about the beauty of the scenery. For example, in the essay "In West Kerry" (Summer 1907), he praises the beauty of the landscape he saw while hiking on a cliff path on Sybil Head, juxtaposing life in the country and in the city in a typically romantic and revivalist way:

> It is a place of indescribable grandeur. East one sees Carrantuohill, in the south the Skellig Rocks many miles away, on the north Loop Head, in the

65

west the full sweep of the Atlantic, and over all, the wonderfully tender and searching colour that is peculiar to Kerry. Looking down the drop of five or six hundred feet, the height is so great that the gannets flying close over the sea look like white butterflies, and the choughs like flies fluttering behind them. One wonders in these places why anyone is left in Dublin or London or Paris, when it would be better, one would think, to live in a tent or hut with this magnificent sea and sky, and to breathe this wonderful air which is like wine in one's teeth. (*TI*, 136)

Although his West Kerry articles strike a balance between these kinds of remarks and keen observations on rural life, beliefs, and customs often narrated in the first person by the people he met during his peregrinations, it is in his private letters to his fiancée, Molly Allgood, that he further indulges in pictorial descriptions. In them, he exploits the landscape of Kerry as a trope for his love in absentia: "Last night I was out on my little hill over the sea about 9 o'clock in the moonlight. It was extraordinary peaceful and grand and I was wondering how you were getting on in the Abbey" (August 30, 1906, *CL1*, 198). His descriptions of Dingle in the letters are passionate and poetic, providing his first impressions and most personal reactions, which were subsequently filtered out in the journalistic pieces to give more room to the local culture. In the articles, Synge's natural descriptions are soon interjected with details regarding the people's lives as well as firsthand testimonies and stories about life in Kerry presented in direct-speech mode. After the contemplation from Sybil Head, for example, Synge meets a young man who had fought in the Boer War and had traveled widely around the world before finally settling in Kerry (*TI*, 136–37). He also bumps into a fisherman, who tells him a story about traditional plant cures (*TI*, 137).

Synge's articles about West Kerry first appeared in the periodical *The Shanachie* in different installments. After his death, they were amalgamated in the *Collected Works* under the composite title *In Wicklow, West Kerry, and Connemara* (*CW2*, 187–343). *The Shanachie* was a biannual little magazine that aimed at showcasing "the shorter work of Irish writers and the work of Irish Artists"[2] who published with Maunsel, which would eventually issue *The Aran Islands* in 1907 with Jack B. Yeats's illustrations. Nicholas Grene explains how "George Roberts, co-owner of Maunsel, tried to enlist Synge as a contributor from the first planning of *The Shanachie*"; Synge would eventually "appear in all but one of the magazine's six issues."[3] *The Shanachie* featured both "literary contents" by writers such as W. B. Yeats, Jane Barlow, Padraic Colum, Lady Gregory, George Fitzmaurice, and Stephen Gwynn as well as "arts contents," such as illustrations and visual artworks by Jack B. Yeats and William Orpen.[4] According to Grene, Synge found more freedom in *The Shanachie*'s editorial policies because the periodical "was prepared to take substantially longer essays than the *Manchester Guardian* . . . allow[ing] for a much more discursive, impressionistic style."[5] Grene also shows how in *The Shanachie* Synge found "an important ally . . . in the culture wars that followed the production of the *Playboy*";[6] in that relationship, the periodical published favorable reviews of *Playboy* and *The Aran Islands*.[7] The longer pieces of journalism Synge produced for *The Shanachie* were written with the aim of eventually being gathered in a book. The West Kerry articles recollect Synge's trips to the Dingle Peninsula, the Blasket Islands, and other West Kerry shores that he took once a year between 1903 and 1907. The annual trips to Kerry followed those to the Aran Islands and, notably, provided inspiration for numerous scenes in his masterpiece *The Playboy of the Western World*.[8] On his West Kerry journeys, he also brought along his camera and took photographs, particularly of the people he stayed with on the Blasket Islands in 1905.

As in the journalistic pieces about the Aran Islands and the Congested Districts, in the Kerry articles Synge explores ethnographic modes of reporting and negotiates participant observation in more extended nonfictional productions. If the emphasis in *The Aran Islands* is essentially more on the repercussions deriving from the conflicting contacts between tradition and modernity, in the West Kerry series Synge's major concern seems to be a rethinking of ways to represent various fieldwork sites, in particular public locales such as fairs, popular entertainment, and train carriages—the latter a privileged space where his interaction with the people and, consequently, his dialogic reporting and ethnographic authority can be negotiated. Synge's perspective in the essays is once more noteworthy and original, particularly if compared with previous travel literature about Kerry compiled by English tourists. This chapter highlights his interest in train carriages and train travel as a "field" in an anthropological sense. His attention to the dynamics of train travel also epitomizes his groundbreaking opening toward a plurality of field-work sites and his attention toward milieus where relations of travel and mobility are explored vis-à-vis relations of inhabitation. Synge's dialogic practice, with its scrupulous attention to detail and great empathy in listening to and recording stories, remarkably takes into account the micro-histories of travel and displacement of those communities served by local railway lines.

This chapter introduces as a useful comparison Robert Lynd's revivalist travelogue *Rambles in Ireland* for its extensive account of his journey in Kerry. Robert Lynd, a Belfast-born but London-resident journalist, was an ardent Sinn Féin supporter and a language activist with the Gaelic League. In 1912, he published *Rambles in Ireland* about his travels to Galway and Kerry undertaken a few years earlier, plausibly during the summer of 1909.[9] The book was published by Mills and Boon and features beautiful illustrations by Jack B. Yeats as well as photographs from the Lawrence Photograph Collection.[10] According to a reviewer in the modernist periodical *Irish Review*, *Rambles in Ireland* presents Lynd's "confession of faith in Irish–Ireland tempered by a realistic note."[11] Throughout the book, Lynd dutifully searches for the Irish Revival.[12] His quest, however, proves to be difficult, and in several circumstances he laments the commodification brought about by centuries-long English tourism. For instance, when he is mistakenly put on a freshly painted train to Killarney instead of on the train to Killorglin, he deems Killarney "a miserable tourist resort that people sing about in the music-halls,"[13] thus adopting the same rhetoric of disdain for the corruptive effect of English culture on Ireland that Douglas Hyde expresses, for instance, in his seminal pamphlet *The Necessity for De-anglicising Ireland*.[14] Lynd's book, as this chapter speculates, owes a debt to Synge's demythologizing gaze as it depicts the harsher reality underpinning the "imagined community" that Irish nationalist activism sought to create. Moreover, Lynd's travelogue also borrows from Synge's ethnographic and dialogic mode of reporting in the West Kerry series but at the same time showcases a number of substantial differences.

As mentioned earlier, Synge's interest in this series lies in the depiction of the vibrant Gaelic-speaking rural lore in the remote fringes of Ireland, away from networks of commodified tourist structures that had been in place since the mid–eighteenth century in nearby Killarney.[15] As a number of historical and sociological studies have shown,[16] since the eighteenth century Killarney had been carefully landscaped and constructed as a romantic tourist resort for the enjoyment of the upper classes.[17] Among the most popular tourist attractions, the history of Inisfallen Abbey on Inisfallen Island in Loch Leane is an interesting example of a studied renovation implemented by Lord Kenmare specifically for tourists. As Finola O'Kane explores, Lord Kenmare had refurbished the abbey as a "banqueting house cum cottage" for the enjoyment of the tourist, who could also benefit from a privileged view of the lakes.[18] Painting created a visual discourse that played a huge role in popularizing Kerry because it fashioned views of the landscape as sublime and picturesque for the visual enjoyment of the tourist.[19] Eóin Flannery maintains that for these reasons "the interplay of aristocratic benevolence, intrepid visitors, and an unruly, sublime landscape at this juncture in Killarney can be viewed as participatory in the flowering of European Romanticism."[20] Among many pictorial examples, Agostino Aglio's painting *Abbey on Inisfallen Island* captures two tourists walking in front of the abbey, pictorially rendered as distinct from two locals, who are painted in traditional Kerry black cloaks.[21] Inevitably, between the end of the eighteenth century and the beginning of the nineteenth, tourist facilities such as villas and hotels sprang up very quickly along the Killarney Lake banks—to the disappointment of a Victorian travel writer, who bitterly remarked in 1875, "Killarney has lost much of the natural charm for which it first became famous. . . . [T]o judge by the company assembled on the platform of the station, there is nothing to distinguish it from a fashionable watering place in Kent, except that the London news is a day older."[22] In 1900, another travelogue by the poet laureate Alfred Austin documented the recent construction of "the hotels in Parknasilla, Kenmare, Waterville, Derrinane [that] will both attract and satisfy numbers of visitors to the exquisite scenery of Kerry."[23] By the first decade of the twentieth century, Kerry was also visited by tourists traveling by motor vehicle, as documented, for example, in Lynd's travelogue

*Rambles in Ireland*, where he mentions "big hotels for motorists" and "a motor char-a-bancs."[24]

In the first half of the nineteenth century, Kerry's notorious scenery had also been co-opted in the nationalist discourse of the Young Ireland movement, as Seán Ryder notes in relation to Thomas Davis's article "Irish Scenery." Davis's piece is in part an exhortation "to the Irish upper classes to spend their holiday in Ireland rather than abroad." Ryder remarks that this home tourism, in Davis's view, "would ensure that Irish wealth is spent within Ireland itself, and would also enable the ruling class to acquaint themselves better with their own country, thereby getting their political loyalties in order. Ireland can offer scenery equal to any nation in Europe, Davis argues, from the lakes of Killarney to the Cliffs of Slieve League. Mont Blanc has nothing on Kerry's 'Carn Tual,' and the river Blackwater rivals the Danube for a cruise."[25] Thus, Killarney lakes remained a favorite tourist destination throughout the nineteenth century and attracted a great variety of both Irish and English visitors.

Kevin J. James's recent study *Tourism, Land, and Landscape in Ireland: The Commodification of Culture* draws attention to popular and leisurely aspects of travel that characterized Kerry tourism throughout the nineteenth century, particularly to the post-Famine tourist experience of Killarney, which transitioned from being a site of engagement with romantic landscapes and the sublime to being a site where modes of "intense sociability, . . . sensorial engagement, . . . and ludic entertainment" prevailed. James amply documents the carnivalesque Gap of Dunloe performance of so-called "Mountain-dew girls" and "Kate Kearney's granddaughters," peasant women who more or less directly embodied a legendary woman sung in odes and stories and whose task was to offer refreshments (goat's milk or the more dangerous *poitín*, an illegally distilled and highly alcoholic spirit) to passing tourists in exchange for a few shillings. These encounters, recounted in many travelogues and tourist guides alike, were "organised around narrative tropes of harassment, disappointment, and frustrated efforts at furtive escapes from a teeming tourist trap." As James puts it, throughout the nineteenth century "Killarney was becoming as famous for its tourist kitsch as for its varied scenery." James's study also highlights that the informal tolls levied by these women had been naturalized as part of the Killarney tour and had perhaps been more widely accepted owing to their performative and interactive nature.[26] However, toward the end of the nineteenth century, because of the growing impact of national-ist movements, official tolls imposed by landlords upon entrance to their demesne attracted loud protests in a variety of tourist publications.[27] As land reforms in Ireland progressed, they were seen—by both nationalist and unionist sides alike—as a negative "symbol of a wider system of land proprietorship that retarded social and commercial progress."[28]

In a way similar to the Aran Islands, Kerry had also been written about by a number of academic observers, in particular botanists and geologists. In 1882, for instance, the Irish writer, revivalist, and amateur botanist Emily Lawless contributed an article on Kerry's biodiversity to the English periodical *Gentleman's Magazine*. Her piece draws attention to yet to be discovered and uncommon aspects of Kerry—namely, its diverse flora and fauna. Lawless's article, like many nineteenth-century travel accounts, also complains about tourists' superficial engagement with place: "What tourist in Ireland (of late years especially) ever lingers one moment longer than he can avoid?" The article closes by criticizing the lack of research about Ireland owing to the "all-pervading and all-invading encroachment of politics" and with a plea to conduct more scien-tific research to the advancement of science.[29] Lawless's microscopic angle, ready to record with detail and precision the autochthonous varieties of small insects and plants, partakes in the scientific discourses and writ-ing of the time. But her piece also borrows some popular travel-writing conventions, quoting poetic extracts from literary travelogues, such as William Makepeace Thackeray's *Irish Sketchbook* of the mid–nineteenth century. Among all the previous travel literature about the area, Synge's West Kerry series is perhaps most indebted to Lawless's scientific perspec-tive, particularly for Synge's own "microscientific" and academic engage-ment with culture and localities.

### Fairs, Circuses, and Train Journeys: Fieldwork as Travel

In the literary journalism about West Kerry, Synge is attracted by the locals' recreational activities such as dances, circuses, fairs, and races. For example, in the article "In West Kerry: To Puck Fair" (*The Shanachie*, winter 1907) Synge walks through the crowded streets of a Kerry town, Killorglin, zigzagging among dealers and beggars during Puck Fair, the traditional August fair. His interest in recreational events is in a broad sense ethnographic, as when he minutely describes the paraphernalia of the fair in the town center. There, he writes, "Puck himself, a magnificent he-goat (Irish *puc*) raised on a platform twenty feet high, [was] held by a chain from each horn, with his face down the road" (*TI*, 159). Synge explains how the goat is the guardian of the fair and how it is "kept in this position, with a few cabbages to feed on, for three days, so that he may preside over the pig-fair, and the horse-fair, and the day of the winding up" (*TI*, 159). Synge also transcribes a ballad dedicated to Puck Fair affixed at the feet of the platform. The ballad presents overt nationalistic references, as in the chorus:

> Where is the tyrant dare oppose it
> Our old customs we will hold up still,
> And I think we will have another—
> That is Home Rule and Purchase Bill. (*TI*, 160)

Elizabeth Malcolm has highlighted the encroachment of nationalist politics on entertainment and popular recreations in relation to the nineteenth-century Fenian and Repeal movements as well as to the Gaelic Athletic Association.[30] However, in this instance Synge does not dwell too much on nationalistic issues but simply transcribes the ballad. His main interest here is to give the full picture of the event with a folklorist eye, such as when he compares the ballad singing in Puck's honor to the "early Greek festivals, since the time of which, it is possible the goat has been exalted yearly in Killorglin" (*TI*, 159), or when he compares another ballad-singing performance about the Russian and Japanese War sung with the alternation of a male voice and a female voice to antiphonic ballad singing he had heard in Dublin (*TI*, 161). These comparativist remarks reflect Synge's absorption of comparative folklore theories foregrounded in the French academy by Henri d'Arbois De Jubainville, whose lectures Synge had attended at the Sorbonne in 1898.[31]

Lynd's travelogue *Rambles in Ireland* features a detailed account of Puck Fair, which comes after his forced detour to Killarney when he is accidentally put on the wrong train. When Lynd finally gets to Killorglin and to the fair, his account indulges in a couple of celebratory moments of "Irish-Irelandism," such as when he is greeted by a sign in Gaelic at the entrance of the town, "an Irish motto of morality and welcome." He then describes the liveliness of the town, with its distinctive sellers and gamblers. However, he also has a few encounters that seem to dispel the Irishness he has actively sought since the beginning of his trip. For instance, he laments the indistinctiveness of the local dress in comparison with the more colorful clothing of people in Galway and Donegal. In an attempt to speak Irish with a local woman who does not speak it, he is mistaken for an English tourist; when he stops in a shop to buy a newspaper, he interacts with a shop owner who is a fan of English monarchs and shows Lynd Queen Alexandra's picture book, declaring that he would believe in nationalism if it paid him.[32] Despite Lynd's efforts and good "nationalist" intentions, these encounters contradict his expectations of the Irish "authenticity" he set out to find. However, they can also be read, perhaps, as a more honest attempt at incorporating multifarious versions of Irishness battling each other in Ireland in the first decade of the twentieth century.

From a stylistic perspective, Lynd and Synge have different ways of showcasing this opening toward multiple notions of Irishness. Lynd essentially still constructs his models in antithesis with English models—as evident, for instance, in his attention to rewriting a nationalist geography, in his regard for the grand narratives of Irish history, in the accounts of famous personalities interspersed throughout the travelogue (e.g., his account of the importance of the Rock of Cashel and Brian Boru), and in his virulent antitourist rhetoric directed against English tourists. Synge, in contrast, adopts a less confrontational approach and does not critique English tourists visiting Kerry. He also focuses mainly on micronarratives and highly localized histories, which intersect with the grand narratives of Irish history. Furthermore, Synge's comparative framework is also wider and informed not only by "English" models but also, more importantly, by Irish and European models. Even on the Blasket Islands, his interactions with members of the local community often highlight connections among the Blaskets and countries such as France and England, particularly with regard to fishing. As Synge recounts in "In West Kerry: The Blasket Islands" (*The Shanachie*, Autumn 1907), he is told that the lobsterpots come from Southampton and that the local lobster trade sells to frequent boats coming from both England and France (*TI*, 148). America, as noted in relation to the Aran Islands, is obviously a constant presence in the lives of the people of West Kerry and the subject of a conversation Synge has with an islander on the Great Blasket (*TI*, 142). Like *The Aran Islands*, the West Kerry series also presents these "contact" moments that showcase a vision of Irish localities as part of a wider transnational framework, particularly from a material and economic standpoint. To borrow Nicholas Allen's words regarding *The Aran Islands*, in Synge the idea of "the national is insufficient," and Aran as well as Kerry are both "local and worldly," a "duality [becoming] archipelagic."[33] Allen's notion of the "archipelagic" as transcending localism to highlight global connections can also be extended to the West Kerry series and is evident in more than Synge's depiction of island life.

Another example of Synge's comparative outlook can be found in the opening article of *The Shanachie* series, "In West Kerry" (Summer 1907), where he describes a colorful scene underneath a circus tent in Ballyferriter. The tent is soaked with rain and shaken by a furious wind. Synge is watching the crowd gathering under the tent when all of a sudden he witnesses a mob at the entrance. Strikingly, a group of women performers quells the mob: "in a moment three or four of the women performers, with long, steaming ulsters buttoned over their tights, ran out from behind the scenes and threw themselves into the crowd, forcing back the wild hillside people, fishwomen, drunken sailors, in an extraordinary tumult of swearing, wrestling, and laughter. These women seemed to enjoy this part of their work, and shrieked with amusement when two or three of them fell on some enormous farmer or publican and nearly dragged him to the ground" (*TI*, 132–33). Synge's interest in the circus can be compared with Jack Yeats's life-long passion for circuses, fairs, and exotic shows, such as the Wild West Show, as exemplified in his numerous pictorial artworks on the subject.[34] Róisín Kennedy, curator of the exhibition of Yeats's work, *Masquerade and Spectacle*, at the National Gallery of Ireland in 2007, has noted how the "traveling circus's ability to perform in remote locations, far from conventional metropolitan centres of popular entertainment[,] meant that it attracted a diverse audience from all social backgrounds." She further argues that "this populist aspect was of great interest to Yeats" and that both Synge and Yeats were enthralled "as much by the relationship of the crowd to the circus people, as by the performance itself," quoting Synge on the same Kerry episode.[35] This performativity aspect of the episode would certainly have appealed as much to Synge the playwright as it captured the painter's attention. In addition, Synge's interest in the scene lies also in the physicality of the performance, expressed through the bodily contact between the crowd and the women performers, which Synge enhances by aural suggestions, "an extraordinary tumult of swearing, wrestling, and laughter." Furthermore, Synge's attentiveness in reporting this particular scene speaks to his carnivalesque interest in challenging gender boundaries and gender social normativity, a strategy that is particularly evident in his female dramatic characters, such as Nora Burke, Mary Byrne, Pegeen Mike, and Deirdre.[36]

Furthermore, it seems to me that the initiative taken by the women performers in their "long, steaming ulsters buttoned over their tights" possibly appealed to Synge for the way it may have evoked the final scene of a story belonging to the epic *Táin Bó Cuailnge*, "The Boyhood Deeds of Cúchulain." In the story, Cúchulain's battle fury (*ríastarthae*) is appeased by "the women of Emain[, who] went forth, with Mugain the wife of Conchobor mac Nesa at their head, and they stripped their breasts at him."[37] Unlike the scene in Ballyferriter, Cúchulain's shyness in front of the women momentarily immobilizes him so that "the warriors of Emain seized him and plunged him in a vat of cold water,"[38] therefore preventing physical contact. Synge was most likely aware of this story that is part of the Ulster Cycle, which he would have known in its entirety from his studies in Paris. Moreover, he also read Lady Gregory's expurgated rendition of Cúchulain's saga in *Cúchulain of Muirthemne* (1902), specifically commenting in a review of that book on how Lady Gregory's version has a "much less archaic aspect than the original text" because she had "omitted certain barbarous features, such as the descriptions of the fury of Cúchulain" (*CW2*, 370).[39] Synge concludes the review by stating that *Cúchulain of Muirthemne* is a revivalist adaptation of the stories and that "students of mythology . . . for their severe studies . . . must still turn to the works of German scholars, and others, who translate without hesitation all that has come down to us in the MSS" (CW2, 370). His description of the women with long, buttoned ulsters and the connection he makes with the epic sagas can be read as another example of the indebtedness of his travel narratives to an indigenous literary tradition, as stressed by critics such as Tony Roche in his comparison between *The Aran Islands* and the Old Irish genres the *immrama* and *echtraí*.[40]

Synge's and Jack Yeats's similar attention to the circus in their work also possesses a salvaging quality in that this attention historically "coincided with [the circus's] gradual decline from being a major form of popular entertainment in the late Victorian era to its eclipse by cinema in the mid twentieth century."[41] Once more, Synge's ethnography analyzes culture on the brink of substantial transformations and captures moments of collision between opposing mindsets. This popular entertainment, the circus, is also a performative space that is itinerant, where the sedentary community encounters various communities of transients. This leitmotif can be found in several of the Wicklow essays dealing with the Travelers' community, but it also surfaces in the Kerry essays in relation to Synge's attention to local and global trajectories of travel and particularly in relation to local train travel. In the West Kerry series, Synge seems to enjoy depicting scenes from a number of train journeys. Attention to train travel is given in three out of the four articles that make up his West Kerry series in *The Shanachie*: "In West Kerry," "In West Kerry: To Puck Fair," and "In West Kerry: At the Races" (TI, 126, 162, 172).

The first article of the series, "In West Kerry" (Summer 1907), starts with a train journey from Tralee to Ballyferriter and opens with Synge in a train carriage packed with "sacks of flour, cases of porter, pots, chairs rolled in straw, and other household goods" (TI, 126). Synge describes the train ride, alternating comments about the landscape view from the window and comments about his fellow passengers. His interest in depicting train rides at this time is not unusual if one thinks about the suggestive piece at the end of part 2 of *The Aran Islands*, when Synge is traveling back to Dublin on the eve of Charles Stewart Parnell's death anniversary. Synge constructs this train journey episode as overtly symbolic. He is traveling at night, and the "tension of human excitement seemed greater in this insignificant crowd than anything I have felt among enormous mobs in Rome or Paris" (*AI*, 75). In the carriage, Synge witnesses a riot between a sailor and the police, and loud noises continue throughout the night journey: "some old men . . . talking in Irish," women "set[ting] up a frantic lamentation," "girls crying out in the carriage next us," and a sailor talking to his fellow passengers for the whole ride (*AI*, 75). Synge's fellow train travelers are symbolically called to embody "the whole spirit of the west of Ireland, with its strange wildness and reserve, . . . moving in this single train to pay a last homage to the dead statesman of the east" (*AI*, 76). First of all, Synge's perspective—from within the interior of a train carriage—is noteworthy in that he depicts himself as part of a multifarious crowd of travelers who are not only tourists but also common people and workers of different ages and genders. In addition, the train's trajectory—from West to East, from the rural periphery to the urban center—seems to unite two opposite and battling realities that have always been constructed as a dichotomy. In the episodes in *The Aran Islands* and in the West Kerry series, Synge's attention and interest in train journeys can be understood if we consider how these journeys allowed him to mingle with a variety of people, from English tourists to more ordinary local travelers and commuters. In the West Kerry series, his recurrent attention to the dynamics of a train journey is part of his narrative strategy, which favors a dialogic practice, as train carriages and train travel become a space where he can be part of a collective of people and negotiate his original perspective in dialogue with his informants. Some of these train episodes also enable him to evoke moments of "history telling"[42] and to deal in an original way with issues and aspects belonging to the grand narrative of Irish social history.

On the differences between train travel and horse-and-coach travel, Mary Banim's travelogue *Here and There through Ireland* offers an interesting perspective and provides an illustration of the horse-drawn vehicle she used to travel around Connemara, a "Bianconi's car," or long car (figure 6). Banim is particularly keen on that vehicle, stressing how it is important to be able to choose which side of the car to sit on, depending on the view. She also praises the long car as an excellent way of touring

6. Matilda E. Banim, *Long Car*, illustration in Mary Banim, *Here and There through Ireland*, series 1 (Dublin: Freeman's Journal, 1891). Image courtesy of the National Library of Ireland, Dublin.

places and "for making acquaintance, for those who journey in this lei-surely way seem far more ready to be kindly and neighbourly and to join in friendly chat than railway travellers."[43] Her predilection for long cars over train carriages is interesting if compared with Synge's penchant for the latter. Banim complains about "the noise of the train[, which] is not conducive to much conversation; then you have a feeling that you will soon be 'there,' and that it is not really worthwhile to put yourself out for your fellow-travelers."[44] Moreover, for Banim, the long-car experience proves to be more rewarding both aesthetically and socially:

> There is time to look at the beauties of nature as we pass; there are surely some amongst the passengers who know all about the route, and some who are eager to learn all the others can tell; the coachman is very com-municative and ready to talk—it is part of his business and his profit to

do so—and he keeps constantly turning round to point this or that point of interest in the landscape. His jokes with all the well-known passers-by on the road are as much for our benefit and amusement as for his own, and altogether the occupants of the car soon fraternise and become a friendly society.[45]

Banim's preference for the long car can be explained by considering issues of readership connected with the periodical where her travelogue was first published. She published in the *Weekly Freeman*, a supplement of the nationalist newspaper the *Freeman's Journal*, so her remarks on modes of traveling are addressing the issue of home tourism and, arguably, are directed toward an educated urban middle class who would have had sufficient means to practice home tourism in order to rediscover the beauties of the aspiring nation.

Furthermore, Banim's ideal of the passengers traveling on board a long car and becoming "a friendly society" epitomizes the rhetoric of a certain commodified type of travel, whereby middle-class tourists travel around not really to engage with new experiences and places but to reproduce in part the same social and material conditions they come from and, more importantly, to do so without upsetting their social conventions. Alfred Austin has brilliantly captured this particular aspect of tourism in his travelogue *Spring and Autumn in Ireland*: "I have observed that many people, in traveling, are anxious, above all things, to meet with a reproduction, as far as possible, for the circumstances and conditions they left at home. That seems odd, since I should have thought absolute novelty was the chief charm of travel."[46] In his trip to the Congested Districts in 1905, Synge would also avail himself of long cars to reach more distant and isolated Western localities such as Belmullet. Unlike Banim's idealization of coach travel on tourist routes, however, Synge's disenchanted account of a dreary night journey to Ballina highlights the routine aspects of the service, such as the changing of horses and the loading of the bag of mail (*TI*, 71). In the concluding article of the Congested District series, he would also argue that these difficult connections partake in keeping the people of the districts poor (*TI*, 96–97).

Robert Lynd's travelogue also displays a keen attention to travel experiences undertaken through various means of transport. In a polemic chapter specifically dedicated to "tourists in Kerry," he articulates a scathing critique of the tourists looking at the Irish scenery from a "rushing motor-car" and internalizing stereotypical assumptions about Ireland and the Irish. According to Lynd, the wilderness of the landscape seen from a motor car rushing through a tourist coastal road would reinforce in the tourist mind the idea of "Irish desolation and poverty." He promptly complains that "this is not Ireland that we see from the tourist motor. Why, the motor is even roofed in such a way that we cannot get a full view of the hills! We are cooped in and protected from the rain and reality." He further satirizes his fellow travelers, who upon seeing a funeral party from the motor car mistakenly refer to it as a "true" Irish eviction,[47] pointing at the scene with a thrill of surprise and delight at having experienced something that they had only previously read about in periodicals in the comfort of their English homes.[48] In another chapter of the travelogue, Lynd describes English tourists with irony: "They had simply the standoffishness of people who did not care for the human race outside their own little social group. They were the most extraordinary spectacle I had yet seen on the West Coast of Ireland. Decent people, kind people, good people, I'm quite sure, Heaven bless them, but you might as well have tried to feel brotherly to a lot of walruses." To these negative remarks about English tourists and the commodification of Kerry, he juxtaposes a number of positive Irish-Ireland-inflected exempla, notably the notice written in Irish that greets him when he finally reaches Killorglin—a sign that welcomes people "not only to the fair [Puck Fair] but to an awakening Ireland."[49] Lynd, as in many English travelogues before his, adopts an antitourist rhetoric but recasts it in nationalist terms.[50] His need to travel for "acculturation"[51] is motivated by a nationalist sentiment, and the off-the-beaten-track experience he is looking for does not simply imply discovering less-trodden localities. Unlike most English travelers, he is searching instead for the Irish Revival. In complaining about the tourist commodification of Killarney, Lynd concedes, "There is a real Killarney, I know, where real people live and work and tell stories around the fire, and think more of the Irish revival than of travelers' tips, but that

Killarney I would have no chance of seeing it from a hotel."[52] Lynd also looks for places and people that embody more fully a distinct national culture, ranging from places charged with Irish history and the memory of political personalities who have fought Ireland's many battles (e.g., Daniel O'Connell and Caheerciveen, defined as "a real place not a tourist resort"[53]) to small towns such as Killorglin that maintain local traditions England has yet to commodify.

Lynd's attention to the dynamics of tourist travel and to the ideological and class bias underpinning these dynamics can be compared with Synge's remarks about car drivers in his series of twelve articles for the *Manchester Guardian*, "In the Congested Districts," from June 10 to July 26, 1905. Synge was diffident toward car men when he traveled to Connemara and Mayo because he felt car men could manipulate the information on the conditions of the people and on the improvements implemented by the Congested Districts Board (see chapter 3 for more discussion of Synge and car men). Lynd's journey in Kerry allows him to mingle both with local people and, albeit reluctantly, with English trippers. Synge's texts, in contrast, avoid discussion of English tourist networks and privilege interactions with local interlocutors along with travel through smaller and more localized tourist infrastructures and transportations (e.g., local train lines, the bicycle) and boarding in local cottages or public houses.

As mentioned earlier, in Synge's Kerry essays the train carriage becomes a privileged area of interaction because it allows him proximity to and exchange with individuals coming from different walks of life. It is a public arena for multiple encounters and negotiations and is revelatory of both the landscape and the people in their everyday lives. In a train carriage, conversation seems to spring up more spontaneously and is less restrained by middle-class codes of respectability and social interaction—the idea of being "kindly and neighbourly and . . . join[ing] in friendly chat" advanced by Banim. In Synge, the train journey is powerfully depicted as a way of bringing people together. In the unpublished article "In West Kerry: At the Races,"[54] Synge finally manages "to get a seat on a sack of flour beside the owner, who has other packages scattered under our feet" (*TI*, 172). He captures the attention of his fellow travelers because "it was too late in the year for even an odd tourist, and on this line everyone is known by sight" (*TI*, 172). Synge occupies the rest of the train journey answering questions from an old man, who posits that Synge speaks and dresses like a Kerryman (*TI*, 172). The train is once more a place where Synge can negotiate his participant observation and shape his original perspective in dialogue with his informants. His interest in train carriages and train travel as a "field," in an anthropological sense, epitomizes his groundbreaking opening toward a plurality of fieldwork sites and his attention to milieus where relations of travel and mobility are explored vis-à-vis relations of inhabitation.

In Synge's foregrounding of anthropological practices typical of twentieth-century anthropology, not only participant observation is to be counted. His attention to depicting relations of travel, mobility, and displacement can be seen as anticipating debates and concerns advanced in contemporary ethnography. In theorizing twentieth-century ethnography, James Clifford notes how the discipline notably "privileged relations of dwelling over relations of travel," arguing that the focus on "fields" of dwelling—such as houses, offices, schools, and shopping malls—can sometimes be problematic because it excludes what gravitates outside them. Namely, what often stays out or is minimized are the complex relations of travel and translation that bring people to dwell in places, "the wider global world of intercultural import–export in which the ethnographic encounter is always already enmeshed." Clifford then analyzes the contemporary tendencies of "an emergent culture-as-travel-relations ethnography," which is embraced in some contemporary works and conceives of fieldwork "as travel encounters." Clifford's critique is asserted not simply to "invert the strategies of cultural localization" but rather to look at dwelling and traveling issues comparatively, "traveling-in-dwelling, dwelling-in-traveling."[55] As such, the series "In West Kerry" and to an extent Synge's travel journalism about Wicklow and the Congested Districts can be read as embodying this idea of "fieldwork as travel encounters." These multiple dislocations of the "field" are important in that they epitomize the angle by which Synge presents his informants' quotidian stories of travel and displacement: from everyday business commute to seasonal and long-term migration. This practice of presenting multiple fields and the way people move among them subverts tropes embedded in ethnographic analysis that see the informant as mainly a static figure, a "homebody" that dwells in his native land. Synge's dialogic practice, with its scrupulous attention to detail and great empathy in listening to and recording stories, instead remarkably also takes into account the micro-histories of travel and displacement of those communities that are served by local railway lines and that are traveling not uniquely for leisure.

Furthermore, Synge also fashions the train as a space where the shift from the "horizontal" to the "vertical" mode of travel starts to take place. Michael Cronin defines the "horizontal" aspect of travel as the linear progression of the trip, roughly from one place to the other. The "vertical" mode, in contrast, is a movement in the depths of time, taking into account a temporal/historical dimension.[56] In his Kerry pieces, Synge manages to intersperse moments of "history telling," and the train journey episodes are often constructed to fulfill this specific task. For example, Synge closes "In West Kerry: To Puck Fair" with an account of his train journey back to Dublin. He had already plunged into historical facts at the beginning of the same piece, where he reports an old man's testimony of his experiences as a migrant worker in England and Wales, where he had moved after the Famine: "I asked him if he remembered the famine. 'I do well,' he said. 'I was living near Kenmare, and many's the day I saw them burying the corpses in the ditch by the road. It was after that I went to England; for this country was ruined and destroyed'" (TI, 153). In the closing sketch of the article, Synge is traveling back to Dublin from a small village in Kerry, which Nicholas Grene identifies as Faranfore, "where the branch line to Valentia met the main Tralee to Killarney line."[57] His train route intersects with other lines and travelers' itineraries directed not only to the big metropolitan center of Ireland, Dublin, but also to Queenstown (now Cóbh), where emigrant ships were leaving for America. Train travel enables Synge to acquire a unique perspective as he finds himself immersed in the middle of the conflicting destinies of several passengers on board the same carriage with him. First, he is assigned the custody of a twenty-year-old girl traveling to Dublin to go to the hospital. The girl's mother escorted her on the trip for only a short while and left her in the care of Synge and someone who had just returned to Ireland from America (TI, 163). While Synge is conversing with the "returned American" "about scenery and politics and the arts . . . and the life of women in America," he is projected to the middle of one of the most dramatic scenes in Irish history when he witnesses people parting ways on the train platform beside his window:

> At several stations girls and boys thronged in to get their places for Queenstown, leaving parties of old men and women wailing with anguish on the platform. At one place an old woman was seized with such a passion of regret, when she saw her daughters moving away from her forever, that she made a wild rush after the train; and when I looked out for a moment I could see her writhing and struggling on the platform, with her hair over her face, and two men holding her by the arms. (*TI*, 163)

Thus, in this final section of "In West Kerry: To Puck Fair," Synge situates Kerry in a specific historical framework and locates his representations of people and places in an Irish-specific temporality that does not ignore social and political issues affecting the rural margins of Ireland at the turn of the twentieth century, such as the plight of emigration.

In the article "In West Kerry: To Puck Fair" as well as in his series "In the Congested Districts," Synge treats the theme of emigration from a nationalist standpoint, portraying immigration to America as traumatic and generally negative and, most importantly, as the consequence of colonial mismanagement.[58] A few years later, in *Rambles in Ireland*, Lynd would also adopt a similar stance and a similar narrative perspective—an encounter with an Irish emigrant in a train carriage. On the train from Killorglin to Caheerciveen, Lynd interacts with a young girl who is returning home after some time spent as a home worker in America. Lynd promptly blames the girl's nostalgia for her life in America—she complains that in Ireland "there was nothing to do on the farm" and that "she would die of dullness"—on the Irish school system, which is guilty of teaching "geography and history on the principle that Ireland is, in the vulgar phrase, the last country God made." Accordingly, he praises "politics and sport" for "keep[ing] some local enthusiasm burning here."[59] This remark is akin to Synge's praise of the IAOS's work and of the Gaelic League's cultural activism in his articles for the *Manchester Guardian*, "the interest made by these local associations" (*TI*, 82–83) being an important but not decisive factor in checking emigration. Lynd shares with Synge the ethnographic approach that Clifford theorizes as "fieldwork as travel encounters"[60] for paying attention to emigration, for depicting the relations of travel that affect the local Kerry communities, and for pointing to the effects of English tourism on the region. However, Lynd's approach is overtly propagandist—his Gaelic Leaguer's quest for the Irish Revival, his anti-English and anticolonial views—and his tone is generally more outspoken. In contrast, Synge's fieldwork strategies in West Kerry are less militant and display empathy toward his interlocutors.

In the West Kerry series, Synge showcases an original perspective that analyzes culture in dialogue with his informants and from a number of diverse fields that also account for the relationship of travel and displacement experienced by local communities. Synge's attention to local train travel is significant as it highlights how communities are not stable constructs but constituted by relations of travel, not just by relations of dwelling. Unlike previous travel writing about Kerry, which was generally concerned with tourist resorts and a peasant culture fabricated ad hoc for the tourist, Synge's essays investigate a residual rural culture orbiting these tourist networks.

# 3

## Traveling Journalist

### *J. M. Synge in the Congested Districts*

In the summer of 1905, J. M. Synge and the painter Jack B. Yeats traveled together in the Congested Districts of Connemara and Mayo under the commission of the English newspaper the *Manchester Guardian* to witness the poverty of the area and to evaluate the work of the governmental Congested Districts Board (CDB). For what would become a most interesting piece of reportage, Synge produced a series of twelve articles that appeared from June 10 to July 26, 1905, under the heading "In the Congested Districts"; Jack Yeats drew a series of pen-and-ink illustrations that were published alongside Synge's articles. While traveling, Synge collected his material and drafted his articles in his indispensable notebooks, while Yeats prepared his illustrations and sketched details of the journey in tiny pocket sketchbooks.

Synge's series "In the Congested Districts" is a remarkable example of investigative reporting that voices the cultural abjection of people living in colonial marginalities. As Declan Kiberd has remarked, Synge's journalism for the *Guardian* has much in common with left-wing engagé writings such as George Orwell's *The Road to Wigan Pier* (1937).[1] Indeed, Synge's series does bear striking resemblance to Orwell's work, not only for the same analytical and investigative slant in dealing with poverty but also for the same efforts to deconstruct events from many perspectives because both writers were keen on accounting for the witnesses' point of view as well as for the narrator's. Synge's journalistic strategy strives to privilege polyphony, letting facts speak for themselves through the testimony of their firsthand observers. Both Synge's and Orwell's disenchantment and lucidity of analysis are striking. As Richard Hoggart suggests in an introduction to *The Road to Wigan Pier*, Orwell "knew that not everyone was filthy, but the filth was the true indication of the cost of capitalist industrialisation in one of its worst forms."[2] With this in mind, Orwell attentively conducts his excavation trying to subvert stereotypes and common assumptions about working-class people, in the same way as Synge would do with "his" rural laborers in the *Guardian* series. Norman Sims emphasizes how literary journalists sometimes operate "outside the centres of power" and "rather than hanging around the edges of powerful institutions . . . attempt to penetrate the cultures that make institutions work."[3] This is exactly what Synge does in his nonfiction: his literary journalism ultimately investigates in a subversive way this differential of marginal and dominant forms—the persistence of backwardness and poverty within the framework of modernizing agents such as the CDB. According to P. J. Mathews, Synge is not concerned primarily with "the major events and significant dates in Irish history." His aim is instead "to break down and devolve abstract ideological issues into micro-contexts where questions of power, personal motivations, psychodynamics, group relations and determinisms of environment can be laid bare."[4] Synge does not adopt this strategy—with a typical literary journalist's attention toward human-interest stories and "a rendering of felt detail"[5] and experience—to avoid history. Rather, he pursues it to narrate another version of history previously kept on the margins but nonetheless deeply intertwined with the predicates of universal, developmental history.

As in chapter 1, this chapter combines a twofold approach whereby visual and textual artifacts are examined. In the first section, I look at Synge's and Jack Yeats's work as traveling artists and journalists. In particular, I retrieve neglected archival sources, Yeats's sketches of the trip, and assess their importance for a fuller understanding of Synge's trip to the Congested Districts. Drawing from Yeats's collection of sketches from the journey, from Synge's notebooks and correspondence, as well as from the published work in the *Guardian*, I examine Synge's approach to travel and travel writing during the trip to Connemara and Mayo. Although in most cases Synge traveled alone, for the Congested Districts trip he traveled and worked in tandem with another artist on a very specific assignment. Yeats's sketches, I argue, add important details to Synge's depiction of life in the Western seaboard, underlining the aesthetic affinities between the two artists evident in both their work in progress and their published work.

In the next section, I analyze Synge's groundbreaking style of reporting, concentrating on the published articles for the *Manchester Guardian*. After contextualizing the CDB's work and historicizing Synge's approach to the *Guardian* commission, I scrutinize Synge's narrative tactics in comparison with those used by previous travelers and reportage about the Congested Districts that appeared in a number of periodicals. I argue that "In the Congested Districts" essentially proposes both a formal and thematic subversion of imperialist rhetorical discourses by adopting a narrative strategy that tends to give voice directly to the people experiencing the distress. This polyphonic practice in particular subverts monophonic modes of journalism and official reports that generally represented the indigent as having no say in the matter of their representation and as being passive recipients of modernizing forces. Some of these reports were aimed at carrying forward ideas of Constructive Unionism, stressing philanthropic efforts and, as a consequence, the need for the people in the West of Ireland to be made even more dependent on their colonial mother country. Unlike in previous journalism about the Congested Districts, in Synge's series "In the Congested Districts" the power of firsthand testimony is in part transferred to the local inhabitants, who voice their concerns in conversation with Synge; in turn, Synge acts as an unobtrusive interviewer and allows them to speak more extendedly. As the final section of the chapter shows, this literary device breaks the "monophonic authority" of omniscient narrators.[6] By privileging a polyphonic and dialogic structure, Synge's reportage clearly frames "from below" his critique of the CDB measures.

### Sketching the Journey: Synge and Yeats on the Road

On June 3, 1905, Yeats and Synge met in Dublin and then set off to the West of Ireland to fulfill their assignment for the *Manchester Guardian*. On the same day, in a postcard to his wife, Mary Cottenham, showing the steamboat the painter had taken to come to Ireland (the "S.S. Scotia running between England and Ireland via Holyhead and Dublin"), Yeats confirmed, "I have just met Synge and wired to you," also promising to write a letter soon.[7] As Yeats's biographer Bruce Arnold reports, Synge and the painter "traveled to Galway by train and then by sidecar to Spiddal";[8] then they continued by several forms of horse-drawn transports. Another postcard that Yeats sent to Mary Cottenham on June 23 from Swinford shows a photograph of a traditional Irish jaunting car, printed at the center of a green-and-gold frame made of harps and shamrocks.[9] A jaunting car will also feature in the small illustration printed at the bottom of the Congested Districts article "Among the Relief Works" (June 17, 1905), depicting Synge and Yeats traveling over one of the many stone bridges connecting the small peninsulas in the Carraroe area. Synge and Yeats's trip to the West started a fruitful collaboration that has been thoroughly explored by Yeats's commentators and biographers, especially in relation to the illustrations that the painter created for Synge's travel book *The Aran Islands* and the sketches of the costumes for his plays.[10]

Critics such as Adele Dalsimer and Tony Roche have also read Synge's prose alongside the pen-and-ink illustrations that appeared in the newspapers. On the two artists' common orientation in the depiction of the distress in the West, Dalsimer argues that Synge's no-frills prose style correlates with Yeats's drawing style for the illustrations published in the *Guardian*. Dalsimer underlines, in particular, a common willingness to give a real depiction of the living conditions without the "allegorizing dimension" of *The Aran Islands*: "Yeats like Synge dispensed the required doses of objectivity and dispassion to the paper's liberal readership, who were certain to help their neighbours across the Irish sea—if they appeared needy and receptive to help."[11] Therefore, in adjusting the tone of the drawings to Synge's journalistic prose, Yeats actively contributed to Synge's unpatronizing representation of the districts. Synge's anti Constructive Unionism is pursued also by Yeats's style of pen-and-ink drawings, and a profound sense of dignity in poverty is what emerges from some of Yeats's finest portraits of men and women of the West. Roche highlights another example of this mutual vision in his analysis of the words and the drawings depicting relief works: "In Jack Yeats's accompanying illustration [for the article "Among the Relief Works" (June 17, 1905)], the picture is dominated by the ganger [labor foreman] in the right foreground, pulling assertively on the lapels of his jacket as his gaze scrutinizes the dozen workers. The latter have been described by Synge as 'a slow, inert procession.' Jack Yeats suggests the loss of bodily energy and individual autonomy in the way the shoulders of all four men are sloped and one body mechanically reproduces the inert shape of the other."[12] In Synge and Yeats's shared artistic vision in the *Guardian* series lies a deliberate statement of resistance against the condescending measures of Constructive Unionism. As I discuss later in this chapter, Synge's series ends by advocating Home Rule as the only way to restore a "renewed life" in Ireland, leading to a series of changes that "would all tend to make life less difficult even in bad years and in the worst districts of Mayo and Connemara" (*TI*, 99).

In reconstructing Yeats's and Synge's similar way of approaching the artistic métier, Ann Saddlemyer describes both authors as "always alert with notebooks and sketchbooks to record the memorable."[13] While traveling to the Congested Districts, both artists produced visual and literary documents: Synge his notebooks, where he drafted the essays, and Yeats his sketchbooks. Despite not having received much critical attention from Synge's scholars to date, Jack Yeats's sketches from this trip in 1905 are an invaluable source not only because they visualize material details of the artists' trip as the journey was unfolding but also because some illustrate significant extracts of Synge's articles, testifying to a shared aesthetic evident in much of their published work, and, more importantly for the purpose of this study, because they offer powerful images of Synge as a travel writer. Owing to the more hurried nature of this trip, the sketches may plausibly have also assisted Synge in drafting some of his articles. Whereas the pen-and-ink drawings published in the *Guardian* are rather essential and concerned primarily with highlighting the political and engagé message of Synge's investigative journalism, the unpublished sketches possess at times a lighter and more picturesque connotation, mirroring in the essays Synge's ethnographic attention to the material culture of the West of Ireland and his love for traveling.

In the Congested Districts, Synge traveled with his trusty notebooks and his typewriter. In his private correspondence with Molly Allgood, he mentions the notebooks a few times in a very interesting and personal way. In a letter dated September 30, 1907, Synge exhorts Molly to get a notebook to keep track of her readings: "By the way, I want you to get a notebook and write down everything you read, who it is by, when he lived, and any particulars that you think you would like to remember. I have a wheelbarrow of such notebooks (everyone who reads seriously keeps them) and you will find it no trouble and the greatest use" (*LM*, 199). In another letter dated May 16, 1907, he suggests that she write articles about the inner workings of theater tours from her perspective as an actress: "Go out when you get this, and buy a good thick square notebook with a strong cover and begin to keep a journal of your tour writing down every-thing as it comes helter-skelter, especially the small things" (*CL1*, 348). This suggestion that Molly keep a journal while traveling with theater practitioners is interesting in this context in that it emphasizes the connection between traveling and writing, between mobility and the creative process.

In the collection of Synge's manuscripts held at Trinity College, four notebooks in particular relate to the *Manchester Guardian* reportage:[14] they contain original impressions, drafts, and fair copies of the articles. However, these notebooks lack more scattered and instinctive impressions like the ones jotted down in the Aran journals, where Synge recorded more random, personal emotions, ballads, readings, colorful linguistic expressions, and turns of phrase. This difference in the later notebook annotations may be attributed to the hastier nature of the Congested Districts journey. Unlike Synge's prolonged and idle stay on the islands, the Congested Districts trip was not only faster but for Synge busier because he had to post the finished articles to Manchester while the trip was still in progress. As he tells Stephen MacKenna in a letter on July 13, 1905, he "sent off 3 articles a week for four weeks running" (*CL1*, 116); they appeared from June 10 to July 26, 1905.[15] In Connemara and Mayo, Synge's mode of travel was different from the mode he employed for the rest of his home journeys, not only because he was not alone on this trip but also because of its more hurried pace. By Synge's own admission, "we had not time in a month's trip to get to the bottom of things anywhere" (*CL1*, 116). According to Saddlemyer, the two did not stay "more than two nights at each place."[16] The Connemara journey therefore involved less-prolonged fieldwork, unlike his trips to Aran and West Kerry, where fieldwork was perhaps the core of Synge's *modus scribendi*. Because of this hastiness, the more creative side of the journey was enjoyed predominantly by Yeats, who seemed to have felt less under pressure and able to give free rein to his artistic inclinations. "I couldn't do anything like what I would have wished to do as an interpretation of the whole life," Synge complains to Stephen MacKenna (*CL1*, 116). In the same letter, the writer also protests ironically against the higher wages that were paid to Yeats, even though Synge had a much more tiring job, having to deal also with unexpected accidents, such as his typewriter breaking down (*CL1* 115, 116).[17] A few letters to his mother during the journey further illuminate a number of adversities, from the difficulty in "rak[ing] up fresh matters for an article every second day" to the often harsh conditions of travel from one place to the other, such as when they had to wait five hours in Athlone for the connecting train and faced a forty-mile drive under a "downpour" (June 24, 1905, *CL1*, 114). In another letter—written on June 16, 1905, at Deehan's Royal Hotel in Belmullet, County Mayo—where he thanks his mother for a parcel with "pyjamas [*sic*] . . . cigarettes and six pounds" (*CL1*, 113–14), he also mentions how he is afflicted by asthma.

The hurried nature of Synge and Yeats's business trip and the faster pace of the world of journalism imposed on Synge a more focused writing discipline, evident also in his notebooks. Overall, his *avant-textes*, to borrow a term used in genetic criticism,[18] reflect a more compositional phase, where a more complex attempt at textualization is already present. Dirk Van Hulle assigns "whatever precedes a first draft (reading notes, marginalia, plans, and schemes) . . . [to a] pre-compositional phase" and clarifies that "the compositional phase is focused on structuring and 'textualisation.'"[19] In the notebooks that make up MS 4400 of the Synge Papers at Trinity College Library in Dublin, Synge jotted down descriptive sentences, already trying to shape the text as a journal article, presumably given the urgency of meeting a deadline for submission every few days.

In it, he wrote at the back of some of the folios a schema of the main points to address in the essay, perhaps in order to recollect them more quickly in one of the other rewritings in the notebooks. In another folio, we have the schema of what will become the first article about Mayo, "The Homes of the Harvest Men" (July 1, 1905): "Arrival in Mayo. Change of / scene, long car / harvesters / turf / Erris head relief / works, cottage interior / women and children."[20] For the last article of the series, "Possible Remedies" (July 26, 1905), Synge clearly numbers his points: "1 Congested Districts / 2 Connemara . . . / 3 Seed Potatoes / 4 Better markets / 5 the carrying on of lace etc. / 6 the encouragement of / local matters (?) like carrageen / moss / 7 of course making life more interesting and / less . . . relief works / state of Ireland."[21] These schemata, however, appear almost only in MS 4400, whereas Synge employed the other three notebooks on the trip to rewrite the articles up to the final fair copy, rewritings that he compiled presumably for his own reference because the typed articles were posted to Manchester for publication. Interestingly, in another manuscript, there is a reference to "Notes Connaught Book," a project Synge wanted to start after the *Guardian* commission but never got around to doing. In some of the notes for this unfinished project, Synge schematizes details such as "evening walk out to the sea, Irises Everywhere, Night in Ballina, sea voyage, stormy evening walk etc."[22] From the letters, we know that Synge wanted to rework the Connemara material in order to give "an interpretation of the whole life" and was ready to use the *Guardian* earnings to go back and do more fieldwork (CL1, 116). Unfortunately, he never made it to the Congested Districts again, nor did this book project make it to the compositional phase. The "Notes Connaught Book" reference remains the only precompositional evidence of Synge's desire to write another travel book along the lines of *The Aran Islands*.

Jack Yeats's work for the *Manchester Guardian* series includes fourteen pen-and-ink drawings and a few additional that were inserted in Synge's Library Edition of *In Wicklow, West Kerry, and Connemara* in 1911,[23] two years after Synge's death. On the road, however, Yeats sketched people and landscapes *en plein air* on tiny sketchbooks.[24] These sketches capture details of local customs and material culture that often complement Synge's data about the conditions on the western seaboard narrated in the articles. In a way, they can be considered visual records of the trip as it was unfolding, similar to Synge's photographs of Aran. To my knowledge, for this Connemara and Mayo tour, Synge did not take any photographs, nor did he take along his camera. Whereas the published pen-and-ink drawings attempt a coherent interpretation of Synge's political message in the articles, Yeats's sketches in part visualize the material conditions in which the artists traveled and provide a glimpse of what first triggered their imagination. In 1981, the artwork that Yeats produced on his trip with Synge in 1905 was creatively reused in a dramatization of their journey, produced, written, and directed by Margy Kinmonth. The film *To the Western World: J. M. Synge and Jack B. Yeats Journey* is a drama documentary powerfully narrated by John Huston, where both sketches and pen-and-ink drawings inspire a large number of reenacted scenes and footage.[25] For example, the small pen-and-ink drawing accompanying the *Guardian* piece "Among the Relief Works" and presenting a landscape view of a stone bridge crossed by a jaunting car with the two artists is re-created from a similar angle in one of the film's initial scenes. Elsewhere in the documentary, Yeats's illustration of the ferryman of Dinish Island for the homonymous article "The Ferryman of Dinish Island" (June 21, 1905) is reenacted from the same perspective: the ferryman is portrayed and filmed by someone who is sitting right in front of him on the boat. The film also animates Yeats's sketch of Synge stretched out on a tree branch and taking a nap.[26] In the scene, Kinmonth's documentary integrates the bidimensional view of the sketch by showing both Yeats while he is sketching Synge and in a subsequent frame the image of the actual artifact from the archive. In a way similar to Kinmonth's cinematic rendition, my analysis attempts to re-create Synge and Yeats's journey from critically neglected visual documents.

Synge's road companion sketched almost everything that stimulated his curiosity. Yeats captured many details of landscapes, objects, and people, including information on his fellow traveler. Thus, in the sketchbooks there are painter studies, such as one of Synge's head; panoramic landscape views, such as the one of Clifden;[27] panoramic town scenes that he sketched from his hotel room;[28] and panoramic views of the hotel rooms

7. Jack B. Yeats, detail of a hotel room in Swinford, 1905, pen-and-ink and water-color. "103 [50] Swinford and London July 1905 [Masefield, Synge]," folios 2v and 3, Jack B. Yeats Archive, National Gallery of Ireland. © Estate of Jack B. Yeats, DACS London / IVARO Dublin, 2017. Photograph courtesy of the National Gallery of Ireland, Dublin.

where Synge and Yeats lodged at night (for example, the one in Swinford shown in figure 7).

Perhaps because funded by the *Guardian*, Synge and Yeats opted for a more comfortable type of accommodation, especially in comparison to Synge's accommodation on Aran. Yeats's sketches, being a sort of behind-the-scenes record of the trip, illustrate fresh impressions and provide a number of interesting images of Synge on the road. Given that Synge claimed not to be fond of being photographed and when traveling took pictures mostly of his interlocutors, these sketches are precious because they visualize Synge as a travel writer. Some of the sketches held in the Henry W. and Albert A. Berg Collection at the New York Public Library portray Yeats's fellow traveler at times in a bohemian way. In one, Synge is sitting on a bench in a walled garden in Carna (figure 8); in another, he is taken in profile, looking at a panoramic view of a Connemara landscape from the side of the sketch (figure 9). In the reenacted scene of the sketch in Kinmonth's film, mentioned earlier, he is shown sleeping outside, presumably during a break from traveling.

In addition to images of Synge, some of Yeats's sketches seem to evoke specific excerpts of a more descriptive nature to be found in Synge's

8. Jack B. Yeats, Synge sitting on a bench in a walled garden in Carna, 1905, pencil and water-color. "V4 Ireland with Synge," folio 26, Henry W. and Albert A. Berg Collection of English and American Literature, New York Public Library. © Estate of Jack B. Yeats, DACS London / IVARO Dublin, 2017. Photo-graph courtesy of the Henry W. and Albert A. Berg Collec-tion of English and American Literature, the New York Public Library, Astor, Lenox and Tilden Foundations.

articles, as attested to in three significant examples. A first parallel relates to the article "The Boat Builders" (June 28, 1905). For publication in the *Manchester Guardian*, Yeats drew one plate, *Boat-Building at Carna*, based on three sketches.[29] The fact that he prepared the final plate with such a significant number of studies and templates arguably mirrors Synge's editorial interest in the same activity—Synge dedicated an entire article to the boat-building industry in the districts. In the album "V4 Ireland with Synge," folio 18, a pencil-and-watercolor drawing that Yeats himself captioned "Boat Builder in Carna," the boat builder leans against a boat, with his shirt open so that one can spot the same hairy chest that Synge refers to in his article: "The old man himself was rather remarkable in appearance, with strongly formed features, and an extraordinarily hairy chest showing through the open neck of his shirt" (*CW2*, 312).

Another parallel between articles and sketches can be drawn with reference to the article "The Small Town" (July 22, 1905), where Synge

9. Jack B. Yeats, Synge's profile overlooking a landscape, 1905, pencil and water-color. "JM, Synge J" written by Jack Yeats in the top left corner. "V5 'Swinford' 1905," folios 10v and 11, Berg Collection, New York Public Library. © Estate of Jack B. Yeats, DACS London / IVARO Dublin, 2017. Photograph courtesy of the Henry W. and Albert A. Berg Collection of English and American Literature, the New York Public Library, Astor, Lenox and Tilden Foundations.

comments on the objects crammed in the window of the local emporium in Swinford: "Inside many of the shops and in the windows one could see an extraordinary collection of objects—saddles, fiddles, rosaries, rat-traps, the Shorter Catechism, castor oil, rings, razors, rhyme-books, fash-ion plates, nit-killer, and fine-tooth combs. Other houses had the more usual articles of farm and household use" (*TI*, 92). Yeats's visual rendition of this passage can be found in his Swinford sketchbook, where he pres-ents a pencil-and-ink drawing of one of these shop windows,[30] along with the head of a little boy sketched in profile, seemingly staring in awe at all the objects cramming the window sill. In the published *Guardian* series, Yeats will give samples of the interior of the crammed shop in the plate that opens the article "The Inner Lands of Mayo—the Village Shop" (July 19, 1905; *TI*, 85).

A final instance of Synge and Yeats's shared vision of the West can be traced in a distinctive remark that appears in the *Guardian* article titled "Erris" (July 8, 1905). In this article, Synge starts by describing the issue of seasonal migration and the seasonal laborers on their way to Scotland for the harvest. He concludes the piece on a more colorful note, describ-ing the market in Belmullet with the following scene: "Once when I looked out, the blacking-brush man and the card trick man were getting up a fight in the corner of the square. A little later was another stir and I saw a Chinaman [sic] wandering about followed by a wondering crowd" (CW2, 327–28). In Jack Yeats's sketches, we have in two folios a pictorial snapshot of that precise moment: the pencil sketch of the "Brush Merchant"[31] and a pencil-and-watercolor sketch of the Chinese man (figure 10) walking among the crowd. He is sketched in profile, with a pipe in his mouth and holding two brushes, one in each hand. Yeats wrote in the caption "brush merchant."

The sketch of the Asian figure seems to me very interesting in relation to Synge's text. He stands in the middle of the picture, wearing traditional light-blue clothes, his black hair tied in a long tress. He holds a little boy in his arms, and beside him there is another child in short white pants, blue shirt, and a hat with a wide brim. Yeats scribbled the word *glory* on the child's hat and wrote a caption at the bottom left of the sketch that purportedly reads "Chinaman in Belmullet." The light-blue color of the Asian man's clothes and his central position on the sheet make him stand out from the rest of the amorphous crowd, which is roughly sketched in brown on the right-hand side of the picture. The emphasis on the word *glory* scribbled on the child's hat seems to recall ironically the moment of glory Synge refers to in his piece, the "stir" among the "wondering crowd." Coincidentally, this figure appeared to be known in Synge's household. In *Letters to My Daughter*, Samuel Synge's memoir of his brother, John, written for his daughter, Edith, Samuel writes about reading John's article in the *Guardian*, where the Chinese man is described. Samuel, who was working in China as a missionary, hypothesizes that the Asian figure is probably a domestic worker of a family acquaintance who was living in China as well. Samuel also remarks how this fact was brought to his brother John's attention.[32]

As the sketches examined here show, Synge and Yeats shared a common ethnographic attention to recording life in the Congested Districts. Moreover, Yeats's ethnographic eye is also evident in seven articles— collectively titled "Life in London" and "Life in Manchester" and published from December 9, 1905, to May 26, 1906—that the painter wrote for another *Manchester Guardian* commission right after his trip with Synge and for which he illustrated a number of sketches about city life. Robert

10. Jack B. Yeats, man in traditional Chinese clothes with children, 1905, pencil and watercolor. "V5 Swinford 1905 Mayo," folio 9, Berg Collection, New York Public Library. © Estate of Jack B. Yeats, DACS London / IVARO Dublin, 2017. Photograph courtesy of the Henry W. and Albert A. Berg Collection of English and American Literature, the New York Public Library, Astor, Lenox and Tilden Foundations.

Skelton argues that Yeats's early journalism for the *Guardian* helped him in creating his experimental drama and fiction a couple of decades later.[33] Arguably, Yeats's pictorial and journalistic eye benefited from the influence of a well-read ethnographer and writer such as Synge. Moreover, Yeats's sketches are also an invaluable treasure for Synge scholars because they offer portraits of Synge as a travel writer and provide a glimpse into what first stimulated his imagination on the road while the journey was progressing.

## "Many Complicated Causes That Keep the People near to Pauperism": Synge and Fellow Journalists in the Congested Districts

The name "Congested Districts" designated the utmost westward localities of rural Ireland, where poverty and distress had been consistent since the Great Famine. However, as historian Ciara Breathnach notes, "the term

'congested' [was] misleading, not all the areas in question were overpopu-
lated. . . . [C]ongestion was a euphemism for relative poverty stemming
from an over-dependency on small holdings."[34] In addition, historian F. S.
L. Lyons has identified in the local shopkeeper's monopoly on the buying
and selling of goods as one of the main factors of an alarming economic
stagnation—what he dubs the "shopocracy."[35] The Congested Districts
were remnants of a previous economic order—landlordism—that was
rapidly changing after the Land War, which began in the late 1870s. Poverty was rampant, and emigration was often the only effective remedy
in areas that had been previously hit by the Great Famine, 1845–49. The
Congested Districts were peripheral and in the process of being economically demarginalized with the modernizing manifesto of the Congested
Districts Board. The CDB was a governmental institution set up by Lord
Arthur Balfour in 1891 aimed at relieving the distress through the implementation of local enterprises and land and holding rearrangements. As
Nicholas Grene has pointed out, "Instituted by a conservative administration, [the CDB] was associated with the politics of Constructive Unionism,
by which the government of the time sought to reconcile Irish people with
the Union by an amelioration in their social condition," thus renovating
public consensus.[36] In other words, as Breathnach points out, Constructive
Unionism implied an effort in "'pacifying' agrarian unrest by a combination of coercive and conciliatory measures."[37] The CDB was active in the
most impoverished areas of the West of Ireland and fostered local enterprises such as fisheries, kelp making, and textile industries. Through the
implementation of new industries and philanthropic activities, England
sought to keep pulling the "colonial" strings of Ireland with "paternalistic schemes [that] turned the locals into dependent provincials," as P. J.
Mathews puts it, thus "stifling rather than fostering a spirit of innovation
and creating an atmosphere of dejection."[38] Hence, within a Constructive
Unionist framework, Ireland was conceived as being in a relationship
of umbilical dependence on the mother country and therefore unfit for
self-government.

The origin of the CDB is connected in an interesting way with
an instance of investigative journalism. The board was set up in 1891
in part as a result of a series of polemic reports written by the Quaker

philanthropist James Hack Tuke about the conditions on the western seaboard. Tuke's pamphlet *Irish Distress and Its Remedies* (1880) caught the
attention of Lord Balfour, who decided to visit the areas personally and
finally in 1891 to set up the CDB to face the emergency.[39] Tuke had been
active in Ireland since the Famine years. As Glenn Hooper observes in a
note to another work by Tuke, Tuke had "worked with the Friends Asylum in York, visited the United States, and supported many charitable
institutions, traveling around Ireland in 1846 and 1857 with the abolition-
ist William Edward Forster to distribute relief funds."[40] The pamphlet
*Irish Distress* would cause a stir and spur many attacks, especially on the
issue of peasant proprietorship, which Tuke advocated for and thought
beneficial in some cases. In his analysis of peasant proprietorship, Tuke
remarks that this measure cannot simply be "possession of land without
the capital required for its proper cultivation."[41] Hooper has related the
sheer poignancy of Tuke's analysis to a sort of Quaker missionary ethos,
whereby the Quakers' "emphasis placed on the 'written word'" pushed
them to address issues to the general media in order to reach a wider
audience, using rhetorically effective language.[42] In addition to denouncing the appalling distress in the West, Tuke also tried to coordinate and
implement a program of assisted emigration with Canada and St. Paul,
Minnesota, from 1880 to 1884.[43] Albeit successful in some cases, the problem of encouraging immigration to America raised a number of cultural
issues—for instance, the antagonism of the Catholic Church, which considered immigration to America debasing for both men and women, who
it assumed would lose their morality in big metropolitan areas.[44] In the
end, however, Tuke was ostracized by the very countries he wanted to
send Irish migrants to, Canada and the United States, and ultimately the
program was interrupted. Next Tuke became involved in a distribution
of potato seeds in 1886 to face the agrarian crisis of that year.[45] In the following years, with the foundation of the CDB, he became one of its com-
missioners.[46] His death in 1896 at the age of seventy-seven prevented him
from effectively evaluating the efficacy of the CDB measures in the long
term. Despite Tuke's analytical mind and excellent problem-solving skills,
his philanthropic work was undeniably used as a tool for Constructive
Unionism, and his pamphlets fully reflect this mindset. For instance, in

the emblematic colonial finale in *Irish Distress and Its Remedies*, Tuke advocates philanthropic action so that Ireland's "union with England (can be) a source of strength and security, instead of one of weakness and danger" and so that Ireland can become "in something more than name, an integral portion of the United Kingdom of Britain and Ireland."[47]

When John Synge and Jack Yeats traveled to the Congested Districts in 1905, after fourteen years of implementations by the CDB and in the aftermath of the Irish Land Act, or Wyndham Land Act, of 1903, there was still strong economic stagnation. According to Richard Vincent Comerford, the Wyndham Land Act was exceptional compared to previous bills not only because it had been drafted in agreement with both landlord and tenant representatives but also because it offered very advantageous terms to both parties. Comerford explains how the annual tenant payments toward purchase were actually lower than their rents, therefore enabling more effectively the tenants' purchase of the land; the option of payments toward purchase were, in turn, made possible through a significant government subsidization to landlords.[48] Retrospectively, according to some historians, the Land Act "spelt the end of the Anglo-Irish Ascendancy class."[49] However, as Patrick Cosgrove maintains, the act also amplified certain difficulties for a number of "landless and land-poor" groups, such as "evicted tenants, agricultural laborers, disinherited farmers' sons, uneconomic smallholders, those living in the Congested Districts, or the landless generally." Cosgrove further explains that the act was financially "unstable and unsound": with "the unexpectedly high volume of sales, administrative and staffing problems, the release of only £5 million annually by the Exchequer for the first three years, and the long delays associated with the distribution of the purchase money and the bonus to landlords, major difficulties arose."[50] Hence, despite a number of material and legislative improvements on the government's part, these utmost westward localities still retained the status of "subaltern spaces," or spaces that exist, as David Lloyd defines them, "in a continuing differential relation to modernity."[51] As subaltern spaces, the districts had the characteristic of being "constituent elements of colonial modernity and agencies in state formation,"[52] in part because the CDB's intervention had been set up with a precise Constructive Unionist agenda. As Synge's series testifies, among the destitute farmers in the districts a sense of spiritual impasse also prevailed in addition to material poverty.

Before heading to the West of Ireland, Synge interacted with the *Manchester Guardian*'s editor C. P. Scott, who had personally contacted him in May 1905 to make arrangements for the assignment.[53] Through several letters, they agreed to the terms of their journalistic partnership and the editorial lines, which Bruce Arnold has reconstructed in his study of Jack Yeats.[54] What emerges from the correspondence between Scott and Synge is Synge's willingness to accomplish the *Manchester Guardian* assignment in his own way; he wrote to Scott that he "would deal with the problem independently, rather than from the point of view of the strictly orthodox Nationist [sic]."[55] Synge also had clearly in his mind the areas he wanted to visit;[56] he had been there previously in 1904 for a cycling trip around the northern coast of Mayo.[57] Although Scott accepted Synge's personal approach without too much resistance, enunciating truthful observation as the only quality he was looking for in a reporter,[58] Synge felt a certain nervousness about the whole project, not considering it fully up to his potential and unwilling to "lift the rags from my mother country, for to tickle the sentiments of Manchester," as he wrote to his friend Stephen MacKenna on May 30, 1905 (*CL1*, 111). Such remarks show how Synge was aware of the political implications surrounding the journalistic project and how he wanted to distance himself from the militant and sensationalist modes of reporting that had characterized previous pamphlets, such as Tuke's. The choice of Jack Yeats as illustrator was made afterward and orchestrated behind the scenes by the poet and dramatist John Masefield. Yeats and Masefield had known each other at least since 1897, and they shared a common passion for boats and model ships.[59] Masefield had already sponsored Synge for a *Guardian* commission in January 1905: on January 24, Synge's article "An Impression of Aran" appeared in the British newspaper, followed by his article "The Oppression of the Hills" on February 15.

C. P. Scott's decision to use Synge and Yeats for a series on Irish distress served a number of purposes on the *Guardian* agenda. To a larger extent, the *Guardian*'s "special commitment to Ireland" was in line with its Whig ethos, endorsing Prime Minister William Gladstone's Home Rule policy.[60] As an encomiastic history of the newspaper has highlighted, "The Irish question was to the *Manchester Guardian* literally and in no figure of speech, a liberal education. Gladstonianism began with the Irish question but it transcended it. . . . It became a feeling for the nationality of other people. From Ireland to South-Africa was a change of scene, but hardly a change of mind."[61] The choice of two personalities connected with the Irish Literary Revival was related both to a political agenda and to dynamics of prestige and authoritativeness—Synge and Yeats were Irish and fairly distinguished voices. These ideas of distinction and authoritativeness very much followed C. P. Scott's inclinations. According to Scott's biographer, the newspaper was developing alongside a city community that was becoming constantly more cosmopolitan and rich thanks to its "rich merchants" and to a lively cultural environment exemplified by Manchester's renowned university and grammar school: Scott "made it his task to put the ordinary citizen of Manchester in touch with the best minds of the day in every department of life and letters. . . . [He] made it one of his special cares to see that his readers could learn all that was to be discovered by highly skilled observers about large problems in any part of the world."[62] Albeit uncritically celebratory, such encomiastic histories suggest that the genre of travel writing with an emphasis on people and locality seen from the perspective of a distinguished observer was in line with the newspaper. Moreover, the same genre would also be employed pervasively in the following years. At the end of 1905 and in 1906, this time at Masefield's suggestion, Jack Yeats would write articles and draw sketches for a series about Manchester, where he had lived at the end of the nineteenth century.[63] In addition, the *Guardian* was directly involved in relief activities in the West, as Synge informs us in the article "Erris," quoting the work done in the village of Aghoos with the funds raised by the newspaper a few years earlier (*TI*, 83). According to a report published in the *New Ireland Review*, the *Guardian*'s philanthropic involvement started around 1898, when the Manchester Relief Fund Committee was set up in Manchester town hall as a consequence of a shocking report on the conditions in the districts that *Guardian* journalist James Long had published in the paper.[64] Like Tuke's writing, Long's work once again exemplify how pamphlets and journalism worked instrumentally (and sensationally) to encourage philanthropic action.

James Long regularly wrote on agriculture for the *Guardian*, contributing a column on farming entitled "Farm Notes."[65] In 1898 and 1899, he also wrote a series about Ireland titled "Cooperation in Agriculture."[66] In these pieces, Long visits a number of Irish creameries and local businesses and generally praises the renowned energy propelled by Horace Plunkett's cooperative society, the IAOS. However, his articles also display a colonial mindset as well as a patronizing attitude toward Irish farmers, who, he claims, are guilty of resisting modernization despite living "within the most advanced culture and civilization" and "within a four-hour journey from the centre of Empire." Long also blames the Irish Celtic nature for hampering progress: "The Irish farmer, who is volatile and lovable son of nature, is, so far as agriculture is concerned, lacking in foresight, thrift, and enterprise, and slow to apply the severe lessons which nature has taught him for his future advantage."[67] He praises elsewhere the work of the CDB in Connemara, and during a visit with a CDB official he notes that renovated holdings enabled a poor tenant to make a fresh start.[68] In the same piece, he remarks about the promising impact that a local cooperative society has, albeit underlining at the same time the need for further education about more up-to-date agricultural techniques, such as the use of artificial fertilizers.

Like previous reporting, Synge's reportage tackles through direct observation "the many complicated causes that keep the people near to pauperism" (*TI*, 87) in the Congested Districts: the shopkeeper's monopoly of the market and the consequent stagnation in commercial activities, technical issues on agriculture and industry, land subdivision, and emigration. His analysis, however, unlike that displayed in his predecessors' work, is formally innovative, avails of dialogic and polyphonic strategies, and is particularly keen on emphasizing that penury and the CDB measures affected the population not only at a material level but also—and more worryingly—at a cultural level. Synge's reportage, in voicing the people's opinions and experiences of the distress and of the effects of the CDB measures, expresses what Raymond Williams describes as "residual ideology"—that is, "a value system that has outlived its own time, . . . unable to function as the dominant ideology in the new social order, but . . . capable of demonstrating the limitations of the ideology that is dominant."[69] Synge subversively uses the people's testimonies that exemplify this "residual" mindset in order to draw attention to the fact that sudden changes and the discourse of progress carried forward by the CDB were perilously affecting the culture of the Irish rural districts. This criticism does not signify that Synge was against material ameliorations that would have improved the daily lives of the people. More precisely, he often points to the way these ameliorations were carried out—with little regard for the existing culture. Ultimately, Synge advocates sustainable ameliorations in line with the local rural culture.

One of the major issues intertwined with the CDB's politics was land redistribution in the aftermath of the Land War in the last three decades of the nineteenth century and the Wyndham Land Act of 1903. The land question in Ireland became inextricably linked with nationalism through the work of the Land League,[70] which encouraged the belief that "tenant proprietorship would promote prosperity," even if "the harsh reality remained that land holdings were too small" and therefore insufficiently productive.[71] This is, essentially, the criticism that Synge advances in the Congested District article "The Smaller Peasant Proprietor" (July 5, 1905), where he explores the CDB process of holdings amalgamation and land purchase. He is very factual in describing the economic inefficiency of some of the new holdings (*TI*, 78). However, he is in favor of land proprietorship in an anticolonial sense—that is, as an empowering device for the farmers and as a first step toward changing the mentality of servility and dependency: "Still no one can deny the good that is done by making the tenants masters of their own ground and consolidating their holdings" (*TI*, 78). Synge also warns that "the state of suspended land purchase" resulting from the post–Wyndham Act difficulties in continuing with the subsidies given to landlords toward land sale, might worsen economic and living conditions once more, and he rightly acknowledges some good work done locally by small CDB grants that went toward house improvements, despite making some of the cottages look "awkward" (*TI*, 79). In "The Boat Builders," Synge further remarks how the new cottages installed with iron instead of thatch roofs are one of the CDB implementations that are "perhaps a little too sudden. It is far better, wherever possible, to improve the ordinary prosperity of the people till they begin to improve their houses themselves on their own lines, than to do much in the way of building houses that have no interest for the people and disfigure the country" (*TI*, 68). This comment displays the typical revivalist ethos of self-help, which Synge advocates also in the article "Erris" when he praises the work of the cooperative movement and the Gaelic League (*TI*, 82). He criticizes how the board's implementations do not take into account the repercussions that these changes have on the people who experience them firsthand and on the people's long-standing traditions.

Synge's personal sensibility can be paralleled to George Orwell's empathy in dealing with an analogous problem in *The Road to Wigan Pier*—the problem of the slums in miners' towns, an issue that was being addressed with the construction of Corporation Estates. Despite the fact that new buildings were put up as a solution to the housing problem, Orwell, like Synge, criticizes the *way* these new buildings were implemented, "in a monstrously inhuman manner." What is "ruthless and soulless about the whole business," in Orwell's view, are the limitations placed on the dwellers' personal possessions (e.g., pets) and strict regulations on the kind of shops that they can open in a Corporation Estate.[72] At the end of the chapter, Orwell sardonically remarks:

> It is a great achievement to get slum-dwellers into decent houses, but it is unfortunate that, owing to the peculiar temper of our time, it is also considered necessary to rob them of the last vestiges of their liberty. The people themselves feel this, and it is this feeling that they are rationalising when they complain that their new houses—so much better, as houses, that those they have come out of—are cold and uncomfortable and "unhomelike." I sometimes think that the price of liberty is not so much eternal vigilance as eternal dirt.[73]

The phrases "monstrously inhuman manner" and "ruthless and soulless" aptly translate what Synge means when stating that the CDB's improvements do not take into account the interests of the people—their active and participatory involvement in these changes as opposed to their objectification in the process of modernization.

As mentioned earlier, one of the major problems that afflicted the districts was the so-called shopocracy,[74] or the control of local markets that shopkeepers exercised through a system of barter and advanced credit at the expense of local farmers. Owing to heavy expenses and poor harvests, farmers were constantly indebted to the shopkeepers, and to repay them they had to trade their labor. In her study on the CDB, Breathnach describes the shopocracy as "a primary factor in rural poverty and shopkeeper's debts [sic] one of the biggest obstacles to rural development."[75] Many contemporaneous commentators negatively assessed the shopocracy as a backward system that placed the districts in an economic limbo. For example, in an article entitled "In Gorumna Island" written by the secretary of the Manchester Relief Fund, E. Keogh, and published in the Irish monthly periodical *New Ireland Review* in June 1898, poverty is sensationalized in ways that not even Tuke's pamphlets had done a decade earlier. Keogh's article can be identified as partaking in the tokenistic process of "affirmation," in which, according to David Spurr, the "rhetorical economy of the media . . . creates a demand for images of chaos in order that the principles of a governing ideology and the need for institutions of order may be affirmed."[76] The ideology being reinforced here is, once again, that of Constructive Unionism. In "In Gorumna Island," after emphasizing the dire straits of the population, Keogh depicts the local inhabitants' state as primitive—the ultimate evidence of that state being, in his opinion, the "total disregard of money for its own sake, i.e. for the purposes of accumulation." He continues: "Here there is no 'love of lucre,' money has resolved itself into its primal essence of a mere token, a convenient medium of exchange. Just as the people in the South Pacific islands treat their pieces of carved stick which represent their method of payment, so the people of Gorumna look upon the coin of realm."[77] Here, Keogh fails to acknowledge that the shopocracy system is a phenomenon that must be ascribed to specific political and social dynamics. Moreover, his alignment of the Irish with the "primitive" population of the South Pacific islands places them both in a subaltern and peripheral position in relation to the central British economic power. His statement reempowers a negative notion of the Irish as primitive and therefore inferior (because of their supposedly self-inflicted poverty) and as a consequence in need of a strong intervention from a mighty economic and colonial power. Furthermore, Keogh defines the Irish people's disinterest in money and their barter with the local shopkeeper as "a happy state of things from a moral standpoint, but taken economically, it is sad, as indicative that each man knows not the day or the hour when he may himself have to fall back on the charity of his neighbour."[78] The emphasis on the Christian syllogism that "poverty equals morality" averts attention from the political and economic factors that generated the same condition, therefore legitimizing the status of poverty as intrinsic to the individual and almost spiritually fulfilling. As Spurr states, this dynamic is a form of idealization, "transforming the other into yet one more term of Western Culture's dialogue with itself."[79] In Keogh's finale, the Constructive Unionist bias is blatantly revealed by the emphasis placed on England's civilizing and modernizing mission toward Ireland: "In this way, without any loss to the State, the people now depressed and demoralised by poverty would be raised into intelligent and useful members of society. By this means they would be enabled to participate in the advantages of our common civilization, and to take their part in the movement of the time which, if it has not retrograded, has certainly stood still in Gorumna Island."[80]

Unlike Keogh's take in the *New Ireland Review*, Synge's approach is less biased and more accurate. In the *Manchester Guardian* series, Synge is meticulous in showing how the shopocracy system is endemic in a problematic way, affecting a number of economic activities that might potentially become fruitful in the districts. For instance, in "The Kelp-Makers" (June 24, 1905) he stresses the connections between kelp making and the shopocracy, showing how the locals were trying to pay off their debts with kelp despite the fact that the kelp market was often monopolized by a single buyer at often unfair prices (*TI*, 63). In the article "From Galway to Gorumna" (June 10, 1905), Synge describes how he meets a Connemara man who laments the scarce fishing activity owing to the lack of good boats,[81] and he emphasizes how instead of building boats the people were exploited by the shopkeepers for cheap labor: "The shopkeeper wants the people idle," the Connemara man states, "so that the shopkeepers can send them for a shilling a day to go out in their hookers and sell turf on Aran or on the coast of Clare" (*TI*, 44). It is in the essay "The Inner Lands of Mayo—the Village Shop" (July 19, 1905) that Synge thoroughly explains the system of credit and the two annual bills compiled by the "gombeen man" (shopkeeper), stressing once more the local inhabitants' helplessness:

> The people keep no passbooks, so they have no check on the traders, and although direct fraud is probably rare it is likely that the prices charged are often exorbitant. What is worse, the shopkeeper in out-of-the-way places is usually the only buyer to be had for a number of home products, such as eggs, chickens, carragheen moss and sometimes even kelp; so that he can control the prices both of what he buys and what he sells, while as a creditor he has an authority that makes bargaining impossible. (*TI*, 86–87)

Nelson O'Ceallaigh Ritschel reads Synge's treatment of the shopocracy phenomenon in the Congested Districts as evidence of his "leftist" and "socialist" leanings as well as of his increasing antagonism toward the Irish nationalist middle class, which he lambasts in his plays.[82] Furthermore, from a stylistic perspective, Synge's strategy in tackling the districts' economic problems also avoids racial and primitivist stereotyping but rather brings to light their possible causes as seen from the point of view of the people who are the victims of the unfair monopoly.

Another example of Synge's groundbreaking attitude is evident when he tackles the governmental system of relief works in the article "Among the Relief Works." This system had notoriously been implemented since the Famine and, according to Synge, was both diminishing for the farmers and unsuccessful in the long run. Farmers worked for one shilling a day and were taken from their households to join the relief system, therefore being subtracted from more remunerative and uplifting works such as farming and kelp making (*TI*, 51). Synge further points out that the relief-works system was not always economically strategic for the state—mentioning the case of a nearby district where a ganger, or foreman, had only two workers under his supervision (*TI*, 51–52). His treatment of relief works shares the same self-help ethos evident, for instance, in an article by Father T. A. Finlay, the editor of the *New Ireland Review* and an active sponsor of self-help ideas. Finlay's article "The Economics of Carna," published in April 1898, is based on his firsthand observation when he was part of the Carna Sub-Committee (connected with the Dublin Committee for the distribution of the Manchester Relief Fund) and on an unpatronizing analysis of the main factors that generated poverty and underdevelopment, including the shopocracy phenomenon. From the start, Finlay's article refuses to comply with a rhetoric of pity, advanced by several other observers, such as E. Keogh: "I do not seek to stimulate sympathy for their condition by pictures of the misery which darkens and degrades human life on our Western Seabord. That has been abundantly and fruitfully done by Mr. Long and other observers."[83] Finlay's endorsement of self-help and cooperation is evident in particular when he addresses the relief-works system:

> Relief Funds and Relief Works are temporary expedients; they may save from death by starvation a people who, always on the verge of want, are pushed over the barrier-line by any accident to their wretched potato crop. But they leave the causes of recurring distress exactly as they found them. Nay, they have a tendency to intensify those causes; they spread abroad the sense of pauperism, they weaken the spirit of self-respect and self-reliance, they teach the suffers to put their trust in charity rather than in the devices of self-help—all this is lamented by those guides and representatives of the distressed folk who, under the stress of imperative necessity, are now appealing to the pity of the world on their behalf.[84]

This point regarding relief works is certainly attuned to Synge's later remarks on the same subject, when he compares the workers to "convicts" presided over by a ganger (*TI*, 51). Moreover, Finlay shares with Synge the belief that the real resources of the West are "the people themselves . . . duly combined and organised, putting their energies and resources together, educating themselves by a common effort, spreading the knowledge by a common public opinion."[85] Overall, Finlay's article reflects a more complete and balanced portrayal of the distress in the West of Ireland. Yet his journalism does not possess the polyphonic qualities or the dialogic approach that characterizes Synge's series. As in most articles on the distress in the West, Finlay's point of view is that of an omniscient narrator and well-informed expert, citing official sources and data. In contrast, Synge adopts a multivocal and dialogic narrative strategy that enables the affected people to speak for themselves, therefore providing the reader with a more rounded understanding of the social and economic issues at stake in the congested West.

Another traveler and organizer who operated in the Congested Districts was Synge's fellow revivalist George Russell (Æ). Russell traveled as bank organizer for the IAOS starting in 1897 and was appointed editor of the *Irish Homestead*, the organization's editorial organ, in 1905. In the *Homestead*, Russell reported on meetings held in the West of Ireland and explained how to organize and run cooperative banks. Although it seems that Synge was aware in general terms of Russell's involvement in the IAOS, he does not appear to have exchanged information or communicated with Russell before heading West with Yeats in 1905.[86] The pieces Russell had to write for the *Irish Homestead* denote how rigorously he fulfilled his task as a propagandist of self-help. In addition to the minutes of organizers' meetings and a dedicated section called "Among the Societies," Russell contributed articles written in a more ornate prose style embellished with catchy literary and philosophical quotes, presumably deriving from his study of theosophy. For example, in an article soliciting house improvements in Irish cottages, some sentences are imbued with Celtic and Orientalist images: "Perhaps the longing for far off things, for fairy and political Tir-na-noges, is incompatible with a care for the here and now, just as the brown fakirs in India squat (with the dirt of twenty years unscraped from their holy skins) in a trance, meditating on the infinite thought, being and joy."[87] His flamboyant sentences shape-shift into a eulogy of peasant life and are followed by practical advice (pinpointed like advertisement slogans) to improve Irish cottages:

> There is no more ideal life than the farmer's, no life which contains more
> elements of joy, mystery and beauty. He has always the scent of the earth
> in his nostrils, pure air, and the perpetual wonder of growing things.
> And it is so easy to make an earthly paradise around every cabin. A
> few lilac bushes, roses, creepers, a little paint on fences and on door and

window, and a pail of creamy whitewash over the walls, will make a home to allure the mighty ones of the earth from the palaces—provided that a tribe of chickens have a place specially set apart for them, and that the pig is not a frequent guest.[88]

This exaltation of only one idealized aspect of the farmer's life—the pastoral symbiosis with nature—arguably leads to a legitimization of poverty and untidiness as inherently part of the peasant condition and therefore once more decontextualizes poverty from a more specific socioeconomic framework. Although Russell had a practical knowledge and political awareness of the whole context of poverty and distress, sometimes his journalistic style indulges in these hyperboles as a propagandist move to persuade his readers.

In contrast, Synge's journalism is deliberately stripped of the frills of hyperbolic strategies. We can juxtapose Russell's Celto-Orientalist images with Synge's more empirical approach, grounded in his own direct observation and demonstrated in the *Guardian* article "From Galway to Gorumna" in his comparison of Ireland and Brittany, whose reality he had come across as a result of a trip to Quimper on the Finistère Peninsula: "One feels . . . that it is part of the misfortune of Ireland that nearly all the characteristics which give colour and attractiveness to Irish life are bound up with a social condition that is near to penury, while in countries like Brittany the best external features of the local life . . . are connected with a decent and comfortable social condition" (*TI*, 41).[89] In another episode, Synge concisely comments about one of the Irish cottages belonging to a family that had just returned from America: "Her cottage was perfectly clean and yet had lost none of the peculiar local character" (*TI*, 94). Whereas Russell projects his aspirations toward the idyllic and the picturesque, Synge prefers to draw a comparison with a reality that is assessed primarily by evidence gathered in loco. Furthermore, Synge's idea of amelioration becomes clearly conceptualized as bearing characteristics of continuity with the past, traditions, and environment, not imported from models that are not significant for the people of the Congested Districts.

Synge's own distancing from a rhetoric of pity and philanthropic attitudes in his analysis of the causes of penury in the Congested Districts can be ideologically traced back to his academic fosterage in Paris. As Ben Levitas has outlined, Synge studied socialist thought, reading, among others, Karl Marx, William Morris, Peter Kropotkin, Victor Considerant, and Paul Lafargue as well as the English economist John Hobson's socio-logical study of poverty, *Problems of Poverty: An Inquiry into the Industrial Condition of the Poor* (1891).[90] Although Hobson's study tackles urban pov-erty more specifically with a critique of the "sweating system," the condi-tion of women workers, and the "influx of population into large towns," it nonetheless offers an interesting insight into the evaluation of the moral aspects of poverty. Hobson exposes the reasons why wealthy people hold the convenient opinion that poverty is an individual shortcoming, mor-ally intrinsic to the individuals it affects:

> In the first place it is a "moral view" and as morality is admittedly the truest and most real end of men, it would seem that a moral cure must be more radical and efficient than any merely industrial cure. . . . Last, not least, this aspect of poverty, by representing the condition of the poor to be chiefly "their own fault" lightens the sense of responsibility for the "well to do." It is decidedly the more comfortable view, for it at once flatters the pride of the rich by presenting poverty as evidence of incom-petency, salves his conscience when pricked by the contrast of misery around him, and assists him to secure his material interests by adopting an attitude of stern repression towards industrial or political agitations in the interests of labor, on the grounds that "these are wrong ways of tackling the questions."[91]

Here, Hobson disagrees with the moralizing and patronizing attitudes held by philanthropists who advance a moral cause for poverty in their implied syllogism that the poor are also "bad" people. The ideas Hob-son expresses here might have constituted the origins of Synge's aware-ness of the sociopolitical dynamics at stake in the Congested Districts that pushed him to counteract such patronizing views in his narratives.

Against these paternalistic schemes and related ideologies, Synge's balanced analysis introduces a number of instances of development and economy, both self-sustaining and capable of sustaining the people and the environment. In these respects, Synge is one of the few commentators displaying a perceptive attention to the intertwined role that people and environment played in those times when modernization and technologization were being cast—often ruthlessly—upon the western seaboard by government agencies. After criticizing obsolete and aberrant relief-work schemes applied with scarce sensibility, he presents alternative measures that tap into what Raymond Williams would call the peasants' "residual culture"—that is, "experiences, meanings and values which cannot be verified or cannot be expressed in terms of the dominant culture [but] are nevertheless lived and practised on the basis of the residue—cultural as well as social—of some previous social formations."[92] It is in this light that Synge presents traditional agricultural chores such as kelp making and thatching as "residual" activities capable of challenging the CDB's rapacious modernization by means of their potential for sustainability. In the article "The Kelp Makers" (June 24, 1905), Synge delineates his case study, the area of Trawbaun, and praises the social aspect of kelp gathering for the whole community, an activity that involved all the inhabitants: "The whole scene, with the fresh smell of the sea and the blueness of the shallow waves, made a curious contrast with the dismal spectacle of the relief workers we had just passed, for here the people seemed as light-hearted as a party of school-boys" (TI, 62).[93]

Furthermore, Synge's critical empathy regarding the people's needs and the cultural impact of the CDB's measures also possesses an ecological sensibility to environmental issues. Specifically, his interest in pointing out the effect of certain measures on the environment and on the people's health as well as in advancing sustainable solutions shows some affinity to contemporary social ecologist concerns. According to Greg Garrard, social ecologists and eco-Marxists share the view that "environmental problems cannot be clearly divorced from things more usually defined as social problems such as poor housing or lack of clean water," a view connected "with environmental justice movements that protest the com mon association of acute environmental degradation and pollution with poverty."[94] Synge's unearthing of the material, social, and political causes of poverty in the Congested Districts may draw from the same works by Marx, Engels, and Kropotkin[95] that inform contemporary socioecological theories and that Synge read while in Paris.[96] In the article "The Inner

Lands of Mayo—the Village Shop," Synge touches on the environmental issue of resource depletion by giving a firsthand account of an old man driving an ass with two panniers full of turf. Synge is told that in twenty years the turf in the area will be extinguished and the people will be left with no less-expensive form of heating (*TI*, 88). Accordingly, Synge's plea to the CDB concerns reforestation of areas such as Carna, an initiative that had been a failure until then and that seems to have been stopped (*TI*, 88). In the same article, when Synge inquires about the conditions of Irish female migrants working in American factories, a local woman replies concernedly that many of them are not in good health because they are "working in factories with dirty air" (*TI*, 87). Through the woman's testimony, Synge seems to hint at the fact that there is a price to pay, in the long run, for rapacious industrialization and emigration.

Synge's attention to the CDB's fast-paced modernization and his projection of environmental scenarios twenty years ahead tap into the idea of "slow violence" theorized by Rob Nixon in his groundbreaking study *Slow Violence and the Environmentalism of the Poor*. Nixon describes the current environmental crisis in its multiple shapes (from climate change to radioactive aftermaths and more) as a "slow violence . . . a violence that is neither spectacular nor instantaneous, but rather incremental and accretive, its calamitous repercussions playing out across a range of temporal scales." In foregrounding the concept of "slow violence," Nixon is keen on drawing attention to the "temporalities of place" and how place is a "temporal attainment,"[97] not uniquely a spatial conception. Synge's awareness of this temporal dimension of place is evident not only in his projection of the districts twenty years ahead but also in the questions he asks the people about the Great Famine, which had plagued the same areas fifty years earlier (*TI*, 76). Nixon also stresses the difficulties in conceptually, visually, and rhetorically conceiving the slow violence of the global environmental crisis as well as the challenges for writer-activists to engage with the invisibility and hard-to-grasp notion of that crisis.[98] Despite not being a contemporary environmentalist grappling with the sword of Damocles that is our twenty-first-century global environmental crisis, Synge pays attention to the exhaustion of resources in the long term and to the repercussions of this process on the poor and thus attempts to articulate the slow violence inherent in some of the CDB's modernizing work. More-over, as the next section examines, Synge's attention to the perspective from which his critique is articulated—his use of the direct-speech mode to show his interlocutors' own experiences of the CDB implementations—can be read as a strategy anticipating those used by contemporary writer-activists in its challenge to "perceptual habits that downplay the damage of slow violence" and in its engagement with "who counts as a witness."[99]

**Polyphony, Critical Empathy, and History Telling**

Synge's subversion of patronizing ideologies is evident not solely at a thematic level but also at a formal level through stylistic strategies and choices that make his literary journalism deviate from the rhetoric used by previous travelers to the Congested Districts. Synge's notorious pen-chant for peasant subjects in his drama and prose has sometimes been dismissed as romantic, idealistic, and unaware of the people's social conditions.[100] This point has been generally argued with a predominant emphasis on the fact that Synge was, for the people he met during his travels, an outsider who belonged to the Protestant Anglo-Irish Ascen-dancy. On the contrary, I argue that despite his higher social status Synge was not only a well-informed observer but also an empathetic and unpa-tronizing reporter. In the *Guardian* articles, he avoids patronizing stylis-tics by intensifying his informants' participation and voicing directly the local people he met on the road. He carefully structures each single piece around more or less extended firsthand storytelling, balancing technical details and descriptive remarks. The use of witness contribution in his series is striking, especially if compared with pamphlets and articles writ-ten earlier, such as Tuke's, Keogh's, and Russell's, where more technical analysis and an omniscient narrator dominate. As this last section in this chapter theorizes, Synge's practice is highly subversive in that it delib-erately foregrounds the Irish farmers' opinions in direct speech mode, unlike previous reporting, which for the most part did not include the farmers or reported about them only in an indirect way.

Throughout the *Guardian* series, Synge refers to a small number of official sources. By "official sources," I mean evidence potentially con-nected with a written, official document and potentially underlying

Synge's interaction with CDB officials. Before heading West, Synge met a Mr. Muldoon, one of the CDB officials in Dublin, around the third week of May.[101] He also mentions officials in passing in the article "Between the Bays of Carraroe" (June 14, 1905) for their distorted vision of the peasantry of Ireland (*TI*, 49). He quotes official sources in "The Kelp Makers" when he mentions a "large volume issued two years ago by the Department of Agriculture and Technical Instruction for Ireland" (*TI*, 60). Synge seemed to be also sufficiently well read on economic issues such as the Raiffeisen system,[102] which he mentions in "Erris," and the current self-help movement. In the Congested District articles, however, he does not quote directly from these official sources, nor does he use statistics or CDB baseline reports to back up his investigation, as Tuke and other commentators did. For example, in *Irish Distress and Its Remedies*, Tuke conducts his investigation using official sources for the most part, with only a few scattered contributions from peasant voices. He must have had a busy meeting agenda: he spoke to the lord lieutenant and the duchess of Marlborough, who established a relief fund bearing her name; he spoke with Relief Committee officials, Poor Law guardians, local government inspectors, dispensary doctors—in his own words, all "gentlemen actively engaged in professional or other work [who] were giving up a large portion of their time to this very important service."[103] This angle completely contrasts with the one adopted by Synge for his series "In the Congested Districts," in which the people who are voiced directly are not officials or philanthropists but rather farmers and laborers. In a manner deliberately different from that of these previous commentators, Synge favors the use of firsthand witnesses from lower social classes, people he personally met on the road and interviewed in every place as his journey progressed. Despite the hasty nature of the trip, Synge manages to include in his articles a considerable range of informants in terms of gender, age, and profession. In "From Galway to Gorumna," he speaks with a begging woman and a returned immigrant back from England; in "Between the Bays of Carraroe," with a man "driving a mare and a foal"; in the homonymous pieces, with relief workers, the ferryman of Dinish Island, and boat carpenters; in "Erris" and "The Homes of the Harvestmen" (July 1, 1905), with harvestmen, their wives, and a car man; and, finally, in "The Inner

Lands of Mayo—the Village Shop," with a one-eyed man sitting at the counter of a public house, discussing his bill with the shopkeeper.

Among all the informants, the car man featured in "The Smaller Peasant Proprietors" (July 5, 1905) comes from a different (higher) walk of life compared to some of the poorest farmers and wanderers encountered elsewhere. In introducing him in the article, Synge immediately identifies the class difference and consequent bias:

> The car-drivers that take one round to isolated places in Ireland seem to be the cause of many of the misleading views that chance visitors take up about the country and the real temperament of the people. These men spend a great deal of their time driving a host of inspectors and officials connected with various Government Boards, who, although they often do excellent work, belong for the most part to classes that have traditional misconception of the country people. It follows naturally enough that the carmen pick up the views of their patrons, and when they have done so they soon find apt instances from their own local knowledge that give a native-popular air to opinions that are essentially foreign. That is not all. The cardriver is usually the only countryman with whom the official is kept in close personal contact; so that, while the stranger is bewildered, many distinguished authorities have been pleased and instructed by this version of their own convictions. (*TI*, 75–76)

These lines are a sharp investigation into and an example of ideological interpellations, to paraphrase Louis Althusser's contention that "ideology interpellates individuals as subjects." This mechanism of ideological interpellation normalizes and renders unmistakably true and unquestionable certain sets of values and statements that are neither "obvious" nor "right" nor necessarily "true."[104] Of relevance here, in particular, is Synge's explanation about how car men legitimate with local "apt instances" those "opinions that are essentially foreign." His preoccupation in exposing these ideological repercussions was in line with a revivalist anticolonial ethos keen on demythologizing stereotypical misrepresentation of the Irish peasantry by a "colonial mindset"—an ethos shared, for example, by Lady Gregory.[105] P. J. Mathews quotes a poignant excerpt from Lady Gregory's essay "Ireland, Real and Ideal," whereby she confirms that stereotypes such as the Irishman are confirmed in front of tourists and visitors by "a car-driver or professional beggar . . . called upon to supply the food he [the tourist] desires."[106] Mathews maintains that Lady Gregory "presaged the thinking of later postcolonial theorists like Said" in believing that Ireland had to find its own identity instead of embracing definitions imposed and reinforced by the dominant power.[107] Nevertheless, despite the car man's different social status and Synge's predilections for the more marginalized, the car man's account is deeply problematized to the point that Synge thinks it "fair to add that the carman is usually a small-town's man, so that he has a not unnatural grudge against the mountain squatter, for whom so much has apparently been done, while the towns are neglected" (TI, 76). He also admits, "The carman may be generally relied on when he is merely stating facts to anyone who is not a total stranger to the country" (TI, 76).

As mentioned earlier, most of Synge's sources in the series are made to speak in direct-speech mode, unlike in the previous travel writing about the region, where people's firsthand feelings on the distress are not considered worthy of any transcription or are noted only in an indirect, paraphrased mode. In Synge, moreover, these firsthand testimonies are not compiled in the shape of an official, question-and-answer journalistic interview but instead disseminated in various articles as part of Synge's own encounters with people on the road. The journalistic interview, as Richard Keeble notes about George Orwell, is "a formalized event in which the reporter assumes a dominant, controlling position over the person being interviewed. . . . In contrast, the conversation, the chat over a meal are more authentic, with all the participants occupying equal status."[108] Accordingly, Synge's conversations with the common people emphasize their vocal presence and become a tool whereby his subjects can operate in a more active role. It is important to acknowledge, however, that the firsthand testimonies are not word-for-word transcriptions but Synge's partial reconstructions of the informants' accounts in conversation with the interviewer. Synge seeks accuracy and balance by combining more technical observations and firsthand impressions of how the changes are experienced by the people concerned.

Synge traveled and talked to the people; perhaps because of his knowledge of the Irish language, he could get people to talk about themselves more easily. As Jack Yeats recollected, "His knowledge of Gaelic was a great assistance to him in talking to the people. I remember him holding a great conversation in Irish and English with an innkeeper's wife in a Mayo inn."[109] Probably because of the intimacy established by a common tongue and Synge's personal sensibility, a "bond of trust" was created between the journalist and his source, so that the interlocutors did not feel too uneasy in offering often heartfelt testimonies.[110] On the courtesy demonstrated by people experiencing utmost poverty, George Orwell offers in *The Road to Wigan Pier* an illuminating consideration that sheds some light on Synge's approach to dealing with his informants. Orwell remarks

> on the extraordinary courtesy and good nature with which I was received everywhere. I did not go alone—I always had some local friend among the unemployed to show me around—but even so, it is an impertinence to go poking into strangers' houses and asking to see the cracks in the bedroom wall. Yet everyone was astonishingly patient and seemed to understand almost without explanation why I was questioning them and what I wanted to see. If any unauthorised person walked into my house and began asking me whether the roof leaked and whether I was much troubled by bugs and what I thought of my landlord, I should probably tell him to go to hell.[111]

A striking episode where Synge shows empathy toward his interlocutors occurs in "Between the Bays of Carraroe" when an old man is telling his personal story and recalling better times. The man seems to be on the verge of experiencing the utmost discomfort, so Synge decides to bring the conversation around to a much lighter topic: "The old man himself was cheerful and seemingly fairly well-to-do, but in the end he seemed to be getting dejected as he spoke of one difficulty after another, so I asked him, to change the subject, if there was much dancing in the country" (*TI*, 48). Synge's decision to change the topic so as not to upset his interlocutor and Orwell's awareness of his own presence as intrusive indicate the two writers' shared sensibility as interviewers.

Synge's artistic choice to construct his informants' direct speech not only gives authoritativeness to their position but also counteracts previous colonial modes wherein the presence of the subaltern usually had to be sought between the lines. In these "monophonic" structures,[112] it was generally the commentator with the mastery of his art and his omniscient, dominant perspective that pointed the bias in a certain direction. However, Synge's partial reconstruction and staging of his informants' accounts might also be read as problematic. As James Clifford has observed in *The Predicament of Culture*, a plurality of narrators and points of view does not necessarily guarantee objectivity. In an anthropological context, this staged plurality sometimes reinforces a series of fake assumptions of objectivity or simply confirms the anthropologist's view because the anthropologist is ultimately the one who organizes the testimonies in the text.[113] In Synge, though, the choice in favor of polyphony seems quite a pioneering attempt toward the "breaking up of monophonic authority,"[114] particularly if compared with previous "monophonic" reporting that often expressed a colonialist bias. Synge's rupture also achieves the value of a political statement, instrumental to the aims of his series, which in the last article, "Possible Remedies—Concluding Article" (July 26, 1905) ends by advocating Home Rule as the only effective remedy to uplift the people from material penury and spiritual dejection: "One feels that the only remedy for emigration is the restoration of some national life to the people" (*TI*, 98). Hence, not only does Synge describe the conditions of the poor in the Congested Districts, but he also quotes the poor directly to give more weight to his critique of the CDB and, as a subversive strategy, to allow the poor to speak for themselves.

Synge's strategy of voicing the rural inhabitants of the West in direct speech shares important implications for similar practices that can be deemed "history telling." The term *history telling* was coined by historian of the Holocaust James E. Young to indicate "a medium that 'works through' the dissonance between impersonal historical narrative and personal 'deep memory,' . . . allow[ing] for a presentation of history that combines events and their representations."[115] In an Irish context, Guy Beiner borrows the term for his study of how historical events that happened during the "Year of the French" (1798) were remembered in folk stories.

"History telling," according to Beiner, has the potential to be extended "beyond biographical oral history accounts, to incorporate oral traditions as recollections of historical events retold over several generations"—for instance, in communal sessions of "*seanchas* storytelling and singing."[116] In the *Guardian* series, Synge adopts a storytelling mode to reminisce on historical events such as the Famine but also to reflect on the broader process of narrating social history by combining both the official events and their perceived impact on the people who experienced them firsthand. In the series, a number of these "history-telling" episodes draw attention not just to the bare historical occurrences but also to the way that these occurrences were felt and retold by the people directly involved.

Synge's excavation of nineteenth-century Irish social history features specific reminiscences of the Great Famine, particularly in the article "The Smaller Peasant Proprietor," where Synge asks his car man whether he has any personal recollections of that time. The car man offers a microhistorical account, describing the building of the Belmullet workhouse in 1857, his father's memories of the dead on the edge of the road, and the horrible sight of corpses piled up on each other (*TI*, 76–77).[117] Synge's dwelling on such historical happenings further contributes to the shaping of the geographical and historical landscape of the Congested Districts as "disheartening," according to Grene, "a desolate landscape of demoralized people."[118] Synge's alternative "history telling," with its emphasis on the felt experience and its linkage with events belonging to macrohistory, not only serves the purpose of historicizing penury in the districts by connecting that penury to previous economic maneuvers, crop failures, and famines that had been plaguing the areas for more than fifty years but also positions Synge's critique of the colonial institution "from below." He rewrites an alternative history from outside the grand narratives of developmental history and combines both "events and their representation,"[119] to borrow Young's words again, as reported by the actors who directly experienced that alternative history.

Another example of this personal history telling occurs in the article "The Ferryman of Dinish Island" (June 21, 1905). If in many of Synge's articles the narration is equally balanced between descriptive and conversational parts, in this piece the conversational takes over, and the whole essay is constructed on the ferryman's long account of his life, past and present. The ferryman had been a seafarer for many years, becoming almost an archetypical traveler-migrant figure whom Synge invests with authoritativeness (*TI*, 55–56).[120] In his firsthand account, the old man tackles a wide range of sociological issues, such as emigration by women because his daughters had been sent to America at around fifteen years of age and in return sent remittances home. He comments on seasonal migration to England and on work at sea; he provides information on practices concerning marriage and land inheritance—for instance, how at thirty-seven he had to come home to inherit the land and get married "after holding out till I was forty" (*TI*, 58). His account, characterized by experiences of poverty and widowhood, ends with him giving vent to his most bitter emotions:

> "If it wasn't for them [his children] I'd be off this evening, and I'd earn my living easy on the sea, for I'm only fifty-seven of age, and I have good health; but how can I leave my young children? And I don't know what way I'm going to go on living in this place that the Lord created last, I'm thinking, in the end of time; and it's often when I sit down and look around on it I do begin cursing and damning, and asking myself how poor people can go on in executing their religion at all." For a while he said nothing and we could see tears in his eyes. (*TI*, 58)

The ferryman's agnostic credo and the desperate tone of his conclusions are perhaps among the most moving lines in the whole series, but, unlike the scenes drawn in previous sensationalist accounts, these tragic personal histories and miserable scenes are not aimed at moving Synge's English audience. Rather, Synge's intent is to present personal life stories as partaking in a shared narrative of displacement and loss immensely common among farmers and laborers of the western seaboard at the turn of the twentieth century. The ferryman's biographical history telling transcends the specificity of the man's own personal experience and reaches a wider historical timeline, connecting the year 1905 with past events that marked the social history of Ireland in the nineteenth century, from the Great Famine to emigration and the Land War.

Although effective Irish peasant proprietorship had been sanctioned through the Wyndham Land Act of 1903, and although the Congested Districts Board and cooperative organizations had set up improvements, Synge's articles highlight how there was still substantial work to do to improve economic conditions in the West of Ireland. More importantly, his series emphasizes how economic improvements need to function alongside the only beneficial remedy in the long term: national sovereignty. As stated earlier, the series "In the Congested Districts" ends up advocating Home Rule as the most effective long-term solution to uplift the people from material penury and spiritual dejection:

> One feels that the only remedy for emigration is the restoration of some national life to the people. . . . If Home Rule would not of itself make a national life it would do more to make such a life possible than half a million creameries. With renewed life in the country many changes of the methods of government and the holding of property, would inevitably take place, which would all tend to make life less difficult even in bad years and in the worst districts of Connemara and Mayo. (*TI*, 98–99)

As Nicholas Grene contends, Synge's blatant pro–Home Rule position in the concluding article "is unlikely a mere gesture towards the *Manchester Guardian*'s Home Rule politics. This is Synge's nationalist declaration against the constructive unionism of the CDB, for all his cautious praise of their [*sic*] work."[121] This clear nationalist statement also aligns with the strategy of staging the informants' testimonies in a direct-speech mode to create polyphonic and empathetic narratives "from below," a strategy that is equally political. Concluding his reportage in such overt terms might seem exceptional, given his tendency toward eschewing dichotomies such as nationalist/Unionist and toward opting instead for a problematization of such binaries. Moreover, Synge's overt endorsement of a nationalist stance may appear unusual in light of the history of his own politics, which has often been summarized in two particular moments. The first moment is a letter to Maud Gonne written on April 6, 1897, when he officially resigned from the Association Irlandaise, her nationalist organization, on this premise: "I wish to work in my own way for the cause of

Ireland and I shall never be able to do so if I get mixed up with a revolutionary and semi-military movement" (*CL1*, 47). The second key moment is embodied in W. B. Yeats's posthumous assessment of Synge's politics in "J. M. Synge and the Ireland of His Time," which describes Synge as "by nature unfitted to think political thought."[122] As P. J. Mathews notes, Yeats's comment removed Synge "from the material domain of quotidian concerns and elevated him to the status of 'a pure artist.'"[123] However, my contention here is that Synge's *Manchester Guardian* commission needs to be considered if not in a history of his politics, then at least as the epitome of his political engagement in "the cause of Ireland." As Synge's subversive analysis in "In the Congested Districts" shows, the future prosperity of the western seaboard needed to be rethought not simply in terms of economic standards but in terms of precise political choices. As this chapter has shown, "In the Congested Districts" voices a specific anticolonial concern both thematically in the way Synge deals with issues of poverty and rural development and formally in the way it subverts narrative strategies belonging to inherited modes of travel writing and journalism that often advanced colonialist and Unionist agendas.

# 4

## J. M. Synge in the Garden of Ireland

### *The Wicklow Essays*

In a poem entitled "Synge's Grave,"[1] Revival writer Winifred Letts pays tribute to John Millington Synge, who died prematurely at the age of thirty-eight in 1909, and celebrates his connection with Wicklow. Letts fashions Synge as deeply embedded in the Wicklow landscape—the Wicklow region being both the place where he holidayed with his family during the summer and a common holiday destination for families of Ascendancy background, such as the Synges. In the poem, Letts is indignant at the fact that Synge was buried in Mount Jerome cemetery in the Dublin suburb of Harold's Cross—"Within the moidher of its thousand wheels" (l. 3), among "alien city graves" (l. 25)—and sets forth to construct the Wicklow environment as Synge's new family, with the wind and the rain becoming Synge's "brothers" (l. 18) and Synge the "free-born son of mountains and wild waves" (l. 27). These pathetic fallacies in the poem deny Synge's belonging to a specific social milieu and once more construct one of the major figures of the Revival as "naturally" part of the Irish landscape. This strategy of naturalization was also efficiently adopted by other Revival writers, who reinscribed themselves in specific places and developed personal narratives as intrinsically embedded in rural locales, notably W. B. Yeats in "The Lake Isle of Innisfree" (1890). Synge's poetry is also not immune from these strategies of place reappropriation and "self-naturalization": in his Wordsworthian poem "Prelude,"[2] Synge paints Wicklow as a spiritual retreat—his art drawing sustenance from the proximity of the natural environment and from the lack of human company:

[I] Lived with the sunshine and the moon's delight.

I knew the stars, the flowers, and the birds,
The grey and wintry sides of many glens,
And did but half remember human words,
In converse with the mountains, moors and fens.[3]

This spiritual bond with the natural world is further emphasized in the same poem by the position of the Wicklow region, described as "far from cities, and the sites of man" (CW1, 32, l. 4), an idea recuperated in Lett's lyric when she describes the valley of Glenmalure as "far off from town-born men" (l. 10).

This contrast between the country and the city is another powerful revivalist trope evident in much poetry of the time and in Synge's personal letters to Molly Allgood, the Abbey Theatre actress to whom Synge was engaged a few years before his death. In these letters, Synge uses the Wicklow landscape as their "love-scape" because it was in Wicklow that they often used to spend time together. In a letter dated May 22, 1907, Synge seems to reenact the Yeatsian moment in "The Lake Isle of Innisfree" when the physical landscape of Ireland materializes in the poet's mind at the time he is dislocated in an urban environment:

It is a wonderfully still beautiful evening, and I feel as if I ought to write verses but I haven't the energy. There is nearly a half moon, and I have been picturing in my mind how all our hooks and glens and rivers would look, if we were out among them as we should be! Do you ever think of them? Ever think of them I mean not as places that you've been to, but places that are there still, with the little moon shining and the rivers running, and the thrushes singing while you and I, God help us, are far away from them. I used to sit over my sparks of fire long ago in Paris picturing glen after glen in my mind and river after river—there are rivers like Annamoe that I fished in till I knew every stone and eddy—and then one goes on to see a time when the rivers will be there and the thrushes and we'll be dead surely. It makes one grudge every evening one spends dully in a town. What wouldn't I give to be out with you now in this rich twilight coming down from Rockbrook or Enniskerry with strange smells and sounds and the first stars and the wonderful air of Wicklow? Is there anything in the world to equal the joy of it? (*LM*, 141)[4]

By juxtaposing the beauty of the Wicklow landscape with the dullness of an urban environment, Synge develops a sense of nostalgia that parallels romantic attitudes to the physical landscape, perceived in romantic texts (and in Synge's) as possessing a regenerative function for humanity. Timothy Clark refers to "a condition of psychic wholeness" that "is understood to be natural in the sense of corresponding to the condition of harmony, stability and health that many (but not all) Romantic writers ascribed to the unspoilt natural world."[5] In both his letters to Molly and his Wicklow poems, Synge yearns for this "condition of psychic wholeness," further emphasized in his remarks about the Wicklow localities defined "not as places that you've been to, but places that are there still, with the little moon shining and the rivers running, and the thrushes singing." On the one hand, this characteristic of Wicklow as existing beyond the ephemeral temporality of human existence can be seen as an immobilizing practice on Synge's part, one where the physical environment is aestheticized, frozen in a static image and disconnected from historical reality. On the other hand, Synge's dismissal of thinking about places "not as places that you've been to" deserves further investigation in light of his experience as a traveler and travel writer because his remark may be taken to gesture toward a concern with place per se.

This concern with place, as this chapter contends, is forcefully expressed in Synge's journalism about Wicklow. His attention to Wicklow's environs as "places that are there still" is read as exemplary of a more invested engagement with localities during his travels and as counteracting more fleeting immersions in place, such as those undertaken by a number of tourists and travel writers affiliated with Revival and Nationalist networks, as presented in this chapter. Synge's comment on the permanence of natural places beyond the human lifespan and his critical nostalgia for them may explain his travel practice of returning to the same place several times and his artistic yearning to go back to a place in order to accomplish a fuller depiction of it. If we think about Synge's whole corpus of travel writing, we notice how it has been produced after many returns: to Aran and Kerry Synge came back four times; to Wicklow he kept coming back nearly every summer of his life. Even in the case of the Congested Districts, to which Synge did not actually have the chance to come back and do more fieldwork, as he had wished, his intentions to return are nonetheless clearly expressed in a letter to his friend Stephen MacKenna dated July 13, 1905: "As soon as I recover from this cold affair I'm off again to spend my £25.4.0 on the same ground" (CL1, 116). Synge's practice of coming back and his dwelling in Irish localities may hint at his refusal to take for granted accepted views of a place and are indicative of his constant questioning of ready-made, received notions of place portrayal in his nonfiction. As I argue, these demythologizing poetics are at the core of Synge's aesthetics in the Wicklow essays.

Nicholas Grene has thoroughly documented Synge's relationship with Wicklow and, drawing from Synge's diaries, has highlighted the writer's extensive knowledge of the Wicklow countryside, where he used to walk, cycle, and fish with members of his Ascendancy family and various friends. Grene describes Synge as "an internal drop-out within a class which he, but not they [his family] saw as defeated and obsolete."[6] On the opposite side of the spectrum of class configurations, another interesting description of Synge in Wicklow portrays the playwright as looking more like a local peasant than a landlord. Karel Mušek, the Czech theater impresario and translator of Synge's works, whom Synge accompanied on an excursion in Wicklow during Mušek's official visit to Ireland in the summer of 1906, recollected his outing with Synge in an article entitled "Z irských glenů" (From an Irish Valley). As Daniel Řehák has documented, Mušek had come to Ireland to make arrangements to translate Synge's works and to meet W. B. Yeats and Lady Augusta Gregory; Synge had to entertain him and took him on a tour "around the Irish counties and the landlords' estates of Wicklow."[7] In the article, Mušek also recalls the story that would inspire Synge for *The Shadow of the Glen*: the story, according to Mušek, is "performed" by a local tailor upon Synge's request during their tour. But Ondřej Pilný notes how Mušek's article is "a shameless collage of passages from Synge's essay 'The People of the Glens' and from *The Aran Islands*" and concludes that, "given the nature of such rare fabulation, . . . Mušek was anxious to present himself as the authentic Czech authority on

Synge."[8] Perhaps in an effort to present the Irish artist as engrained in the landscape and subject matter of his work, Mušek comments on how Synge was dressed like a local peasant and argues that the homespun clothes were perhaps what made him so well acquainted with the locals:

> Připomínám, že Synge svým zevnějškem se od venkovanů valně nelišil, liboval si v těžkých botách a šatech z nejhrubší domácí příze. Proto snad byli k němu důvěřivějšími než k jiným návštěvníkům svých údolí.

> I recall how Synge's appearance did not differ much from that of the general villagers. He enjoyed wearing heavy boots and rough wool homespun clothes. Therefore [that is why] he might have been more trustworthy to the locals than other visitors in their valleys.[9]

In Pilný's opinion, Mušek's portrayal of Synge is not too farfetched and "may likely be trusted,"[10] even if Mušek clearly inflated the portrait of a foreign artist for his Czech audience, and even considering the more official revivalist role that Synge had been asked to perform to comply with networking directives that emanated from Lady Gregory.[11] Synge's "peasantlike" clothing (if we are to take Mušek's description at face value) does not work as a disguise because his Ascendancy identity is known to many of his interlocutors in Wicklow.[12] The image of Synge in homespun clothes and his status as "an internal drop-out" of the Ascendancy class frame him as inhabiting two social and cultural spaces simultaneously. Mušek's remarks about Synge's abilities as mediator and ethnographer between different cultures and social formations seem therefore highly appropriate.

Synge's unpatronizing way of dealing with his informants is evident, for instance, in his approach to describing nomadic life in Wicklow, which he experienced through his interaction with the Travelers' community and various vagrants. All of them, as Mary Burke contends, are treated "as equals worthy of being listened to."[13] She also maintains that Synge's experience of wandering life stands in drastic opposition to practices and discourses in vogue in the late nineteenth century, such as the gypsylorist surveillance conducted by field clubs and the baroque camouflage of certain artists tramping Ireland on "gipsy" carts dressed up in Travelers' clothes: "Synge, by contrast, . . . did not merely depict the wandering life, but lived in it in a manner that did not involve the hiring of ostentatious conveyances that might unwittingly mock those he moved amongst."[14] Synge's empathetic attempt at understanding nomadic cultures in Ireland derives from his belief that nomadism is an intrinsically human condition that enables a deeper sensorial (and artistic) experience. As he writes in a lyrical fragment that he reworked into parts of the essay "The Vagrants of Wicklow," published in the periodical *The Shanachie* in the autumn of 1906,

> Man is naturally a nomad . . . and all wanderers have finer intellectual and physical perceptions than men who are condemned to local habitations. The cycle, automobile and conducted tours are half-conscious efforts to replace the charm of the stage coach and of pilgrimages like Chaucer's. But the vagrant, I think, along with perhaps the sailor, has preserved the dignity of motion with its whole sensation of strange colours in the clouds and of strange passages with voices that whisper in the dark and still stranger inns and lodgings, affections and lonely songs that rest for a whole life with the perfume of spring evenings or the first autumnal smoulder of the leaves. (CW2, 196–97)

In his traveling around and writing about the environment of Wicklow, Synge looks up to nomadic people, whom he constructs as an antidote to the local people's threatened connection with their milieu in that the itinerants' slow mode of travel and immersion in locality seem to enable that "condition of psychic wholeness" that Synge yearns for in his poetry.[15] Synge's penchant for nomadic subjects is evident not only in his dramatic repertoire and in the essays but also notably in his private letters to Molly Allgood, often signed "your old tramp." Far from being an artistic facade, his tributes to nomadism in his work indicate, rather, an intellectual nomadism or mobility on his part—his capacity to straddle different cultural and social systems. Moreover, his remarks about tourism and modes of transportation, "the cycle, automobile and conducted tours," as modern substitutes for older modes of travel can be taken to signal the importance of travel and travel writing in shaping his aesthetic of nomadism and his intellectual mobility.

Even if Synge's poems and love letters share a more romanticized view of Wicklow, whose landscape and natural environment seem untainted by the hustle of modern urban environments, in his Wicklow essays he keeps this romantic impetus more carefully at bay and offers a more subtle portrayal of place. Whereas in his poetry Synge fashions Wicklow as a powerful symbol of the potency of the physical environment on the poetic imagination, following at times well-established revivalist tropes of place reappropriation, in the travel essays he subverts inherited modes of Revival travel literature, which essentially rewrote the Wicklow region in eulogistic nationalist terms. The "psychic wholeness" aspired to in his private letters and poems cannot be attained in the essays, which instead expose the psychic disconnect experienced by people inhabiting Wicklow's most isolated margins. In the Wicklow essays, Synge's main preoccupation is to explore in a dialogic fashion the local inhabitants' perceptions of place and to depict Wicklow as a contested space where historical forces such as colonization and agrarian agitation have profoundly altered the landscape and its inhabitants' apprehension of it. His opening toward a plurality of testimonies expressed in a dialogic way further contributes to shaping the Wicklow environment as "a process rather than a constant," to borrow Lawrence Buell's words.[16] Synge's strategy points to a multilayered representation of the Wicklow landscape and can be connected with the notion of the "plural landscapes thesis," advanced by Buell and drawing from Barry Lopez's work on indigenous storytelling. The "plural landscapes thesis" sees the narrative "as wrought by the interplay between the 'outer landscape' and the story-teller's 'interior landscape' which by implication is mediated by the 'cultural landscape.'"[17] Similarly, Synge's Wicklow articles blend his own perceptions of the environment with his informants' recollections and knowledge of the locality.

Synge wrote his articles about Wicklow sporadically from 1903 to 1908 and for different periodicals, such as *The Gael*, *The Shanachie*, and the *Manchester Guardian*. These articles are preoccupied mostly with the impact that the natural and social milieu have on the daily lives of the people, and, unlike many travelogues of the time, they do not eulogize the countryside or famous tourist spots such as Glendalough. This chapter historicizes Synge's Wicklow essays within Revival travel narratives of nationalist sympathies, such as those compiled by Katharine Tynan, Mary Banim, and William Bulfin, in order to show how Synge moves away from a more overt nationalist rhetoric that tends to depict Wicklow either as a site with a distinct Irish patriotic history or as a tourist resort for the future nation. Synge's Wicklow essays, in their dialogic approach and interest in certain features of the physical environment (from the edges of Wicklow with its most isolated glens to landlords' gardens and the felt presence of coercive institutions) can in contrast be read as an attempt to articulate what Buell terms the "environmental" unconscious—the complexities of the environment and of its not always fully expressed effects on the locals. They accordingly can also be read as an attempt to "retrieve the environment from dormancy to salience"[18] and to expose the cultural disconnect experienced by communities inhabiting marginal localities, where place has been redefined in hegemonic terms. This chapter concentrates in particular on Synge's attention to Wicklow's social landscape of coercive institutions—workhouses and "lunatic asylums"—as profoundly embedded in his storytellers' "interior landscape." Synge's representation denounces how the vitality of Irish rural life has been jeopardized by mechanisms of colonial surveillance. His Wicklow essays and his articles about the Congested Districts are more than simply preparatory sketches for his Wicklow plays.[19] They attend to the complexities of place representation by deploying polyphonic narrative strategies and, if read alongside travel writing of the Revival period, can be seen as engaging with early-twentieth-century Irish historical dynamics.

## Wicklow, the Garden of Ireland

It is widely acknowledged that since the eighteenth century Wicklow had become a popular tourist resort. In *Ireland and the Picturesque*, Finola O'Kane identifies the Wicklow tour (the Dargle Valley and Glendalough) as one of the principal tourist itineraries of eighteenth-century Ireland, in addition to Killarney and the Giant's Causeway. What made Wicklow fashionable, O'Kane suggests, was Wicklow's proximity to Dublin and its measured quality as a recreational site, "not too wild and too extensive." For these reasons, she continues, sites such as the Dargle "always had more the character of a leisure landscape than a tourist one,"[20] especially if compared with Killarney, where tourist networks and infrastructures had to be more developed from early on owing to Killarney's greater distance from urban centers. In *Wicklow through the Artist's Eye*, Patricia Butler and Mary Davies show how Wicklow in the nineteenth century had also become a "favorite sketching destination" not simply for artists but also for common tourists as well, with its scenic spots made accessible by means of transportation such as mail coach, private carriage, and post chaise.[21] Enhanced transportation and the concomitant expansion of Bray as a seaside resort from the 1850s also increased access to Wicklow, introducing "a new type of visitors, a seaside holiday-maker who wanted a day out in the country."[22] In the nineteenth century, a renovated interested in Wicklow's famous archaeological sites (e.g., Glendalough), in its majestic landscaped gardens and demesnes (e.g., Powerscourt), and in scenic spots such as the Meeting of the Waters glorified in Thomas Moore's *Irish Melodies* further contributed to the establishment of Wicklow as a prime tourist destination. Nicholas Grene describes Wicklow as "a favorite site for gentleman's residences, landed estates with fine houses and picturesque views owned by aristocrats . . . or people like the Synges themselves, who had made their money in the city and invested in land as a sign of status."[23] Synge, despite his status as regular Ascendancy "holiday-maker" in Wicklow, chose peripheral sites for his travels—and for his travel articles—avoiding more popular tourist localities. Moreover, as in his West Kerry essays and the Congested Districts series in the *Manchester Guardian*, in his Wicklow pieces he is committed to sharing the inhabitants' perspectives—a commitment not always present in other Irish travel accounts of the time.

Synge rejects and complicates the too simplistic and one-dimensional portrayals of the Wicklow region as "the Garden of Ireland," a popular nickname gained in the nineteenth century and omnipresent in travel literature of the time.[24] Travel literature compiled by Irish artists affiliated with Revival and nationalist networks reframed Wicklow as a paradise for the emerging nation and as a site of nationalist commemoration. This is the case, for instance, in the early work of the Irish poet, novelist, and journalist Katharine Tynan. In a travel article published in the American newspaper *Providence Sunday Journal* on November 21, 1890, and titled "Mr Parnell Not at Home. About and Around Avondale. The House in

the Wicklow Hills," Tynan uses the epithet "Garden of Ireland" to immediately locate Charles Stewart Parnell's residence, Avondale House: "Here
in the garden of Ireland—and in the garden of the garden so to speak, for
Avondale lies at the heart of an earthly paradise—there is no levelness."
Tynan's hyperbole clearly positions Wicklow as the quintessential site of
patriotic history for being Parnell's county and for its connections with
the Irish Rebellion of 1798. Tynan reminisces about a teenage Parnell—"an
adventurous boy climbing, as we are told, a high tower, and dropping hot
lead there from in the hope it would form bullets, a shot is made, and per-
forming many other such feats, always purposeful, be sure"—carefully
constructing Wicklow as an environment that nurtures patriotism and a
nationalist spirit in the same way that it nurtured Parnell's own sense of
nationality and made him a man with a "deep and romantic enthusiasm
. . . never tired of talking of the rebellion, of its scenes and personages, of
Holt and Michael Dwyer." For the American readers, Tynan portrays Parnell's leaders in the description of his hunting cabin, a frugal but dignified environment in the Avondale demesne, where Parnell hosts hunting
companions such as William O'Brien (whom Tynan acknowledges as a
source for her article). The cabin environment reinforces Parnell's "sense
of comradeship," and Parnell is described as an industrious leader of the
estate, "an excellent farmer and an advanced one, using methods to make
his sleepy agricultural neighbors rub their eyes," working even during
leisurely moments, with a treatise on trigonometry open in the hunting
cabin, and interrupting a conversation with his friends "to confer with
an engineer who is constructing some works at Avondale to relieve his
turbine from winter floods." Thus, the Avondale estate in the Wicklow
hills—"the garden of the garden" of Ireland—becomes a perfect nationalist synthesis of human-built and natural environment, where "the whirr
[of the sawmills] seems to fill a pause in the music of the birds and the
ewes, and the stone quarries away near Arklow . . . are hewing out pav-
ing setts for the Dublin streets. He is an admirable man of business."[25]
Tynan's article celebrates Parnell's symbiotic connection with his land and
constructs his legacy as a modern and advanced leader, notwithstanding
the political split and his absence from Avondale alluded to in a couple

of instances throughout the article, including in the headline "Mr Parnell Not at Home."

This contribution on Parnell to the *Providence Sunday Journal* can be read as an example of Tynan's "unsophisticated and emotional" Parnellism, according to Tynan's biographer, Ann Connerton Fallon. Fallon documents how Tynan had worked for the Ladies Land League, formed by Parnell's sister Anna, but plays down her political views, noting how she possessed a "weak understanding of historical movements in Ireland or in any other country, no interest in political theory of any kind, and . . . did not involve herself in any real political activity."[26] Similarly, Marilyn Gaddis Rose notes how the eighteen years Tynan spent in England from 1893 to 1911 distanced her from "the Irish Renaissance in the paths their patriotism was taking them" and accounted for her "dual loyalty" to both Britain and Ireland.[27] Against this notion of "dual loyalty," more recent criticism of Tynan's poetic work has highlighted her ability to appeal to culturally and politically adverse audiences, such as the English in relation to the Irish question. Donna Potts argues that Tynan's apparent unwillingness to transgress gender binaries, her appeal to a traditional sense of Irish womanhood, as well as her use of sentimentalism and Catholic piety in her work were all ways in which she asserted her patriotism and sought compassion for the plight of her country without alienating audiences normally not sympathetic to it.[28] Tynan's ability to appeal to her readers was evident from the time this early article for the *Providence Sunday Journal* was published. "Mr Parnell Not at Home" can be read not uniquely as an example of her acerbic Parnellism influenced by the early Irish Revival social circles she frequented in her father's house in Dublin but also as the work of a journalist conscious of writing for an American audience sympathetic to Ireland, starting with the journal editor Alfred Williams, an American of English origins interested in Irish culture and literature. Tynan's appeal to her audience is also evident when she plays up Parnell's American descent by listing the Native American artifacts in his house: "on the walls curiously side by side with glaring Land League addresses are Indian clubs and bows, snowshoes and such like, reminisces of Mr Parnell's American ancestry."[29]

Tynan's efforts to gauge and appease potentially adverse audiences are evident in another travel piece, her travelogue *Ireland*, published in 1909 and written for the popular series "Peeps at Many Land" of the London-based publishers Adam and Charles Black and aimed at the young reader. From the beginning, Tynan defines herself as "an Irish exile home-returning," and she makes it clear that she is keen on treading familiar terrain, such as the Irish brogue and the Irish sense of hospitality and friendliness.[30] These rather unproblematic topics allow her to moderately discuss accounts of Irish patriotic history such as the Irish Rebellion of 1798 in Wicklow,[31] while maintaining a conciliatory tone when comparing the virtues and flaws of the Irish and English characters. Overall, although careful not to estrange her English readers, she offers a positive image of Ireland, and her travelogue ends with a romantic image of freedom and transgression—albeit domesticated for her audience. In stressing the Irish people's lack of punctuality and respect for regular meal times, Tynan concludes with an anecdote about an Irishman settled in England, "who always has the motor round for a spin as soon as the dinner-bell rings. He cannot keep his English servants, and is grieved at their perversity, which would keep him chained to a hot dining-room on an ideal evening for a motor-run. His guests stay their hunger with sherry and biscuits while they await his return."[32] Even if this Irishman is no enlightened statesman in the Garden of Ireland, with this image Tynan seems to create a sense of anticipation for what can be taken to signify the return of Ireland—if not necessarily as a nation, then at least as a strong cultural presence.

In a way similar to Tynan's expression of cultural concerns, Mary Banim's travelogue also conflates Wicklow as a tourist resort for the emerging nation, to be appreciated by Irish visitors and not solely by English tourists. In the account of her Wicklow tour, Banim brands Wicklow once again the "Garden of Ireland" and offers a sympathetic account of the region commodified for the tourist: "'April Showers bring forth May flowers.' Watching the process, and noting the wonderful verdure and floweriness of this spring, it has occurred to me that to few parts of the land would a visit be so delightful, this month of the wild flowers, as to the Garden of Ireland—Wicklow."[33] Banim offers advice on the best time for traveling in Wicklow "before any tourists make their appearance" and

advances a neat distinction between the tourist and the traveler: the for-
mer is a more superficial and hurried gazer. She advocates an alternative,
more relaxed way of seeing things and experiencing places:

> Stop at a farm-house; go here and there as the fancy takes you; chat with
> the people; watch their daily lives; see them in their every-day dress,
> and make an every-day acquaintance with the ins and outs, the ups and
> downs of country life. . . . Stay if you can, long enough even to know the
> dogs and cats, the cows, calves, and pigs; to take a lively interest in the
> donkey's misdemeanours, in the effect of the thunder on the last setting
> of eggs. . . . By this time you will have got a vivid picture in your mind
> . . . and each picture will be framed in some pleasant, kindly association
> that will make you feel you have had a real country trip, and that you
> know more about the place than all the mere passing tourists who visit it
> in a summer could, even were they rolled into one.[34]

Even if Banim encourages a more prolonged engagement with locales, the
emphasis nevertheless seems to remain on the transience of the tourist-
traveler experience. In opposition to Synge's idea of "places that are there
still," the focus of Banim's tourist-traveler is still on "places that you have
been to," as the "pictures" framed in her mind seem to suggest. In other
words, rather than a more sustained consideration for place per se, Banim's travel aesthetic continues to be an aesthetic of tourist consumerism.
Furthermore, in this particular extract her rhetorical strategies pinpoint
and reinforce steps in the tourist's mythical quest for authenticity.[35] Her
account successfully contributes to creating stereotypical markers of Irish
authenticity for tourists, such as wool products; home-made artifacts; the
proverbial Irish hospitality of the *bean an tí* (woman of the house), proudly
described as "roundiest, cosiest, prettiest old woman you could wish to
see" and readily associated with men's demands and traditional gender
expectations, such as taking care of the home: "No one knows better than
an Irish woman, be she of low or high degree, how to give an hearty welcome: our Wicklow hostess made no exception to the rule."[36] Mary Banim's account eulogizes the *bean an tí* for the visitors, admirably debunking
colonial stereotypes and praising Irish artifacts over the English ones in
line with a cultural-nationalist and revivalist "self-help" ethos. Yet her

representation contributes somehow to reinforcing and essentializing the cultural formation of the "Ireland as a woman" trope and to further relegating women to the domestic space.[37]

Another travelogue of nationalist sympathies where the Wicklow region is repackaged for the emerging nation is William Bulfin's cycling narrative *Rambles in Éirinn*, published in 1907. In his cycle through Wicklow, Bulfin, like Banim, creates a dichotomy between the "cheap trippers" and more engaged travelers—for Bulfin, the latter are the tough cyclist and the tireless pedestrian tourist, the only figures who can access and fully grasp the beauties of Wicklow and a clear embodiment of Irish nationality. Bulfin, who had lived in Argentina since 1884, was an active promoter of both the Gaelic League and Sinn Féin and contributed articles in the advanced nationalist press. His cycling tour around Ireland allowed him a deeper apprehension and understanding of the Irish landscape, to the point of making it visually translatable in "Illustrations, and Maps specially made under the author's direction," as the front cover of the book notes. This visual materials accompany the first editions of *Rambles in Éirinn* and are justified by the fact that, according to Bulfin, maps included in tour guides of Ireland published in England had left out important landmarks, such as hills connected with Irish mythology and graves of Irish patriots.[38] *Rambles in Éirinn* also showcases a protoenvironmentalist awareness that pushes Bulfin to promote afforestation against the "evils" of deforestation "eloquent of the foreign rule in Ireland."[39] As in Synge's attention to Wicklow marginal localities, Bulfin stays away from major Irish tourist resorts for English tourists, nor does he depict traditional Revival destinations, such as Galway and the West of Ireland. Rather, he rediscovers places neglected by most tourist publications. The emphasis on the Midlands, for instance, is a tribute to an area that was the birthplace of many Irish immigrants to Buenos Aires.[40] Bulfin's account of his rambles in Wicklow is particularly interesting from a documentary perspective, especially his narration of his encounter with three young men in the Martello tower at Sandycove—James Joyce, Oliver St. John Gogarty, and Samuel Chenevix Trench, who will come to literary life in Joyce's novel *Ulysses* (1922) as, respectively, Stephen Dedalus, Buck Mulligan, and Haines.[41] Martin Ryle speculates that Joyce was aware of

Bulfin's text and draws a parallel between the "drinkers' grandiloquent discourses" and parody of Sinn Féin rhetoric in the "Cyclops" episode of *Ulysses*, on the one hand, and Bulfin's hyperbolic style and nationalistic rhetoric in *Rambles*, on the other.[42]

Bulfin's ramble in Wicklow continues with a decolonizing Ireland invective when he complains about place-names deemed "un-Irish" for their irrelevance to the actual environment.[43] Further into his trip, however, he slips into romantic pastoralism when he describes the bucolic scene of a shepherd "smoking a pipe and looking dreamily into the wild waste of peaks which overlook the valley of Glencree. What a large inheritance he was enjoying there!"[44] In this passage, the landscape is aestheticized, and the description of the shepherd is devoid of any sociopolitical context. Later on, he depicts the landscape as an Eden, which the nationalist observer repossesses by deploying a vocabulary similar to the sexualized language typical of arrival scenes in imperial travel writing: "No plough has ever furrowed those virgin hills, no spade has ever turned a sod along them. The heather and the blue water and the moss-grown rocks looked just as they do now when a human eye first beheld them. . . . It seems to lead you out of the present and take you back to the ages when the Druids wove their spells."[45] According to Bulfin's own admission, the sublimity of the landscape transports the viewer into a remote and undefined Celtic past. His descriptions of the untamed Wicklow landscape are reminiscent of the stereotypical constructions present in certain imperial and colonial travel writing. In these typologies of travel writing and in Bulfin's prelapsarian Wicklow, the writer usually positions himself as the "monarch of all I survey" and describes the physical environment both in gendered (feminine) terms and uniquely in terms of resources to be exploited by the male gazer. Such descriptions, to borrow Eóin Flannery's words, "confine [the landscape] to the political inert domains of leisure and legend,"[46] even if Bulfin's travelogue elsewhere showcases an anticolonial and revisionist impetus.

The equation of both nature and woman as "colonized others" has been thoroughly investigated by ecofeminist critics such as Val Plumwood, Maria Mies, and Vandana Shiva.[47] In "Androcentrism and Anthropocentrism: Parallels and Politics," Plumwood defines five processes and positions that align the "feminine Other" with "nature as (colonized) other." In addition to radical exclusion, homogenization, backgrounding/ denial, and incorporation, she discusses "instrumentalism" as the binding relationship taking place when "the [feminine] Other's independent agency is downgraded or denied . . . [or] subsumed within the agency of the male." Through the process of "instrumentalism," "nature's agency and independence of ends are denied and are subsumed in, or remade to coincide with, those of the human."[48] Bulfin's instrumentalist processes of feminization and othering of the Wicklow landscape are informed and influenced by contemporary discourses, such as Celticism and nationalist rhetoric and iconography, in which Ireland is commonly represented as a woman.[49] By rewriting and transvaluating imperialist and colonial tropes, Bulfin's travelogue constructs a reinvigorated sense of masculinity for the Irish national subject, which was too often denigrated in foreign travelogues, but he achieves this objective through the disempowerment of the feminine-natural.

These travelogues' recurrent use of the epithet "Garden of Ireland" for Wicklow and their multifarious and symbolic engagement with the idea of the garden can be read as a further example of what Sharae Deckard deems the "resilience" of paradise discourse. In her book *Paradise Discourse, Imperialism, and Globalization*, Deckard notes how the myth of paradise lived on, becoming increasingly secularized and shape-shifting into a consumer Eden that "could be accessed not through religious piety but through the accumulation of money and status . . . a state of consumption."[50] In these nationalist reappropriations of paradise discourse, the Wicklow paradise becomes for Tynan a utopian dream of industrial exploitation and natural sublimity; for Banim a tourist site to be rediscovered by Irish tourists; and for Bulfin a new Celtic Arcadia. Differently from all of these travel writers, however, Synge exploits the stereotype of Wicklow as the "Garden of Ireland" in more subversive ways.

### Synge's Own Garden of Ireland

A direct counterpoint to Tynan's Parnellism in her piece for the *Providence Sunday Journal* is offered in Synge's essay "A Landlord's Garden in County Wicklow," composed ten years after Tynan's article, in 1900, but not published until July 1, 1907, in the *Manchester Guardian*. Synge's piece sets the scene for a critical examination of the decline of the Ascendancy class from the specific site of a neglected garden in a manorial estate. As P. J. Mathews points out, Synge's both "elegiac" and "critical" piece is "levelled against his own class,"[51] and it hints in many ways at Parnell's relationship with Ireland. Mathews draws a parallel between Synge's essay and Joyce's story "Ivy Day in the Committee Room" in *Dubliners* (1914) for their common "attempt to reflect on the legacy of Parnell more than a decade after his death" and for their frequent evocation of moments of paralysis.[52] Notably, in the last scene of the article, Synge, breathless after a chase, tries in vain to upbraid a boy who had erupted into the garden to steal apples. Synge's choice of an abandoned landlord's garden as the main setting for his essay allows him to connect the Wicklow region with the historical forces and human agents that have invariably shaped Ireland and deeply transformed its landscape. His strategy in "A Landlord's Garden in County Wicklow," as in his travel essays, is to engage with the grand narratives of Irish history from a microscopic and localized perspective. Mathews further contextualizes Synge's sociological tendencies in his Wicklow nonfiction as "in line with a wider intellectual rapprochement that was taking place in the European academy at the end of the nineteenth century between the natural and human sciences" and as being influenced by the emerging field of early-twentieth-century French human geography, with Paul Vidal de la Blache among its chief proponents.[53] Despite being "a patchwork of bits and pieces derived from experiences over a number of years" and avoiding "the specifics of historical time and place," as Grene describes them,[54] the Wicklow essays recollect historical temporalities in different ways. For instance, they do so through a multivocal topography that is interested primarily, according to Mathews, in "the progress of nineteenth-century Irish history in Spenserian terms, as the outworking of a dysfunctional relationship of atrophying mutual dependence promoted by coercive power by means of enclosure."[55]

Synge's simulacrum of the abandoned garden, in addition to serving as an oblique critique of the dereliction and social fractures of rural Ireland at the turn of the twentieth century, also highlights how demesnes, in Terence Reeves-Smyth's words, played a crucial "role in the development of Irish agriculture, horticulture, sylviculture and field sport, [making] a distinct contribution to the natural history of Ireland." Furthermore, Reeves-Smyth has documented how the shaping of the manorial land was conditioned by different trends and fashions throughout the centuries, from "formal geometric layouts which sought to prove that man could subdue nature" to "naturalized parklands, . . . the Arcadian parkscape of supposedly 'untouched nature.'"[56] Within the demesne's territory, gardens certainly played an important part in supplying both vegetables and fruits as well as flowers and plants for ornamental purposes,[57] becoming status symbols and the kind of consumer Eden theorized by Deckard.[58] Synge's description of the walled garden in County Wicklow highlights the pretentiousness in the practice of floriculture and horticulture there, especially when he mentions seeing, among the ruined flowerbeds, "remnants [of] beautiful and rare plants" to be appreciated only by "anyone who had the knowledge" (*TI*, 122). Synge's garden is a place "that had been left to itself for fifteen or twenty years" (*TI*, 122), where wild plants had slowly begun to take over again. The trope of derelict demesnes is not unusual in popular travel writing and appears, for instance, in Mary Banim's series. In *Here and There through Ireland*, Banim explores an old demesne in Connemara that had belonged to a notable landlord in the area, Dick Martin. She concentrates on the ruined and "ghostly" gates at the main entrance, whose pillars are surmounted by urns that "look exactly like funeral urns," with "wild and tangled" trees and weeds growing all around the entrance. Banim's run-down landscape functions as the background for her romanticizing attitudes toward the history of the landed gentry as she tells her readers, "I had often listened with rapt interest to the sad and romantic story of this lady, as told by one who never tired of weaving wonderful romances for her youthful audience. The story-teller was a great embroideress; so how much of Miss Martin's story was real I have never discovered, beyond the fact that her life began in much style and splendour, and ended very sadly."[59] In the subsequent chapters describing her Connemara tour, Banim intersperses various anecdotes concerning the Martins[60] with a selection of topics and an approach reminiscent of those criticized by Synge in "A Landlord's

Garden": "The desolation of this life is often of a peculiarly local kind, and if a playwright chose to go through the Irish country houses he would find material, it is likely, for many gloomy plays that would turn on the dying away of these old families, and on the lives of the one or two delicate girls that are left so often to represent a dozen hearty men who were alive a generation or two ago" (TI, 123). Unlike Banim, Synge does not give vent to these decadent anecdotes but rather concentrates on a marginal yet allegorical episode about a petty theft in order to ponder social and historical change in early-twentieth-century rural Ireland. In the concluding part of the essay, Synge portrays himself as the last defender of the order, willing to punish a young thief who had stolen an apple from the garden's orchard, only to realize the absurdity of his position at the end of a frantic chase (TI, 125). After letting the boy go, he remarks: "Yet it must not be thought that this young man was dishonest; I would have been quite ready the next day to trust him with a ten pound note" (TI, 125). In addition to a sense of stasis, this final episode is another example of Synge's contact strategy, which emphasizes moments of collision between opposite social and cultural formations. In the essay, Synge is preoccupied with showing how landscape is mediated by culture and shaped by history: he reconfigures the physical environment not as a stable, immutable construct but rather "as a process" continually shaped by historical and human dynamics from both inside and outside.[61]

Synge's alternative topography of Wicklow becomes polyphonic in a typescript draft of the essay "The Oppression of the Hills"—an alternative that was subsequently omitted in the version that appeared in the *Manchester Guardian* on February 15, 1904—when he records an old man's embittered remark about the region that directly speaks back to the popular epithet "Garden of Ireland": "'I suppose there are some places where they think that Ireland is a sort of garden,' he laughed bitterly, 'and I've heard them say that Wicklow is the garden of Ireland. I suppose there's fine scenery for those that likes [sic] it, but it's a poor place in the winter and there's no money moving in the country.'"[62] Synge's noting of this man's view, if taken at face value, can be read as providing an insight into the locals' take on the tourists' denomination of Wicklow. More importantly, it shows Synge's deliberate attempt to voice his critique from the point of view of people living in the so-called Garden of Ireland on a daily basis. His alternative historicization in the Wicklow essays is keen on demystifying representations of Wicklow as solely a site of leisure and tourism. His prose does not lapse into a eulogy of grand narratives, such as accounts of the Irish Rebellion or descriptions of landmarks of patriotic history. His representation instead follows an alternative trajectory, focusing on the local inhabitants' perceptions of place as well as on neglected sites. In the Wicklow essays, Synge is interested in describing both human-built and nonhuman environments in their interrelation and in providing a plurality of testimonies and perceptions of environments from the perspective of the people more directly involved with them. His quest for a "psychic wholeness" in his poetry and private letters shifts in his journalism into a concern for the psychic disconnect experienced by the Wicklow inhabitants he encounters in his travels.[63] In particular, the Wicklow essays expose the psychic disconnect experienced by people inhabiting physical landscapes that bear the marks of coercion, surveillance, and marginalization.

In the two essays written for *The Shanachie*, the biannual magazine published by Maunsel, where the West Kerry series was also published, Synge emphasizes how human-built environments are embedded in the natural spots of Wicklow and affect certain types of social phenomena, such as vagrancy. In "The Vagrants of Wicklow," published in *The Shanachie* in the autumn of 1906, he comments, "Some features of County Wicklow, such as the position of the principal workhouses and holiday places, on either side of the coach road from Arklow to Bray, have made this district a favourite with the vagrants of Ireland" (*TI*, 100). These human-built environments, although not directly visited by Synge, resurface in his informants' accounts when describing the desolation of some of the remotest part of the region, as in *The Shanachie* article "The People of the Glens" (March 1907): "When they [the people of the glens] meet a wanderer on foot, these old people are always glad to stop and talk to him for hours, telling him stories of the Rebellion, or the fallen angels that ride across the hills, or alluding to the three shadowy countries that are never forgotten in Wicklow—America (their El Dorado), the union, and the madhouse" (*TI*, 107). The landscape of Wicklow in Synge's work is not simply naturalized as Irish and patriotic, as in previous travelogues of nationalist sympathies: it is instead depicted as bearing traces of colonial surveillance by means of a focus on institutional sites that populated Wicklow alongside its tourist resorts. In the Wicklow essays, Synge is concerned with articulating the disturbing psychological effects that life in harsh mountain spots and remote valleys has on the locals. Moreover, he is also deeply preoccupied with the landscape of coercive institutions that seem to affect the locals' mental health—workhouses and "lunatic asylums," where place has been redefined in hegemonic terms. Detailed descriptions of these coercive institutions is generally absent in his articles, but their presence is nevertheless profoundly embedded in the interior landscape of Synge's informants and storytellers and in their apprehension of locality. The narrative focus on the psychic repercussions of sites of coercion in the locals' accounts represent Synge's original way of denouncing how mechanisms of colonial surveillance had affected and jeopardized the vim of rural Ireland.[64]

In addition to derelict Ascendancy gardens, Synge evokes another forceful simulacrum: Wicklow's mental institutions, recollected in many stories told to Synge during his travels. In "An Autumn Night in the Hills," first published in April 1903 in *The Gael/An Gaodhal*, a monthly bilingual literary periodical printed in New York, the narrative unravels from a specific visit that Synge paid to one of the families living in an isolated cottage in order to collect a wounded pointer dog belonging to his brother-in-law, Harry Stephens.[65] In the piece, the story of the wounded dog is intertwined with local lore about haunted places. The whole narrative seems to be specifically haunted by Mary Kinsella, a young mother with two children who "went wrong in her head" (*TI*, 23) and died after having been hospitalized in the Richmond Asylum.

The Richmond Asylum was erected in 1814 and was the first "purpose-built public institution" to treat mental illness. According to some commentators, from 1817 on "the Irish administration in Dublin was empowered to impose asylums at will, and twenty-one county institutions were erected before 1871."[66] In *Madness and Civilization*, Michel Foucault theorizes how the asylum, in its relationships among patient, keepers, and physicians and during the therapeutic treatment, mimics and reappropriates "the massive structures of bourgeois society and its values: Family–Child relations centered on the theme of paternal authority; Transgression–Punishment relations, centered on the theme of immediate justice; Madness–Disorder relations, centered on the theme of moral and social order."[67] Furthermore, as historian Oonagh Walsh has exposed, "asylums and prisons in Ireland were intimately linked, with the Inspector General of Prisons acting simultaneously as the asylum inspector." Walsh also observes how in nineteenth-century Ireland the situation worsened as a result of the Dangerous Lunatics Act of 1838, whereby "individuals admitted to Irish asylums were automatically criminalised, as they had threatened violence towards others." She demonstrates how very often the person deemed insane was hospitalized in one of these facilities after the committal by two justices of the peace who were "acting on a sworn statement by a third party—in Ireland, [usually] a relative."[68] Very often this practice was open to abuse, with family interests in arranged marriage, land transmission, and inheritance playing a huge part in the commitment process.[69] Thus, according to Walsh, to a large extent the asylum was "perceived by contemporaries as means of control, not cure."[70] This bond between lunacy and criminality was in all respects another official tool of surveillance adopted by the English administration.

Synge does not provide further details about Mary Kinsella's hospitalization in the Richmond Asylum and her subsequent death. His interlocutor, an old woman, describes Kinsella as "a young woman with two children [who] a year and a half ago went wrong in her head, and they had to send her away. And then up there in the Richmond asylum maybe they thought the sooner they were shut of her the better, for she died two days ago this morning" (TI, 23). The old woman's remark may be interpreted as embodying the community ostracism of the insane. Certainly, this view can be considered a product of the ideology behind the institutions of surveillance, such as prisons and lunatic asylums, whose distinction, as noted earlier, was often blurred and whose function was reduced to population control. The most common reasons for committing women to asylums were deeply tied to stress that was often due to puerperal mania and more generally "linked to the uncertainty of their condition of poverty."[71] Mary

Kinsella's mental issues, we may speculate, might have fallen within these two categories.[72]

It is this initial image of Mary Kinsella's death in an asylum that seems to trigger all the ghost stories and anecdotes that compose "An Autumn Night in the Hills." Her story resurfaces again in the concluding moment of the essay. While Synge is making his way home during a heavy storm, in a gloomy landscape made "unreal and dismal" by the rough weather, he catches a glimpse of "the shadow of a coffin, strapped in the rain, with the body of Mary Kinsella" (*TI*, 28). The coffin had been left in the rain outside the local pub while the men in charge of collecting it at the station were drinking. Nicholas Grene has defined the ending of "An Autumn Night in the Hills" as a "Gothic conclusion" and notes how Synge had previously titled the piece "The Body of Mary Kinsella" but had changed it later for publication.[73] This gothiclike atmosphere and Synge's deployment of gothic-inspired features in his scene construction can be read as a strategy that draws attention to the uncanny return not only of repressed emotions but also, symptomatically, of repressed controversial issues afflicting rural Ireland at the beginning of the twentieth century, such as mental illness and institutionalization. Synge's interest in the social landscape of mental institutions within the natural landscape of Wicklow is his acute way of exposing the threat that mechanisms of colonial surveillance had on the vitality of rural Ireland. In truth, asylums' attempts "to 'cure' the native properly," to apply Frantz Fanon's words to the Irish context, meant "seeking to make him thoroughly a part of a social background of the colonial type."[74]

In Synge's attempt to create a multivocal portrayal of place, other types of impressions regarding mental institutions are included. In "The People of the Glens," a woman in a public house tells Synge about her brother coming home after seven years in the Richmond Asylum. This account seems to offer a more positive experience of the asylum, to Synge's utmost surprise. The woman informs the writer how her brother was at the asylum "walking about like a gentleman, doing any light work he'd find agreeable" (*TI*, 110). She also adds a comment that her own son made after a visit to the uncle at the asylum: "'You'll never see Michael again,' says he when he came back, 'for he's too well off where he is.' And indeed it was well for him, but now he's come home" (*TI*, 110). This different account of asylum experience seems nevertheless to be in line with typical expectations of the asylums that family members had in relation to the person hospitalized. Walsh notes that relatives of those deemed insane regarded the asylum in a utilitarian way as "a resource, one which could be assessed in terms of its efficacy, and used as they felt appropriate."[75] These references to the impact of mental institutions on the people of Wicklow, exposed through lived experiences and constructed in the form of direct accounts, showcase once again Synge's plural and dialogic approach to reporting. Synge multiplies the narrative perspectives rather than sticking to a more simplistic and "monophonic"[76] representation of the Wicklow landscape as a patriotic Eden or nationalist Arcadia.

In his portrayal of the Wicklow region, Synge is also interested in presenting episodes of resistance to those mechanisms of colonial surveillance. In a letter to Jack Yeats dated July 22, 1907, he writes about his sojourn with a local family in a cottage in Lough Bray, Enniskerry, informs Yeats about a visit he paid to a local reformatory near his cottage, and chronicles a couple of curious incidents he witnessed on those premises:

> Glen Cree Reformatory—that you might have heard of—is a mile off townwards—and I went through it a week or two ago and saw an admirable cake-walk danced by one of the convicts—and a roomful of the youngsters with a hag—a lay hag—over them knitting stockings for the institutions. <and> When we went in the young divils [*sic*]—God help them—blushed scarlet at being caught at such ungaolbirdlike employment. It is told that one of them a while ago made himself a nun's outfit— he was a tailor apprentise [*sic*]—and escaped in it, and then before he was caught went round Dublin and collected 40 pounds for foreign missions.[77]

The performance of the cakewalk in contrast with its setting as well as the anecdote of the picaresque jailbreak may have certainly intrigued Synge as an example of the Irish peasant's resilience against the abasement of patronizing measures such as relief assistance, reformatories, and philanthropic associations—all apparatuses utilized by the hegemonic power to exercise more or less direct forms of control. In a paragraph subsequently omitted in the essay "The People of the Glens," Synge, rather than resorting to the paternalism toward the Irish country people evident in much Revival rhetoric, comments on their sense of humor at the expenses of the tourist and praises this irony as a tool of resistance:

> When a benevolent visitor comes to his cottage, seeking a sort of holy family, the man of the house, his wife and all their infants, too courteous to disappoint him, play the part with delight. When the amiable visitor, however, is out once more in the boreen, a storm of good-tempered irony breaks out behind him, that would surprise him could he hear it. This irony I have met with many times . . . and I have always been overjoyed to hear it. It shows that, in spite of relief-works, commissions, and patronizing philanthropy—that sickly thing—the Irish peasant, in his own mind, is neither abject nor servile. (TI, 116)

Synge critiques essentialist constructions of Irishness advanced by nationalists in Dublin, whose custom was "to exhalt the Irish peasant into a type of almost absolute virtue, frugal, self-sacrificing, valiant, and I know not what" (TI, 116).

Synge's Wicklow journalism departs from stereotypical representations of the area to be found in popular travelogues of nationalist sympathies by instead exposing the causes of the cultural disconnect and identity crisis of people inhabiting colonial marginalities. Synge uses several strategies of resistance: firsthand testimonies to build a multivocal account, a focus on human-built locales that have invariably shaped both the natural and the human history of the Wicklow region, and an interest in examining the psychological impact of the environment on its inhabitants. His sensitive attention to the representation of the entanglement between the environment and its inhabitants can be seen as an attempt to articulate what Lawrence Buell names the "environmental unconscious" embedded in people, communities, and texts. Buell defines the environmental unconscious as "the necessarily partial realization of one's embeddedness in environments as a condition of personal and social being."[78] His concept draws from a number of theories, but particularly from those of human geographer Robert Sack, whose idea of the *homo geographicus* "envisions human situatedness as produced by the interaction of social

construction, territorial physicality, and phenomenology of perception."
Most notably, Buell also draws from Frederic Jameson's theory of the
political unconscious of literary texts and their evocation, rewriting, and
restructuring of previous ideological frameworks. More forcefully than
ideology, however, Buell considers "embeddedness in spatio-physical context [to be] even more constitutive of personal and social identity." According to Buell, the term *environmental unconscious* in its positive connotation
implies "a residual capacity (of individual humans, authors, texts, readers,
communities) to awake to fuller apprehension of physical environment
and one's interdependence with it." In its negative implication, it "refers
to the impossibility of individual or collective perception coming to full
consciousness at whatever level."[79] Synge's articulation of the effects of
mental institutions on the Wicklow inhabitants by means of a polyphonic
narrative can be read as his attempt to draw attention to and to voice the
environmental unconscious of the Wicklow region. In contrast to the travelogues discussed earlier in this chapter, Synge's portrayal of Wicklow
focuses not solely on "natural" spots but also on human-built sites of coercion and hegemony, such as workhouses and mental institutions, where
cultural loss and disconnect emanate more strongly.

In another significant episode in the Wicklow essays, Synge depicts
a moment of reawakening and reappraisal of the material environment
as an antidote to that physical and psychological disconnect. In "The
Oppression of the Hills," a girl seems to have been seized by a sort of
panic attack generated by the presence of a bog: "Intense nervousness is
common also with much younger women. I remember one night hearing someone crying out and screaming in the house where I was staying. . . . That afternoon [the girl's] two younger sisters had come to see her,
and now she had been taken with a panic that they had been drowned
going home through the bogs, and she was crying and wailing and say-
ing she must go to look for them. It was not thought fit for her to leave the
house alone so late in the evening so I went with her" (*TI*, 38). After exposing the girl's psychological disequilibrium generated by the bog, Synge
presents an evocative description of the night walk in the bog with her.
During the walk, the girl seems to calm down, and both make their way
back home. In the account of the night ramble, Synge conveys a sense of

place by mentioning precise sensory details about the volatile fauna of the bog ecosystem. The reader, together with Synge and the girl, hears the Nightjars clapping their long wings in the dark. The two night ramblers also encounter another inhabitant of the bog, the Ground-Nester Snipe, whose "well-known calls and cries," according to Peter Foss and Catherine O'Connell, "are an evocative part of the atmosphere of the wild boglands."[80] Through the unfolding of details about the natural environment, Synge's narrative mimics the girl's process of rediscovery of the natural premises and her coming to terms with her fears, which—at least temporarily—seem to be exorcised: "I could see that the actual presence of the bog had shown my companion the absurdity of her fears, and in a little while we went home" (TI, 39). Although Synge does not dwell on this episode too much, the experience of a girl scared by the isolated mountains and boglands can be read as igniting a process of rediscovery of (self-)identity that is intimately linked with the rediscovery of the physical landscape. Rediscovering the environment and making sense of it can be interpreted as an alternative remedy to the coercive measures of the colonial power—that is, the claustrophobic environments of lunatic asylums, workhouses, relief work schemes, and reformatories—whose only interest has always been to shape the native identity according to the colonizer's terms. Synge's "awakening to full apprehension"[81] of the natural environment as antidote to the displacement and misplacements caused by social and cultural practices of a colonial type is also exposed by means of another powerful construct: the nomadic figures of tramps and "tinkers" sketched in the Wicklow articles and powerfully reimagined in his drama.[82] As noted at the beginning of this chapter, Synge cherishes these nomadic people for their nonconformism and vitality, qualities found in artists, too. Against the sedentary community inhabiting the edges of the "Garden of Ireland" and experiencing the repercussions of a cultural and psychological disconnect, Synge juxtaposes these peripatetic subjects who embody a different way of dwelling and are represented as an alternative way to reconnect people to their environment.

In conclusion, in contrast to Synge's poetry and lyrical prose fragments, his literary journalism about Wicklow examined in this chapter is critical of essentialist constructions of the Irish landscape and its inhabitants and showcases a profound qualitative engagement with locales, in opposition to popular representations of Wicklow that deal with places in passing and superficially. Synge portrays the physical environment not simply as a background for human actions but also as an agent mutually intertwined with the human community. In the Wicklow articles, he engages with a plurality of locales, both natural premises and social landscapes, such as the coercive institutions and manorial estates belonging to the Ascendancy class. His literary journalism offers a dynamic interplay between his informants' inner and outer landscapes to expose the historical and social fractures in rural Ireland at the turn of the twentieth century. Through a polyphonic and dialogic narrative—which includes perceptions of place filtered from his informants' firsthand testimonies—and by his attempts at articulating the "environmental unconscious" of the so-called Garden of Ireland, his essays move away from previous modes of travel writing with nationalist sympathies to denounce the cultural disconnect provoked by colonial practices of surveillance that remapped places in their own hegemonic terms.

# Epilogue

## *"Turning Home"*

In 1908 during a trip to Coblenz, John Millington Synge wrote the poem "(Abroad)," published posthumously in the *Collected Works*:

Some go to game, or pray in Rome
I travel for my turning home
For I've been six months abroad
Faith your kiss would brighten God! (CW1, 62)

According to Robin Skelton, the editor of the collected volume of poems, Synge adapted the poem from a Gaelic original with clear religious connotations.[1] Synge's version subverts the original by irreverently turning the sacred into the profane. Critics have long explored his subversive "turning home" in his dramatic production. However, they have given comparatively less attention to the subversive qualities of his nonfiction. This book has illuminated Synge's craft as a nonfiction writer by examining his corpus of travel texts about Ireland in its own right. It historicizes his travel book *The Aran Islands* and his series of travel essays about West Kerry, Wicklow, and the Congested Districts of Connemara and Mayo in relation to the genre of Irish travel writing at the turn of the twentieth century by various Irish writers and activists connected with Revival groups.

"(Abroad)" quoted by permission of Oxford University Press, © Oxford University Press.

Synge's critical outlook in his travel writing destabilizes inherited modes of travel literature about Irish localities through a number of ground-breaking narrative strategies.

Synge's travel book and journalism are in part unleashed from dominant and essentializing discourses. Far from endorsing imperial or purely nationalist interests, as some of the travel narratives analyzed in this study do, Synge's travel nonfiction interrogates those grand narratives through the deployment of a "contact perspective." Synge's contact perspective is expressed through his singular method of writing about place, travel, and the communities he visited. This contact angle focuses on moments of cultural collision and is interested in the depiction of how opposite cultural formations come into contact and function within those moments of forced proximity. Throughout this book, I have discussed several contact moments—for instance, the arrival of the peddler on the Aran Islands; the intrusion of the golf ball interrupting Synge's reveries; the boy proudly teaching Synge Irish but not willing to be photographed in his homespun clothes; the car man who drives CDB officials and reminisces about the Famine. In all of these moments and many more, Synge interrogates ideological formations, representations of Irish places, language, and history. He also often queries issues of cultural translation and the rewriting of Irish culture by Revivalists and foreign visitors. As Gregory Castle notes, one of the important consequences of Synge's problematizing discursive practice is the fact that his texts write and read culture and its representations not as stable, singular constructs but rather as processual and plural configurations.[2]

Synge's contact strategy in his narratives provides an infrastructure in which a plurality of stories, encounters, and representation of locales reverberate in a dialogic way. These micro- and polyphonic histories, whereby the testimonies of Synge's informants are constructed in direct-speech mode, conduct a critical and empathetic mediation between clashing cultural, social, and historical formations as they intersect with broader macrodynamics. This tactic draws attention not simply to the so-called facts but also, more importantly, to the perception of those facts by the people more directly affected by them. In this book, I have referred to this aspect of Synge's work as "history telling," particularly with regard to the journalistic series "In the Congested Districts," whereby the local inhabitants' perceptions of the modernizing changes imposed by the CDB take center stage and interact with major events in Irish history (e.g., the Great Famine).

Synge's nonfiction does not simply excavate the everyday memories of the communities among which he traveled and dwelled. He writes about places and communities with the awareness of his impact on and interaction with them. His persona in his travel writing often works as a vehicle that connects and brings into play and coexistence different cultures and representations. For example, the scene in *The Aran Islands* in which the islanders gather around Synge to look at his photographs of the islands functions as a kind of performative act of recognition at both an individual and a communal level. In 2009 at the launch of the exhibition *John Millington Synge, Photographer*, discussed in chapter 1, Synge's photographs reenacted a similar performance of recognition and were unproblematically embraced as part of the community's cultural memory. For its ability to share people's lives rather than to observe them,[3] and for its prerogative to strike a balance between elegy and critique,[4] Synge's travel nonfiction takes part in the narration of an alternative history that restores significant memories of particular rural communities on the fringes of Irish life—physically and socially—during the Revival.

Another important concern of this study has been to demythologize the romantic notion of Synge as the aloof intellectual or aesthete, detached from everyday material and political concerns, interested uniquely in his dramatic art. This demythologization has, of course, already occurred in much scholarship about his drama, which often uses his travel writing as evidence for documenting his social realism.[5] Aligning with this criticism, this book has foregrounded Synge's nonfiction, in particular his travel journalism, as the chief instance where his concerns for the material, social, and political conditions of Ireland are first and most directly articulated. For instance, as argued in chapter 3, Synge's series of essays on the Congested Districts for the *Manchester Guardian* deeply engage with social change and with the political debates of the time, advocating national self-determination as the only way in the long run to solve chronic distress in the West of Ireland. Furthermore, his journalism about the Congested Districts prefigures contemporary ecological concerns in its attention to the impact of the CDB's modernizing measures on the environment and its natural resources.

Finally, Synge's corpus of travel writing works as a critique of a certain Revival idealism championed by a number of revivalist associations. Synge's travel journalism shares with many other Irish travelogues of the time a deep attachment to Irish locales and the search for a distinctive cultural identity. However, as shown in chapters 1, 2, and 4 through a direct comparison of Synge's work with revivalist travel narratives, Synge is also critical of grand narratives of cultural and linguistic purity. Like his plays, Synge's travel writing is equally a powerful instance of his cultural criticism of the Revival even as it was unfolding.

Notes • Bibliography • Index

# Notes

## Introduction

1. John Millington Synge, *Letters to Molly: John Millington Synge to Maire O'Neill, 1906–1909*, ed. Ann Saddlemyer (Cambridge, MA: Belknap Press of Harvard Univ. Press, 1971), 152, subsequently cited parenthetically in the text as *LM*.

2. James Clifford, *Routes: Travel and Translation in the Late Twentieth Century* (Cambridge, MA: Harvard Univ. Press, 1997), 66.

3. See the bibliography for a complete list of Synge's periodical articles.

4. See Catherine Wilsdon, "Daring to Be European: J. M. Synge Transformative Travels," PhD diss., Univ. College Dublin, 2015.

5. See John Millington Synge, *In Wicklow, West Kerry, and Connemara, Collected Works*, vol. 2: *Prose*, ed. Alan Price (Gerrards Cross, UK: Colin Smythe, 1982), 187–343; this volume of the Collected Works is subsequently cited parenthetically in the text as *CW2*. Among other editions, these essays are also collected in John Millington Synge, *In Wicklow, West Kerry, and Connemara*, with essays by George Gmelch and Ann Saddlemyer, photography by George Gmelch (Dublin: O'Brien Press, 1980).

6. This approach is evident, for instance, in Thomas J. Morrissey, "Prose," in *A J. M. Synge Literary Companion*, ed. Edward Kopper (New York: Greenwood Press, 1988), 15–24, where Synge's travel nonfiction is dealt with alongside his other prose; his Wicklow essays, in particular, are deemed "excellent companion pieces to the plays" (21). A similar angle is also evident in Nicholas Grene, "On the Margins: Synge and Wicklow," in *Interpreting Synge: Essays from the Synge Summer School 1991–2000*, ed. Nicholas Grene (Dublin: Lilliput Press, 2000), 20–40.

7. For *The Aran Islands* and island ethnographies, see Declan Kiberd, "Synge's *Tristes Tropiques*: *The Aran Islands*," in *Interpreting Synge*, ed. Grene, 82–110; Gregory Castle, "'Synge-on-Aran': *The Aran Islands* and the Subject of Revivalist Ethnography," in *Modernism and the Celtic Revival* (Cambridge: Cambridge Univ. Press, 2001), 98–133; and Veerendra Lele, "Reading Dialogic Correspondence: Synge's *The Aran Islands*," *New Hibernia Review* 11, no. 4 (Winter 2007): 124–29. , for a detailed comparison between Synge's work and the scientific

writing about the Aran Islands by anthropologists Alfred Cort Haddon and Charles R. Browne, see also John Brannigan, *Archipelagic Modernism: Literature in the Irish and British Isles, 1890–1970* (Edinburgh: Edinburgh Univ. Press, 2015).

8. Mary Louise Pratt, "Fieldwork in Common Places," in *Writing Culture: The Poetics and Politics of Ethnography*, ed. James Clifford and George E. Marcus (Berkeley: Univ. of California Press, 1986), 27.

9. Tony Roche, "J. M. Synge: Journeys Real and Imagined," *Journal of Irish Studies* 16 (Sept. 2001): 85.

10. Cited in Oona Frawley, "Synge, *The Aran Islands*, and the Movement towards Realism," in *Irish Pastoral Nostalgia and Twentieth Century Irish Literature* (Dublin: Irish Academic Press, 2005), 97.

11. John Millington Synge, diary entry, June 9, 1898, MS 4419, folio 71, Papers of John Millington Synge, Trinity College Library, Dublin. For a comparison between the Synge of *The Aran Islands* and French regionalists such as Anatole le Braz and Pierre Loti, see John Wilson Foster, "'Certain Set Apart': The Romantic Strategy—John Millington Synge," in *Fictions of the Irish Literary Revival: A Changeling Art* (Syracuse, NY: Syracuse Univ. Press; Dublin: Gill and MacMillan, 1987), 94–113.

12. Synge crossed out in the typescript and omitted in the final publication his reference to Loti: "The general plan of the book . . . largely borrowed from Pierre Loti, who has I think treated this sort of subject more adequately than any other writer of the present day" (MS 4344, folio 4, Synge Papers, Trinity College Library).

13. See also Patrick Lonergan, ed., *Synge and His Influences: Centenary Essays from the Synge Summer School* (Dublin: Carysfort Press, 2011), and Ben Levitas, "J. M. Synge: European Encounters," in *The Cambridge Companion to J. M. Synge*, ed. P. J. Mathews (Cambridge: Cambridge Univ. Press, 2009), 77–91.

14. Shawn Gillen, "Synge's *The Aran Islands* and Irish Creative Nonfiction," *New Hibernia Review* 11, no. 4 (Winter 2007): 129.

15. Nicholas Grene, introduction to John Millington Synge, *J. M. Synge: Travelling Ireland, Essays 1898–1908*, ed. Nicholas Grene (Dublin: Lilliput Press, 2009), xiv, xiii–xiv; *Travelling Ireland* is hereafter cited parenthetically in the text as *TI*.

16. See John Millington Synge, *The Works of John M. Synge* (Dublin: Maunsel, 1910).

17. Robert Lynd, extract from review of J. M. Synge, *The Aran Islands*, *Sunday Sun*, quoted in a marketing blurb for Synge's book in *The Shanachie*, no. 4 (Winter 1907): front matter.

18. P. J. Mathews, *Revival: The Abbey Theatre, Sinn Féin, the Gaelic League, and the Co-operative Movement* (Cork: Cork Univ. Press in association with Field Day, 2003), 2, 3.

19. Kevin Rafter, ed., *Irish Journalism before Independence* (Manchester, UK: Manchester Univ. Press, 2011).

20. Karen Steele, *Women, Press, and Politics during the Irish Revival* (Syracuse, NY: Syracuse Univ. Press, 2007); Karen Steele and Michael de Nie, eds., *Ireland and the New Journalism* (Basingstoke, UK: Palgrave Macmillan, 2014).

21. Catherine Morris, *Alice Milligan and the Irish Cultural Revival* (Dublin: Four Courts Press, 2012).

22. See Philip O'Leary, *The Prose Literature of the Gaelic Revival, 1881–1921* (University Park: Pennsylvania State Univ. Press, 1994); Regina Uí Chollatáin, "Newspapers, Journals, and the Irish Revival," in *Irish Journalism before Independence*, ed. Rafter, 160–73.

23. See Luke Gibbons, "Synge, Country and Western: The Myth of the West in Irish and American Culture," in *Transformations in Irish Culture* (Notre Dame, IN: Univ. of Notre Dame Press in association with Field Day, 1996), 23–37; Frank Shovlin, *Journey Westward: Joyce, Dubliners, and the Literary Revival* (Liverpool: Liverpool Univ. Press, 2012).

24. Mary Louise Pratt, *Imperial Eyes: Travel Writing and Transculturation* (London: Routledge, 1992), 4.

25. Glen Hooper, ed., *The Tourist's Gaze: Travellers to Ireland, 1800–2000* (Cork: Cork Univ. Press, 2001); John P. Harrington, ed., *The English Traveller in Ireland: Accounts of Ireland and the Irish through Five Centuries* (Dublin: Wolfhound, 1991).

26. Raphaël Ingelbien, *Irish Cultures of Travel: Writing on the Continent, 1929–1914* (Basingstoke, UK: Palgrave Macmillan, 2016).

27. See Harriet Martineau, *Letters from Ireland by Harriet Martineau*, ed. Glenn Hooper (Dublin: Irish Academic Press, 2001), and Asenath Nicholson, *Annals of the Famine in Ireland*, ed. Maureen Murphy (Dublin: Lilliput Press, 1998). See also Kevin J. James, *Tourism, Land, and Landscape in Ireland: The Commodification of Culture* (London: Routledge, 2014), on the development of County Kerry as a tourist resort in the nineteenth century.

28. See Stephen Gwynn, *The Fair Hills of Ireland* (Dublin: Maunsel, 1906) and *Highways and Byways in Donegal and Antrim* (London: Macmillan, 1899).

29. Seaton Milligan and Alice Milligan, *Glimpses of Erin* (London: Ward, 1888).

30. Joseph Campbell, *Mearing Stones: Leaves from a Note-book on Tramp in Donegal* (Dublin: Maunsel, 1911).

31. James Joyce, *Scritti Italiani*, ed. Gianfranco Corsini and Giorgio Melchiori (Milan: Arnoldo Mondadori Editore, 1979).

32. Within this time frame, the only exception is perhaps Robert Lynd's travel book *Rambles in Ireland* (London: Mills and Boon, 1912). Lynd discusses trips that most likely happened a few months after Synge's death, during the summer of 1909, as C. J. Woods has speculated in *Travellers' Accounts as Source-Material for Irish Historians* (Dublin: Four Courts Press, 2009), 196. Lynd's travelogue is examined in this book nonetheless for its extensive account of Kerry and in particular for its detailed description of Puck Fair.

33. Carl Thompson, *Travel Writing* (London: Routledge, 2011), 57.

34. Ríona Nic Congáil, "Editor's Introduction," in Agnes O'Farrelly, *Smaointe ar Árainn / Thoughts on Aran*, trans. and ed. Ríona Nic Congáil (Syracuse, NY: Syracuse Univ. Press for Arlen House, 2010), 74.

35. David Fitzpatrick, "Synge and Modernity in *The Aran Islands*," in *Synge and Edwardian Ireland*, ed. Brian Cliff and Nicholas Grene (Oxford: Oxford Univ. Press, 2012), 125.

36. Tim Robinson, "Place/Person/Book: Synge's *The Aran Islands*," introduction to J. M. Synge, *The Aran Islands*, ed. Tim Robinson (London: Penguin Books, 1992), xv.

37. Peter Collins, "Railway," in *The Oxford Companion to Irish History*, ed. S. J. Connolly (Oxford: Oxford Univ. Press, 1998), 471, 472.

38. See chapter 2 for a discussion of the transportation Banim and Synge used in their travels.

39. Brian Griffin, "'As Happy as Seven Kings': Cycling in Nineteenth-Century Ireland," *History Ireland* 22, no. 1 (Jan.–Feb. 2014): 33, 34.

40. Brian Griffin, *Cycling in Victorian Ireland* (Dublin: Nonsuch Press, 2006), 145, 147.

41. Ibid., 149.

42. Esme Coulbert and Tim Youngs, "Introduction," in "Travel Writing and the Automobile," edited by Esme Coulbert and Tim Youngs, special issue of *Studies in Travel Writing* 17, no. 2 (2013): 111.

43. Esme Coulbert, "The Romance of the Road: 'Narratives of Motoring in England, 1896–1930,'" in *Travel Writing and Tourism in Britain and Ireland*, ed. Benjamin Colbert (New York: Palgrave Macmillan, 2012), 202.

44. Henry Sturmey, cofounder and editor of *The Autocar*, also wrote a travel book entitled *On an Autocar through the Length and Breadth of the Land in 1899* (Coulbert, "The Romance of the Road," 202).

45. Michael Myers Shoemaker, *Wanderings in Ireland* (New York: Putnam's, 1908).

46. Giulia Bruna, "'In the Heart of the Roman Metropolis': An Italian Prologue to Synge's Investigative Journalism," *Studi Irlandesi: A Journal of Irish Studies* 1, no. 1 (2011): 147–56.

47. Chris Morash, "Synge's Typewriter: The Technological Sublime in Edwardian Ireland," in *Synge and Edwardian Ireland*, ed. Cliff and Grene, 24.

48. Sligo, Leitrim, and Northern Counties Railways, *By-laws and Regulations* (Belfast: R. Carswell & Son, Printers, 1905), NLI EPH F6, Prints and Drawings Department, National Library of Ireland, Dublin.

49. Caitríona Clear, "Homelessness, Crime, Punishment, and Poor Relief in Galway 1850–1914: An Introduction," *Journal of the Galway Archaeological and Historical Society* 50, no. 1 (1998): 131, 130.

50. Brian Griffin, "The Tourist Gaze: Cycling Tourists' Impressions of Victorian and Edwardian Ireland," *Irish Studies Review* 25, no. 3 (2017): 305.

51. Susan Bassnett, "Travel Writing and Gender," in *The Cambridge Companion to Travel Writing*, ed. Peter Hulme and Tim Youngs (Cambridge: Cambridge Univ. Press, 2002), 233–34.

52. Pratt, *Imperial Eyes*, 215.

53. Andrew J. Garavel, "*Beggars on Horse Back*: The Irish Cousins in Wales," *Studies in Travel Writing* 18, no. 2 (2014): 161.

54. James Pethica, editor's note in Augusta Gregory, *Lady Gregory's Diaries, 1892–1902*, ed. James Pethica (Oxford: Oxford Univ. Press, 1996), 18.

55. Gregory, like her male counterparts, including Synge, prepared for the trip to the Aran Islands by reading Emily Lawless's novel about an Irish peasant woman of the islands, *Grania: The Story of an Island*, and Jane Barlow's fictional sketches of Connemara, *Irish Idylls*, both published in 1892 (James Pethica, "Editor's Introduction," in Gregory, *Lady Gregory's Diaries 1892–1902*, xx).

56. Gregory, *Lady Gregory's Diaries, 1892–1902*, 18.

57. Synge visited Inishmore May 10–24 and June 9–25, with an interval on Inismeáin from May 24 to June 9 (Pethica, editor's note in Gregory, *Lady Gregory's Diaries, 1892–1902*, 187).

58. See Augusta Gregory, "'A Garden Enclosed' Inisheer: 'A Cloughaun,'" in "Lady Gregory Sketchbook 3033TX," NLI PD 3033 TX 33, Prints and Drawings Department, National Library of Ireland, at http://catalogue.nli.ie/Record/vtls000048975; Augusta Gregory, "[Hearth]," in "Lady Gregory Sketchbook 3033TX," NLI PD 3033 TX 37, Prints and Drawings Department, National Library of Ireland, at http://catalogue.nli.ie/Record/vtls000048996.

59. O'Farrelly, *Smaointe ar Árainn / Thoughts on Aran*, 37.

60. J. M. Synge to Lady Gregory, Sept. 11, 1904, in John Millington Synge, *The Collected Letters of John Millington Synge*, vol. 1: *1871–1907*, ed. Ann Saddlemyer (Oxford: Clarendon Press, 1983), 93; this volume is subsequently cited parenthetically in the text as *CL1*; see also Saddlemyer's introduction to *CL1*, 63. Of this trip to Sligo and North Mayo in 1904, no private correspondence or travel writing seems to have been recorded. After the letter to Lady Gregory dated September 11, 1904, Synge's letter writing resumed in November (*CL1*, 95–96). His notebooks include only a few pages of annotations and transcriptions of words and phrases; see John Millington Synge, *The Synge Manuscripts in the Library of Trinity College Dublin*, a catalogue prepared on the occasion of the Synge Centenary Exhibition (Dublin: Dolmen Press, 1971), 46.

61. For studies on postcolonialism and travel writing, see Edward W. Said, *Orientalism: Western Conceptions of the Orient* (1978; reprint, London: Penguin, 1991); Pratt, *Imperial Eyes*; and Clifford, *Routes*, and *The Predicament of Culture: Twentieth-Century Ethnography, Literature, and Art* (Cambridge, MA: Harvard Univ. Press, 1988). In an Irish context, see Kiberd, "Synge's *Tristes Tropiques*"; Castle, "'Synge-on-Aran'"; David Lloyd, *Ireland after History* (Cork: Cork Univ. Press in association with Field Day, 1999) and *Irish Times: Temporalities of Modernity* (Cork: Field Day in association with the Keough-Naughton Institute for Irish Studies at the Univ. of Notre Dame, 2008).

62. For example, Norman Sims, "The Literary Journalists," introduction to *The Literary Journalists: The New Art of Personal Reportage* (New York: Ballantine Books, 1984), 3–25, and "The Art of Literary Journalism," in *Literary Journalism: A New Collection of the Best American Nonfiction*, ed. Norman Sims and Mark Kramer (New York: Ballantine Books, 1995), 3–19; Richard Keeble, "On Journalism, Creativity, and the Imagination," introduction to *The Journalistic Imagination: Literary Journalists from Defoe to Capote and Carter*, ed. Richard Keeble and Sharon Wheeler (London: Routledge, 2007), 1–14; and Thomas B. Connery, "A Third Way to

Tell the Story: American Literary Journalism at the Turn of the Century," in *Literary Journalism in the Twentieth Century*, ed. Norman Sims (Oxford: Oxford Univ. Press, 1990), 3–20.

63. See Rafter, *Irish Journalism before Independence*, and Steele, *Women, Press, and Politics during the Irish Revival*.

64. Robinson, "Place/Person/Book," xxxix.

65. See, respectively, Frantz Fanon, *The Wretched of the Earth* (1961; reprint, London: Penguin, 1990), and Lawrence Buell, *Writing for an Endangered World: Literature, Culture, and the Environment in the United States and Beyond* (Cambridge, MA: Belknap Press of Harvard Univ. Press, 2001) and *The Future of Environmental Criticism: Environmental Crisis and Literary Imagination* (Oxford: Blackwell, 2005).

66. Michel Foucault, *Madness and Civilization: A History of Insanity in the Age of Reason* (London: Routledge, 1993).

67. Oonagh Walsh, "Lunatic and Criminal Alliances in Nineteenth-Century Ireland," in *Outside the Walls of the Asylum: The History of Care in the Community 1750–2000*, ed. Peter Bartlett and David Wright (London: Athlone Press, 1999), 132–52.

68. See the following works by Justin Carville: "*My Wallet of Photographs*: Photography, Ethnography, and Visual Hegemony in John Millington Synge's *The Aran Islands*," *Irish Journal of Anthropology* 10, no. 1 (2007): 5–11; "Visible Others: Photography and Romantic Ethnography in Ireland," in *Irish Modernism and the Global Primitive*, ed. Maria McGarrity and Claire A. Culleton (New York: Palgrave Macmillan, 2009), 93–114; "'With His Mind-Guided Camera': J. M. Synge, J. J. Clarke, and the Visual Politics of Edwardian Street Photography," in *Synge and Edwardian Ireland*, ed. Cliff and Grene, 186–207.

### 1. "The Cuckoo with Its Pipit"

1. Andrew McNeillie, *An Aran Keening* (2001; reprint, Madison: Univ. of Wisconsin Press, 2002), 32–33.

2. Synge, *The Aran Islands*, ed. Robinson, 23, subsequently cited parenthetically in the text as *AI*.

3. Levitas, "J. M. Synge"; Lonergan, *Synge and His Influences*.

4. David Fitzpatrick, "Synge and Modernity in *The Aran Islands*," in *Synge and Edwardian Ireland*, ed. Cliff and Grene, 124.

5. Nicholas Allen, "Synge, Reading, and Archipelago," in *Synge and Edwardian Ireland*, ed. Cliff and Grene, 159, 166, 168.

6. See Robinson, "Place/Person/Book," xv–xvi, and his note in Synge, *AI*, 137–38, for a detailed excursus on all the academic visitors to the Aran Islands.

7. Elaine Sisson, "*The Aran Islands* and the Travel Essays," in *The Cambridge Companion to J. M. Synge*, ed. Mathews, 58.

8. Nicola Gordon Bowe, *Art and the National Dream: The Search for Vernacular Expression in Turn of the Century Design* (Dublin: Irish Academic Press, 1993), quoted in Sisson, "*The Aran Islands* and the Travel Essays," 58.

9. Martin Haverty, "The Aran Isles; or a Report of the Excursion of the Ethnological Section of the British Association from Dublin to the Western Islands in September 1857," in *An Aran Reader*, ed. Breandán Ó hEithir and Ruairí Ó hEithir (Dublin: Lilliput Press, 1999), 43, 46.

10. Breandán Ó hEithir and Ruairí Ó hEithir, introduction to excerpts in *An Aran Reader*, ed. Ó hEithir and Ó hEithir, 13.

11. As Tim Robinson documents, Irish-language activists and nationalists who visited Aran included Patrick (Pádraic) Pearse, Thomas MacDonagh, Eoin MacNeill, and Father Eugene O'Growney ("Place/People/Book," xvi).

12. Dame Columba Butler, O.S.B., "The Life of Mary E. L. Butler," NLI, MS 7321, National Library of Ireland, Dublin, quoted in Nic Congáil, "Editor's Introduction," 77.

13. Nic Congáil, "Editor's Introduction," 77.

14. Pratt, *Imperial Eyes*, 6.

15. C. L. Innes, "Postcolonial Synge," in *The Cambridge Companion to J. M. Synge*, ed. Mathews, 118, 120.

16. In a lecture entitled "Taking the Long View: The Irish Revival" given at the Irish Seminar 2010, University of Notre Dame, Dublin, in June 2010, David Lloyd discussed the concepts of "transvaluation" and "transformation" in the framework of cultural production and postcolonial theory. He defined "transvaluation" as a process whereby the meaning of a value judgement is completely subverted—for instance, a positive concept is transposed into a negative one and vice versa. Among the examples he gave, he mentioned the Négritude literary movement, which transvaluated ideas of race and "blackness" from negative to positive—from "black is bad" to "black is good." However, as Lloyd further maintained, this transfer of value often reverts to essentialism, entrapping identities in stereotypical notions.

17. Banim's travelogue was illustrated by her sister, Matilda, and was first serialized in the late 1880s in the nationalist magazine the *Weekly Freeman and Irish Agriculturist* (a compendium to the *Freeman's Journal*).

18. "Mary Banim," in *The Oxford Companion to Irish Literature*, ed. Robert Welch (Oxford: Clarendon Press, 1996), 30.

19. See the bibliography for a complete list of Mary Banim's work; the *Providence Sunday Journal* is collected at the Rockefeller Library, Brown Univ., Providence, RI.

20. During a visit to Ireland in 1887, where Williams stayed with the Banim sisters in Dalkey, he met Tynan and "perhaps the rest of a small band of writing people in Dublin" (George Potter, *An Irish Pilgrimage* [Providence, RI: Providence Journal Company, 1950], 10).

21. Mary Banim, *Here and There through Ireland*, series 2, with illustrations by Matilda E. Banim (Dublin: Freeman's Journal, 1892), 122, 143.

22. Ibid., 2:147.

23. William Reed, *Rambles in Ireland; or Observations Written during a Short Residence in That Country* (1815), excerpted in *The Tourist's Gaze*, ed. Hooper, 19.

24. Ibid., 19.

25. Mathews, *Revival*, 142.

26. Ibid., 143.

27. Susan Cannon Harris, "Synge and Gender," in *The Cambridge Companion to J. M. Synge*, ed. Mathews, 107. Arthur Griffith was the founder of the Sinn Féin party in 1905. He became president of the Irish Free State in 1922.

28. Frawley, "Synge, *The Aran Islands*, and the Movement towards Realism," 98.

29. Said, *Orientalism*, 93.

30. Banim, *Here and There through Ireland*, 2:103–4. In addition, Banim refers to Crusoe when contemplating a desolate spot in Connemara (*Here and There through Ireland*, series 1, with illustrations by Matilda E. Banim [Dublin: Freeman's Journal, 1891], 162).

31. Quoted in Anthony Purdy, "'Skilful in the Usury of Time': Michel Tournier and the Critique of Economism," in *Robinson Crusoe: Myths and Metamorphoses*, ed. Lieve Spaas and Brian Stimpson (Basingstoke, UK: Macmillan, 1996), 184–85.

32. Lee Morrissey, "The Restoration and Eighteenth Century 1660–1780," in *English Literature in Context*, ed. Paul Poplawski (Cambridge: Cambridge Univ. Press, 2008), 286.

33. David Spurr, *The Rhetoric of Empire: Colonial Discourse in Journalism, Travel Writing, and Imperial Administration* (Durham, NC: Duke Univ. Press, 1993), 48.

34. Said, *Orientalism*, 93, 94.

35. Arthur Symons, *Cities and Sea-coasts and Islands* (New York: Brentano, 1896), 305.

36. Ibid., 302.

37. Thompson, *Travel Writing*, 55.

38. Symons, *Cities and Sea-coasts and Islands*, 303, 314.

39. See the citations in notes 11, 12, and 13 in the introduction.

40. Roche, "J. M. Synge," 83. Roche also argues that Synge's scholarly grounding in the Irish language and early Irish literary tales was his personal motivation for his interest in the islands, independently of W. B. Yeats's famous advice to him to visit the islands to find his literary vocation (85).

41. Banim, *Here and There through Ireland*, 2:144.

42. Thompson, *Travel Writing*, 10.

43. Catherine Nash, "'Embodying the Nation': The West of Ireland Landscape and Irish Identity," in *Tourism in Ireland: A Critical Analysis*, ed. Barbara O'Connor and Michael Cronin (Cork: Cork Univ. Press, 1993), 87.

44. Symons, *Cities and Sea-coasts and Islands*, 306, 310.

45. Ibid., 324.

46. Edith Somerville and Martin Ross, "An Outpost of Ireland," in *Some Irish Yesterdays* (London: Longman, Greens, 1906), 12, 16.

47. Ibid., 32.

48. James F. Knapp, "Primitivism and Empire: John Synge and Paul Gauguin," *Comparative Literature* 41, no. 1 (Winter 1989): 53.

49. Sinéad Garrigan Mattar, "The Passing of the Shee: John Millington Synge," in *Primitivism, Science, and the Irish Revival* (Oxford: Oxford Univ. Press, 2004), 147.

50. According to Neal Garnham, golf was first introduced in Ireland in 1881 and "grew steadily in popularity, encouraged by the availability of land and the patronage of landowners." Garnham also notes that "the social level of players was kept high by the cost of fees and equipment" ("Golf," in *Oxford Companion to Irish History*, ed. Connolly, 223).

51. Knapp, "Primitivism and Empire," 64.

52. Alan Sinfield, "Cultural Materialism, *Othello*, and the Politics of Plausibility," in *Literary Theory: An Anthology*, eds. Julie Rivkin and Michael Ryan (Oxford: Blackwell, 2004), 752, 756, 757.

53. Pratt, *Imperial Eyes*, 6, 7.

54. Tenant evictions were performed by bailiffs and police forces if rent payments were delayed. Tim Robinson explains that the eviction narrated by Synge (in Synge, *AI*, 43–47) seems to have been the last eviction on the islands (*AI*, 143 n. 23).

55. Banim, *Here and There through Ireland*, 2:119, 120.

56. For further discussion about notions of time, history, and temporality related to concepts of tradition and modernity, see Lloyd, *Irish Times*.

57. Banim, *Here and There through Ireland*, 2:119.

58. Ibid., 2:118.

59. Somerville and Ross, "An Outpost of Ireland," 17, 21–22.

60. Nic Congáil, "Editor's Introduction," 77.

61. Ibid., 73, 84.

62. O'Farrelly, *Smaointe ar Árainn*, 101.

63. Ibid., 52 (Irish), 101 (English).

64. Anne Markey, "'The Price of Kelp in Connemara': Synge, Pearse, and the Idealization of Folk Culture," in *Synge and Edwardian Ireland*, ed. Cliff and Grene, 214, 212.

65. Carville, "Visible Others," 107–8, 109.

66. Carville, *"My Wallet of Photographs,"* 9.

67. Typescript draft of *The Aran Islands*, MS 4344, folio 517, Synge Papers, Trinity College Library. I thank Seán Hewitt for bringing to my attention these variants in Synge's typescript drafts.

68. Typescript draft of *The Aran Islands*, MS 4344, folio 143, Synge Papers, Trinity College Library.

69. Castle, "'Synge-on-Aran,'" 132.

70. Lele, "Reading Dialogic Correspondence," 125, 126.

71. Robinson, "Place/Person/Book," xvii.

72. Michael Cronin, *Across the Lines: Travel, Language, Translation* (Cork: Cork Univ. Press, 2000), 23.

73. Pádraic Pearse, from an article in *Fáinne an Lae* (1898), excerpted in Ó hEithir and Ó hEithir, *An Aran Reader*, 96.

74. Mary Burke, "Synge, Evolutionary Theory, and the Irish Language," in *Synge and His Influences*, ed. Lonergan, 64.

75. Pádraic Pearse, "A Visit to Inis Mór and Inis Meáin, August 1898," *Fáinne an Lae*, 1898, excerpted in Ó hEithir and Ó hEithir, *An Aran Reader*, 93.

76. O'Farrelly, *Smaointe ar Árainn*, 38 (Irish), 92 (English).

77. Nic Congáil, "Editor's Introduction," 81–82, 84.

78. In the article "Le mouvement intellectuel Irlandais," written for the French periodical *L'Européen* and published on March 15, 1902, Synge describes the "fort mauvais Irlandais" (loud bad Irish) of the Gaelic League audience attending the first performance of Douglas Hyde's play *Casadh an tSúgáin* and their patriotic rapture in singing traditional Irish songs during the interval (*CW2*, 381–82). This scene is another instance of Synge's "contact perspective" and a poignant metaphor for the clash between the ancient tradition on the verge of extinction and its artificial reinvention. Despite his post-*Playboy*-riots invective against what is "senile and slobberish in the doctrine of the Gaelic League" (*CW2*, 382), Synge also rightly acknowledges the League's excellent work in revitalizing the western seaboard ("Erris," *TI*, 82).

79. Alan Titley, "Synge and the Irish Language," in *The Cambridge Companion to J. M. Synge*, ed. Mathews, 95.

80. Gerald Vizenor, "Fugitive Poses," in *Fugitive Poses: Native American Scenes of Absence and Presence* (Lincoln: Univ. of Nebraska Press, 1998), 154.

81. Lloyd, *Ireland after History*, 88.

82. Declan Kiberd, *Inventing Ireland: The Literature of a Modern Nation* (Cambridge, MA: Harvard Univ. Press, 2002), 171–72.

83. Diarmuid Ó Giolláin, "Folklore and Poverty," in *Locating Irish Folklore: Tradition, Modernity, Identity*, ed. Diarmuid Ó Giolláin (Cork: Cork Univ. Press, 2000), 159.

84. Kiberd, *Inventing Ireland*, 171.

85. Patrick Lonergan, "J. M. Synge, Authenticity, and the Regional," in *Regional Modernisms*, ed. Neal Alexander and James Moran (Edinburgh: Edinburgh Univ. Press, 2013), 78.

86. Maurice Bourgeois, *John Millington Synge and the Irish Theatre* (London: Constable, 1913), 82.

87. Kiberd, "Synge's *Tristes Tropiques*," 89.

88. For further discussion on polyphony, see chapter 3.

89. Eilís Ní Dhuibhne, "The Best Field Worker: Synge and Irish Folklore," in *Synge and His Influences*, ed. Lonergan, 93–110, and "Synge's Use of Popular Material in 'The Shadow of the Glen,'" *Béaloides: Journal of the Folklore of Ireland Society* 58 (1990): 167 (quotation).

90. Castle, "'Synge-on-Aran,'" 133.

91. Gregory Dobbins, "Synge and Irish Modernism," in *The Cambridge Companion to J. M. Synge*, ed. Mathews, 137.

92. Tim Youngs, "Travelling Modernists," in *The Oxford Handbook of Modernisms*, ed. Peter Brooker, Andrzej Gąsiorek, Deborah Longworth, and Andrew Thacker (Oxford: Oxford Univ. Press, 2010), 272.

93. Neal Alexander and James Moran, "Introduction: Regional Modernisms," in *Regional Modernisms*, ed. Alexander and Moran, 3, 8, 6–7.

94. In the catalog *The Synge Manuscripts in the Library of Trinity College Dublin*, see in particular the listings for MS 4344, containing manuscripts and typescripts of *The Aran Islands*, and for MSS 4382, 4384, 4385, 4387, with notes from Synge's diaries and notebooks.

95. See the copies of Synge's Aran photographs in Parcel 38, Jack B. Yeats Archive, National Gallery of Ireland, Dublin.

96. Clare Hutton, "The Extraordinary History of the House of Maunsel," in *The Irish Book in English 1891–2000*, ed. Clare Hutton (Oxford: Oxford Univ. Press, 2011), 551.

97. Synge's amateur snapshots would be printed posthumously in John Millington Synge, *My Wallet of Photographs: The Collected Photographs of J. M. Synge*, arranged and introduced by Lilo Stephens (Dublin: Dolmen Editions, 1971).

98. Grene, introduction to Synge, *TI*, xxxvii–xxxviii.

99. On Haddon and Browne's anthropometry, see Justin Carville, "Resisting Vision: Photography, Anthropology, and the Production of Race in Ireland," in *Visual, Material, and Print Culture in Nineteenth Century Ireland*, ed. Ciara Breathnach and Catherine Lawless (Dublin: Four Courts Press, 2000), 158–75.

100. John J. Burke, "A Stronghold of the Gael," *The Gael*, Dec. 1903, 415.

101. Christopher Pinney, quoted in Carville, "Visible Others," 93.

102. Carville, "Visible Others," 94.

103. Edward Chandler, *Photography in Ireland in the Nineteenth Century* (Dublin: Edmund Burke, 2001), 29.

104. Ibid., 90.

105. Carville, "'With His Mind-Guided Camera,'" 193.

106. John Bertolini, "Shaw on Photography, Review," *English Literature in Transition, 1880–1920* 33, no. 4 (1990): 478.

107. Ibid., 480.

108. Morash, "Synge's Typewriter," 24–26. See also the introduction for an excursus on technological ameliorations in transportation.

109. Ibid., 24, 29–30.

110. Introduction to Synge, *The Synge Manuscripts in the Library of Trinity College Dublin*, 9.

111. John Millington Synge, diary, entry for May 17, 1898, MS 4419, folio 62, Synge Papers, Trinity College Library.

112. W. J. McCormack, *Fool of the Family: A Life of J. M. Synge* (London: Weidenfeld and Nicolson, 2000), 203.

113. For instance, in a letter to a relative, Rosie L. Calthrop, Synge asked for a photograph of her baby, Synge's godson, and informed her that he had not taken many photographs lately (August 27, 1900, in CL1, 51).

114. McCormack, *Fool of the Family*, 185, 203.

115. Carville, *"My Wallet of Photographs."*

116. See Morash, "Synge's Typewriter," and Carville, "'With His Mind-Guided Camera.'"

117. Carville, *"My Wallet of Photographs,"* 7.

118. Carville, "Visible Others," 107–8, 109.

119. McCormack, *Fool of the Family*, 253.

120. Carville, "Resisting Vision," 168.

121. Elizabeth Edwards, *Raw Histories: Photography, Anthropology, and Museums* (Oxford: Berg 2001), 69.

122. On the topic of race in Irish literature, see John Brannigan, *Face Value: Race in Irish Literature and Culture* (Edinburgh: Edinburgh Univ. Press, 2009). See also Brannigan's book *Archipelagic Modernism* on how scientific and ethnographic discourses influenced the representation of the Aran Islands in various fictional and nonfictional accounts.

123. Edwards, *Raw Histories*, 69.

124. Carville, "'With His Mind-Guided Camera,'" 187, 189, 204.

125. Luke Gibbons, "Mirrors of Memory: Ireland, Photography, and the Modern," in *The Moderns*, exhibition catalog, ed. Enrique Juncosa and Christina Kennedy (Dublin: Irish Museum of Modern Art, 2011), 339.

126. On "fugitive poses," see Vizenor, "Fugitive Poses."

127. Kiberd, "Synge's *Tristes Tropiques*," 87.

128. Gregory Castle, "Yeats, Revival, and the Temporalities of Modernism," *UCD Scholarcast*, series 12, "Modalities of Revival," podcast transcript, ed. Giulia Bruna and Catherine Wilsdon, 2015, 4, at http://www.ucd.ie/scholarcast/transcripts/Yeats_Revival_Modernism.pdf.

129. Catherine Morris, "Republican *Tableaux* and the Revival," *Field Day Review*, Dec. 2010, 144.

130. Ibid., 144, 163.

131. Nic Congáil, "Editor's Introduction," 82.

132. Ibid., 82–83.

133. McCormack, *Fool of the Family*, 253.

134. See Paige Reynolds, "Synge's Things: Material Culture in the Writings of Synge," in *Synge and His Influences*, ed. Lonergan, 73–92.

135. John Millington Synge, photograph, Y1/JY/14/13 (verso), Parcel 38, Jack B. Yeats Archive, National Gallery of Ireland.

136. Lilo Stephens, introduction to Synge, *My Wallet of Photographs*, vii.

137. Nic Congáil, "Editor's Introduction," 82.

138. Kiberd, "Synge's *Tristes Tropiques*," 88.

139. Ibid., quoting John Berger.

140. O'Farrelly, *Smaointe ar Árainn*, 33.

141. See, for instance, Lady Gregory's sketches mentioned in the introduction, Somerville and Ross's travelogue, and the illustrations for Mary Banim's travelogue *Here and There through Ireland*, which include a number of landscape views.

142. Sisson, "*The Aran Islands* and the Travel Essays," 61.

143. Ciarán Walsh quoted in Deirdre McQuillan, "Pictures of the Western World," *Irish Times*, May 16, 2009.

144. George Bernard Shaw, "Group of Children Overlooking Skelligs" (1908), Artwork 7, *The Moderns*, exhibition, Irish Museum of Modern Art Virtual Tour, at http://imma .gallery-access.com/intl/en/tour.php?a_id=406.

145. George Bernard Shaw, "Man with Camera, Tripod, Skelligs (1908)," Artwork 6, *The Moderns*, Irish Museum of Modern Art Virtual Tour, at http://imma.gallery-access.com /intl/en/tour.php?a_id=405.

146. George Bernard Shaw, "Bridge, Paris (1904)," Artwork 9, *The Moderns*, Irish Museum of Modern Art Virtual Tour, at http://imma.gallery-access.com/intl/en/tour.php ?a_id=408, and "Trees, France (1904)," Artwork 8, *The Moderns*, Irish Museum of Modern Art Virtual Tour, http://imma.gallery-access.com/intl/en/tour.php?a_id=407.

147. George Bernard Shaw, "A Portrait of Unknown Woman, Ayot," n.d., Artwork 10, *The Moderns*, Irish Museum of Modern Art Virtual Tour, at http://imma.gallery-access .com/intl/en/tour.php?a_id=409; "Self-Portrait, (Young Man) in Chair (1904)," Artwork 15, The Moderns, Irish Museum of Modern Art Virtual Tour, at http://imma.gallery-access .com/intl/en/tour.php?a_id=414; "Nude Self-Portrait, Setting Up a Camera" (1910), Artwork 16, The Moderns, Irish Museum of Modern Art Virtual Tour, at http://imma.gallery-access .com/intl/en/tour.php?a_id=415.

148. Michael Laffan, "Casement, Sir Roger David," in *Dictionary of Irish Biography*, ed. James McGuire and James Quinn (Cambridge: Cambridge Univ. Press, 2010), at http://dib .cambridge.org.ucd.idm.oclc.org/viewReadPage.do?articleId=a1532.

149. Roger Casement, "Group of Putumayo Girls, Facing Away from the Camera (1910)," Artwork 5, *The Moderns*, Irish Museum of Modern Art Virtual Tour, at http://imma .gallery-access.com/intl/en/tour.php?a_id=404.

150. Gibbons, "Mirrors of Memory," 333.

## 2. Reimagining Travel and Popular Entertainment

1. Glenn Hooper, preface to *The Tourist's Gaze*, ed. Hooper, xxiv.

2. *The Shanachie*, no. 1 (May 1906), a note on this first number.

3. Grene, introduction to Synge, *TI*, xlii.

4. For "arts contents," see *The Shanachie*, no. 1 (May 1906).

5. Grene, introduction to Synge, *TI*, xliv.

6. Ibid., xlv.

7. See George Roberts, "A National Dramatist," *The Shanachie*, no. 3 (Mar. 1907), quoted in Grene, introduction to Synge, *TI*, xlv. See also *The Shanachie*, no. 5 (Autumn 1907), and no. 6 (Winter 1907).

8. Grene, introduction to Synge, *TI*, xx.

9. Based on a number of references to King Edward, who died in May 1910, and to the old-age pension introduced in 1909, C. J. Woods speculates that Lynd most likely undertook his trip during the summer of 1909 (*Travellers' Accounts*, 196).

10. The Lawrence Photograph Collection is a historical collection of mid-nineteenth- to early-twentieth-century photographs taken mostly by photographer Robert French (1841–1917). The collection is named after a successful photography studio in Dublin and is now held in the National Library of Ireland, Dublin.

11. S. O'C., "A Rambler's Notebook" (review), *Irish Review* 2, no. 24 (Feb. 1913): 671.

12. For further discussion of Lynd's propagandist travelogue, see Giulia Bruna, "The Irish Revival en Route: The Travel Writing of William Bulfin and Robert Lynd," in "Irish Travel Writing," ed. Éadaoin Agnew, Michael Cronin, and Raphaël Ingelbien, special issue of *Studies in Travel Writing* 20, no. 2 (June 2016): 162–75.

13. Lynd, *Rambles in Ireland*, 141.

14. Douglas Hyde, *The Necessity for De-Anglicising Ireland*, in *Poetry and Ireland since 1800: A Source Book*, ed. Mark Storey (London: Routledge, 1988), 78–84.

15. Finola O'Kane, "Agostino Aglio, *Abbey on Inisfallen Island, Killarney, County Kerry*," in *Painting Ireland: Topographical Views from Glin Castle*, ed. William Laffan (Tralee, Ireland: Churchill House Press, 2006), 98–99.

16. See in particular Colbert, *Travel Writing and Tourism in Britain and Ireland*, and James, *Tourism, Land, and Landscape in Ireland*.

17. On Killarney in the eighteenth century, see O'Kane, "Agostino Aglio," 98–99.

18. Ibid.

19. See also Mary Jane Guinness, *Glena Cottages, County Kerry*, and Eliza Jane, Lady D'Oyly, *The Lower Lake, Killarney*, in *Painting Ireland*, ed. Laffan, 100, 101.

20. Eóin Flannery, "Ireland of the Welcomes: Colonialism, Tourism, and the Irish Landscape," in *Out of the Earth: Ecocritical Readings of Irish Texts*, ed. Christine Cusick (Cork: Cork Univ. Press, 2010), 99.

21. O'Kane, "Agostino Aglio," 98–99.

22. Reverend W. J. Loftie, "Gems of Home Scenery: Views of Wicklow and Killarney" (1875), quoted in Anne Hodge, "Mary Jane Guinness, *Glena Cottages, Killarney, County Kerry*," in *Painting Ireland*, ed. Laffan, 100.

23. Alfred Austin, *Spring and Autumn in Ireland*, excerpted in *The Tourist's Gaze*, ed. Hooper, 158. Despite listing the hotel as the emergent and fashionable type of accommodation for tourists, Austin would argue in favor of inns for their homely feel.

24. Lynd, *Rambles in Ireland*, 145, 172.

25. Seán Ryder, "The Politics of Landscape and Region in Nineteenth-Century Poetry," in *Ireland in the Nineteenth Century: Regional Identity*, ed. Leon Litvack and Glenn Hooper (Dublin: Four Courts Press, 2000), 178.

26. James, *Tourism, Land, and Landscape in Ireland*, Kindle ed., chaps. 1 and 2 passim.

27. Ibid., chap. 5.

28. Ibid.

29. Emily Lawless, "In the Kingdom of Kerry," *Gentleman's Magazine* 28 (1882): 542, 553.

30. Elizabeth Malcolm, "Popular Recreation in Nineteenth-Century Ireland," in *Irish Culture and Nationalism, 1750–1950*, ed. Oliver MacDonagh, W. F. Mandle, and Pauric Travers (London: Macmillan, 1983), 40–55.

31. Ann Saddlemyer, introduction to Synge, *CL1*, xxi.

32. Lynd, *Rambles in Ireland*, 147, 148, 149, 166.

33. Allen, "Synge, Reading, and Archipelago," 167.

34. Roísín Kennedy, "Masquerade and Spectacle: An Introduction," in *Masquerade and Spectacle: The Circus and the Travelling Fair in the Work of Jack B. Yeats*, exhibition catalog, edited by Roísín Kennedy (Dublin: National Gallery of Ireland, 2007), 12–23.

35. Ibid., 13, 14.

36. For an analysis of gender subversion in Synge's female heroines, see Cannon Harris, "Synge and Gender."

37. Thomas Kinsella, trans., *The Táin* (Oxford: Oxford Univ. Press, 1969), 92. For the story "The Boyhood Deeds of Cú Chulaind," see Jeffrey Gantz, trans., *Early Irish Myths and Sagas* (London: Penguin, 1981), 134–46.

38. Kinsella, *The Táin*, 92.

39. John Millington Synge, "An Epic of Ulster" (review of Lady Augusta Gregory, *Cúchulain of Muirthemne*), *The Speaker*, June 7, 1902.

40. Roche, "J. M. Synge," 81–83.

41. Kennedy, "Masquerade and Spectacle," 12.

42. See chapter 3 for more discussion of the concept of "history telling."

43. Banim, *Here and There through Ireland*, 1:120.

44. Ibid.

45. Ibid.

46. Austin, *Spring and Autumn in Ireland*, 158.

47. Lynd, *Rambles in Ireland*, 177, 178.

48. See my discussion of Said's book *Orientalism* in chapter 1.

49. Lynd, *Rambles in Ireland*, 179, 147.

50. For further discussion of antitourism in English travel writing, see James Buzard, *The Beaten Track: European Tourism, Literature, and the Ways to Culture 1800–1914* (Oxford: Clarendon, 1993).

51. Ibid., 8.

52. Lynd, *Rambles in Ireland*, 141.

53. Ibid., 170.

54. Nicholas Grene states that "though Synge did not live to publish this final essay in his West Kerry series, a more or less complete draft under this title is to be found in MS 4344, ff. 156r–172r" (note in Synge, *TI*, 165). The unpublished piece appeared posthumously in the edition of the *Collected Works* published by Maunsel in 1910.

55. Clifford, *Routes*, 23, 26, 67, 36.

56. Cronin, *Across the Lines*, 18, 19.

57. Grene, note in Synge, *TI*, 162.

58. Synge's depiction of emigration as problematic is clear, especially in the *Manchester Guardian* series. In "Possible Remedies—Concluding Article," *Manchester Guardian*, July 26, 1905, Synge contends that long-term emigration can be solved only with "the restoration of some national life to the people" (*TI*, 99).

59. Lynd, *Rambles in Ireland*, 169, 170.

60. Clifford, *Routes*, 67.

## 3. Traveling Journalist

1. Kiberd, "Synge's *Tristes Tropiques*," 84.

2. Richard Hoggart, introduction to George Orwell, *The Road to Wigan Pier* (London: Penguin, 2007), vi.

3. Sims, "The Literary Journalists," 3.

4. P. J. Mathews, "Re-thinking Synge," in *The Cambridge Companion to J. M. Synge*, ed. Mathews, 10.

5. Connery, "A Third Way to Tell the Story," 6.

6. For "monophonic authority," see Clifford, *The Predicament of Culture*, 50.

7. Jack Yeats to Mary Cottenham, postcard, June 3, 1905, Y1/JY/6/1/54, Jack B. Yeats Archive, National Gallery of Ireland.

8. Bruce Arnold, "John M. Synge 1905–1909," in *Jack Yeats* (New Haven, CT: Yale Univ. Press, 1998), 136.

9. Jack Yeats to Mary Cottenham, postcard, June 23, 1905, Y1/JY/6/1/54, Jack B. Yeats Archive, National Gallery of Ireland. For this photograph, see the cover of this book.

10. See, for instance, the sketches for Christy Mahon's character reproduced in Arnold's biography of Jack Yeats (Arnold, "John M. Synge 1905–1909," 133).

11. Adele M. Dalsimer, "'The Irish Peasant Had All His Heart': J. M. Synge in the Country Shop," in *Visualising Ireland: National Identity and the Pictorial Tradition*, ed. Adele M. Dalsimer (London: Faber & Faber, 1993), 223.

12. Roche, "J. M. Synge," 91.

13. Ann Saddlemyer, "Synge and Some Companions, with a Note Concerning a Walk through Connemara with Jack Yeats," *Yeats Studies* 2 (1972): 29.

14. See MS 4397, 4398, 4399, 4400, Synge Papers, Trinity College Library.

15. Synge perhaps handwrote the final drafts, the "fair copy" of the articles, in the notebooks in order to keep a copy of his work before typing everything up to send to Manchester.

16. Saddlemyer, editor's note in *CL1*, 113. For further details on the route and transports that Synge and Yeats followed in Connemara and Mayo, see Grene, introduction to *TI*, xxv–xxvi.

17. Synge mentions the breaking down of his typewriter in J. M. Synge, Deehan's Royal Hotel, Belmullet, to Kathleen Synge, Saturday, c. June 24, 1905, *CL1*, 114.

18. With the compound *avant-texte*, genetic critics indicate generally "all the documents that come before a work when it is considered as a text and when those documents and the text are considered as part of a system" (Jed Deppman, Daniel Ferrer, and Michael Groden, "Introduction: A Genesis of French Genetic Criticism," in *Genetic Criticism: Texts and Avant-Textes*, ed. Jed Deppman, Daniel Ferrer, and Michael Groden [Philadelphia: Univ. of Pennsylvania Press, 2004], 8). Although contemporary studies in genetic criticism have further problematized the term, for the purpose of this essay I use it in this more general sense.

19. Dirk Van Hulle, *Textual Awareness: A Genetic Study of Late Manuscripts by Joyce, Proust, and Mann* (Ann Arbor: Univ. of Manchester Press, 2004), 5.

20. MS 4400, folio 17v, Synge Papers, Trinity College Library.

21. MS 4400, folio 35r, Synge Papers, Trinity College Library.

22. MS 4398, folios 48v and 47v, Synge Papers, Trinity College Library.

23. John Millington Synge, *In Wicklow, West Kerry, and Connemara* (Dublin: Maunsel, 1911).

24. Jack Yeats produced at least seven tiny sketchbooks, from which he drew inspiration for the pen-and-ink drawings that accompanied Synge's articles. Hilary Pyle has catalogued these sketchbooks in Jack B. Yeats, *Jack B. Yeats: His Watercolours, Drawings, and Pastels*, ed. Hilary Pyle (Dublin: Irish Academy Press, 1993). The sketchbooks I examined in the National Gallery of Ireland and in the New York Public Library are very small, pocket size, and ring bound; they were fabricated by G. Rowney & Co., with the exception of a slightly bigger, blank exercise book, "Vere Foster's Drawing Book National School Edition," from Blackie and Sons.

25. Margy Kinmonth, dir., *To the Western World: J. M. Synge and Jack B. Yeats Journey* (Foxtrot Films, 1981; DVD, 2009).

26. Jack B. Yeats, a sketch of John Synge, "Λ103 [50] Swinford and London, July 1905," folio 4, Jack B. Yeats Archive, National Gallery of Ireland, © Estate of Jack B. Yeats, DACS London / IVARO Dublin, 2017.

27. Jack B. Yeats, landscape view of Clifden, "97 [A4] Synge 1905" (coast scenes, some certainly done in the West of Ireland at Clifden), folios 31v and 32, Jack B. Yeats Archive, National Gallery of Ireland, © Estate of Jack B. Yeats, DACS London / IVARO Dublin, 2017.

28. Jack B. Yeats, town scene, Erris, with "Erris Hotel" scribbled on the central door of the red building, "100. [A13] Belmullet. Undated, prob 1905," folios 2v and 3, Jack B. Yeats Archive, National Gallery of Ireland, © Estate of Jack B. Yeats, DACS London / IVARO Dublin, 2017.

29. Jack B. Yeats, sketches of the boat builders, pen and watercolor, "V4 Ireland with Synge," folios 17v, 18, 19, 19v, sketchbooks, looseleaf, 1900–1908, Jack B. Yeats Collection, Berg Collection, New York Public Library, © Estate of Jack B. Yeats, DACS London / IVARO Dublin, 2017.

30. Jack B. Yeats, sketch of a boy looking at a shop window, pencil and ink, "V5 'Swinford' 1905 Mayo," folio 23v, sketchbooks, looseleaf, 1900–1908, Jack B. Yeats Collection, Berg Collection, New York Public Library, © Estate of Jack B. Yeats, DACS London / IVARO Dublin, 2017.

31. Jack Yeats, brush merchant, pencil, "V5 Swinford 1905 Mayo," folio 8v, sketchbooks, looseleaf, 1900–1908, Jack B. Yeats Collection, Berg Collection, New York Public Library, © Estate of Jack B. Yeats, DACS London / IVARO Dublin, 2017.

32. Samuel Synge, *Letters to My Daughter: Memories of J. M. Synge* (Dublin: Talbot Press, 1931), 124.

33. Robert Skelton, introduction to Jack B. Yeats, "Sketches of Life in London and Manchester," typescript, Box 20-13, folio F, Y1/JY/2/4/13, Jack B. Yeats Archive, National Gallery of Ireland.

34. Ciara Breathnach, *The Congested Districts Board of Ireland, 1891–1923: Poverty and Development in the West of Ireland* (Dublin: Four Courts Press, 2005), 11.

35. F. S. L. Lyons, *Culture and Anarchy in Ireland, 1890–1939* (Oxford: Clarendon Press, 1979), 7–13, quoted in in Breathnach, *Congested Districts Board of Ireland*, 14.

36. Grene, introduction to Synge, *TI*, xxiii.

37. Breathnach, *Congested Districts Board of Ireland*, 11.

38. Mathews, *Revival*, 127.

39. Breathnach, *Congested Districts Board of Ireland*, 22, 24.

40. Glenn Hooper, note in Jack Hack Tuke, *A Visit to Connaught in the Autumn of 1847* (1847), excerpted in *The Tourist's Gaze*, ed. Hooper, 85.

41. James Hack Tuke, *Irish Distress and Its Remedies: The Land Question. A Visit to Donegal and Connaught in the Spring of 1880* (London: Hodges, Figgis, 1880), 109.

42. Glenn Hooper, "Trekking to Downfall, 1820–1850," in *Travel Writing and Ireland 1760–1860* (Basingstoke, UK: Palgrave Macmillan, 2005), 141.

43. Tuke, *Irish Distress and Its Remedies*, 92.

44. Ibid.

45. Ibid., 63.

46. In 1889, Tuke, along with Major Robert Routledge-Fair, drew up a study for the railway system that Balfour wanted to implement on the western seaboard. Tuke promptly

addressed the issue to a wider audience through letters that appeared in the *Times* on May 20 and 28 and June 29 and were later collected in his pamphlet *The Condition of Donegal: Letters with Further Suggestions for the Improvement and Development of the Congested Districts of Ireland and Promotion of Light, Railways, Fisheries etc.* (London: Ridgway, 1889).

47. Tuke, *Irish Distress and Its Remedies*, 116.

48. Richard Vincent Comerford, "Land Acts," in *The Oxford Companion to Irish History*, ed. Connolly, 295.

49. "Wyndham Land Act," in *The Oxford Companion to Irish Literature*, ed. Robert Welch (Oxford: Clarendon Press, 1996), 606–7.

50. Patrick Cosgrove, "The Wyndham Land Act, 1903: The Final Solution to the Irish Land Question?" (thesis abstract), *Irish Economic and Social History* 36, no. 1 (Oct. 2009): 96.

51. Lloyd, *Ireland after History*, 84.

52. Ibid.

53. Grene, introduction to Synge, *TI*, xl.

54. Arnold, "John M. Synge 1905–1909," 134.

55. J. M. Synge to C. P. Scott, May 22, 1905, John Ryland Library, Univ. of Manchester, reprinted in *Irish University Review* 45, no. 1 (Spring–Summer 2015): 28–29. See also Arnold, "John M. Synge 1905–1909," 134.

56. Arnold, "John M. Synge 1905–1909," 134.

57. Saddlemyer, introduction to Synge, *CL1*, xxiv, and commentary on 63.

58. J. L. Hammond, *C. P. Scott of the* Manchester Guardian (London: Bell, 1934), 53 n.

59. Skelton, introduction to Yeats, "Sketches of Life in London and Manchester," unpublished typescript. This interest is also reflected in numerous sketches that Yeats painted in Connemara, which are full of details about different types of boats and their components—illustrations of everything from *pookawn*s (small fishing boats) to masts, rudders, decks, and sails. See 97 [A4] Synge 1905, folio 30, Jack B. Yeats Archive, National Gallery of Ireland (item 98 in Hilary Pyle's classification in Yeats, *Jack B. Yeats*).

60. Grene, introduction to Synge, *TI*, xl.

61. William Haslam Mills, *The* Manchester Guardian: *A Century of History*, with a special introduction for the American edition by Charles Prestwich Scott (New York: Holt, 1922), 129.

62. Hammond, *C. P. Scott of the* Manchester Guardian, 52–53.

63. Arnold, "John M. Synge 1905–1909," 148.

64. Charles Stevenson, secretary of the Manchester Relief Fund Committee, reconstructed the whole story retrospectively in a detailed report published in the *New Ireland Review*: "Mr Long is a strong protestant, Churchman and Unionist. He went to Ireland to study the agricultural question, steeped in prejudice against the Irish, and believing that the popular cries of distress were greatly exaggerated and hardly worth consideration. What he saw and recorded led him to modify his opinion very considerably, and as has

been already said, these letters roused Manchester, and led to the opening of a fund which embraces contributions from Liverpool and surrounding towns" ("West of Ireland Distress," *New Ireland Review* 10, no. 4 [Dec. 1898]: 192).

65. These notes dealt primarily with English agriculture and appeared fairly regularly from the mid-1880s on.

66. James Long, "Cooperation in Agriculture," *Manchester Guardian*, Dec. 26 and 27, 1898, and Jan. 3, 7, 16, 20, 1899.

67. James Long, "Cooperation in Agriculture: I," *Manchester Guardian*, Dec. 26, 1898.

68. James Long, "The Solution of the Land Question in the West of Ireland," *Manchester Guardian*, Aug. 10, 1898.

69. Quoted in Heather Laird, *Subversive Law in Ireland, 1879–1920* (Dublin: Four Courts Press, 2005), 139.

70. The Land League "was an emergency organization with exclusively agrarian purposes, but it was informally connected to the parliamentary Home Rule movement. It acted as a radicalizing force which destabilized rural Ireland and politicized the rural Catholic population around the land and national issues" (Stephen Ball, "Crowd Activity during the Irish Land War," in *Crowds in Ireland c. 1720–1920*, ed. Peter Jupp and Eoin Magennis [London: Macmillan, 2000], 212).

71. Breathnach, *Congested Districts Board of Ireland*, 18–19.

72. Orwell, *The Road to Wigan Pier*, 65–66.

73. Ibid., 67.

74. Lyons, quoted in Breathnach, *Congested Districts Board of Ireland*, 14.

75. Breathnach, *The Congested Districts Board of Ireland*, 160.

76. Spurr, *Rhetoric of Empire*, 109.

77. E. Keogh, "In Gorumna Island," *New Ireland Review* 9, no. 4 (June 1898): 194.

78. Ibid.

79. Spurr, *Rhetoric of Empire*, 128.

80. Keogh, "In Gorumna Island," 200.

81. Synge will develop the issue of the boat-making activity in "The Boat Builders," *Manchester Guardian*, June 28, 1905 (*TI*, 176).

82. Nelson O'Ceallaigh Ritschel, *Shaw, Synge, Connolly, and Socialist Provocation* (Gainesville: Univ. Press of Florida, 2011), 58, 59–60.

83. T. A. Finlay, "The Economics of Carna," *New Ireland Review* 9, no. 2 (Apr. 1898): 66.

84. Ibid., 74.

85. Ibid., 75–76.

86. Russell had been on the Aran Islands in 1898 to set up a cooperative bank two months before Synge's first visit (see W. B. Yeats to George Russell, from Crossmolina, Feb. 10, 1898, in George Russell, *Letters from Æ*, ed. Alan Denson [London: Abelard-Schuman, 1961], 26–28). William L. Daniels's article "Æ and Synge in the Congested Districts" (*Éire-Ireland* 11, no. 4 [Winter 1976]: 14–26), despite a detailed reconstruction of Russell's and

Synge's similar routes in the districts, does not document any direct exchange of information between the two on the subject and only speculates: "This was the life that Æ had been immersed in for seven years and that Synge must have learned about from him before going out with Jack Yeats in 1905" (18–19). In letters, Synge mentions Russell only once briefly to Lady Gregory and W. B. Yeats about theater matters. From Russell's letters, we know that in 1897 Synge wrote a note to Russell, presumably to arrange a meeting and to ask how to reach Yeats in London. Russell's reply is written from Belmullet, County Mayo, on Christmas Day in 1897, while Russell was on his very first IAOS assignment, but it omits details of his work there so as not to make a Christmas letter full of miserable stories (Russell, *Letters from Æ*, 23). Synge's diaries, according to David H. Grene, highlight only four meetings between Russell and Synge in the late 1890s (editor's note in Russell, *Letters from Æ*, 229).

87. George Russell, "The Irish Cottage," in *Selections from the Contributions to the Irish Homestead by G. W. Russell—Æ*, vol. 1, ed. Henry Summerfield (Gerrards Cross, Ireland: Colin Smythe, 1978), 49–50.

88. Ibid., 50.

89. Synge traveled to Brittany from April 3 to April 16, 1899 (Saddlemyer, introduction to Synge, *CL*1, xii).

90. Levitas, "J. M. Synge," 82.

91. John A. Hobson, *Problems of Poverty: An Inquiry into the Industrial Condition of the Poor* (London: Methuen, 1891), 171–72.

92. Raymond Williams, "Base and Superstructure in Marxist Cultural Theory," in *Problems in Materialism and Culture: Selected Essays* (London: Verso, 1980), 40–41.

93. A similar description of kelp making is also given in Synge, *AI*, 282.

94. Greg Garrard, *Ecocriticism* (London: Routledge, 2004), 30. Garrard differentiates between the two theories, stressing perhaps a more pragmatic approach endorsed by so-called social ecologists, who "in place of a workers' revolution . . . promote exemplary lifestyles and communities that prefigure a more general social transformation and give people practice in sustainable living and participatory democracy" (30).

95. Ibid., 28.

96. Levitas, "J. M. Synge," 82.

97. Rob Nixon, *Slow Violence and the Environmentalism of the Poor* (Cambridge, MA: Harvard Univ. Press, 2011), 18.

98. Ibid., 5, 14–16.

99. Ibid., 15, 16.

100. See Foster, "'Certain Set Apart.'"

101. Arnold, "John M. Synge 1905–1909," 134.

102. Raiffeisen cooperative societies had strong Christian ethic principles and were designed to help farmers. According to Anthony Quinn, "agricultural credit societies were disproportionately based in the poorer areas especially in the western seaboard; voluntarily

communal effort kept interest rates much lower than those charged by ruthless local shop-keepers" (*Credit Unions in Ireland* [Dublin: Oak Tree Press, 1999], 12–13).

103. Tuke, *Irish Distress and Its Remedies*, 1.

104. Louis Althusser, "Ideology and Ideological State Apparatuses," in *Literary Theory: An Anthology*, 2nd ed., ed. Julie Rivkin and Michael Ryan (Oxford: Blackwell, 2004), 698.

105. For "colonialist mindset," see Mathews, *Revival*, 11–12.

106. Quoted in ibid., 11–12.

107. Ibid., 12.

108. Keeble, "On Journalism, Creativity, and the Imagination," 11.

109. Jack Yeats, "Appendix: A Letter about J. M. Synge by Jack Yeats. Published in the *Evening Sun* (New York) of 20 July 1909," in Synge, *CW2*, 401.

110. The phrase "bond of trust" comes from Joseph Nocera, quoted in Sims, "The Art of Literary Journalism," 6.

111. Orwell, *The Road to Wigan Pier*, 68.

112. Clifford, *The Predicament of Culture*, 50.

113. Ibid.

114. Ibid.

115. As explained in Guy Beiner, *Remembering the Year of the French: Irish Folk History and Social Memory* (Madison: Univ. of Wisconsin Press, 2007), 82.

116. Ibid.

117. Moreover, in "Among the Relief Works" Synge immediately connects road build-ing with relief measures generally adopted during famine years (*TI*, 51).

118. Grene, introduction to Synge, *TI*, xxiii.

119. As explained in Beiner, *Remembering the Year of the French*, 82.

120. Nicholas Grene has identified this man as "probably Robert Audley, a widower of 50 with two children at the time of the 1901 Census" (editor's note in Synge, *TI*, 56).

121. Grene, introduction to Synge, *TI*, xlii.

122. W. B. Yeats, "J. M. Synge and the Ireland of His Time" (1910), quoted in Mathews, "Re-thinking Synge," 7.

123. Mathews, "Re-thinking Synge," 7.

**4. J. M. Synge in the Garden of Ireland**

1. Winifred Letts, "Synge's Grave" (1913), in *Poetry by Women in Ireland: A Critical Anthology 1870–1970*, ed. Lucy Collins (Liverpool: Liverpool Univ. Press, 2012), 181–82.

2. On Synge's poetry and poetic influences, see Alex Davis, "Learning to Be Brutal: Synge, Decadence, and the Modern Movement," *New Hibernia Review* 14, no. 3 (2010): 36.

3. John Millington Synge, "Prelude," in *Collected Works*, vol. 1: *Poems*, ed. Robin Skel-ton (Gerrards Cross, Ireland: Colin Smythe, 1982), 32, ll. 5–8; this volume is subsequently cited parenthetically in the text as *CW1*.

4. In a notebook with drafts of the Wicklow essay, Synge also expresses the regret of spending time in cities and of consequently missing the experience of the Wicklow countryside: "At such moments one regrets every hour that one has lived outside Ireland and every night that one has passed in cities" (CW2, 220).

5. Timothy Clark, *The Cambridge Introduction to Literature and the Environment* (Cambridge: Cambridge Univ. Press, 2011), 16.

6. Nicholas Grene, "Synge and Wicklow," in *Wicklow History and Society: Interdisciplinary Essays on the History of an Irish County*, ed. Ken Hannigan and William Nolan (Dublin: Geography Publications, 1994), 697, 698.

7. Daniel Řehák, "Irsko jako téma a obraz v české literatuře 19. století" (Ireland as Topic or Image in the Czech Literature of the Nineteenth Century), in *Cizí, jiné, exotické v české kultuře 19. století* (The Foreign, the Different, and the Exotic in Nineteenth-Century Czech Culture) (Prague: Academia/KLP, 2008), 156. Řehák also reports a most interesting exchange at Coole Park of views regarding the Czech and Irish political situations. Mušek was asked if the national theater was getting public funding, and when he confirmed it, the revivalists were astonished: "'Are you getting from this empire funding for this national theatre . . . what else do you want? You have the national congress, what else do you want again, we had a whole century of fighting for Home Rule" (165).

8. Ondřej Pilný, "The Translator's Playwright: Karel Mušek and J. M. Synge," in *Synge and His Influences*, ed. Lonergan, 166.

9. Karel Mušek, "Z irských glenů" (From an Irish Valley), *Zlatá Praha* 33, no. 43 (1916): 512, trans. Alex Zeryk and Eva Kokogiannaki. I acknowledge with gratitude Dr. Ondřey Pilný for providing these two important sources—Řehák's and Mušek's articles.

10. Pilný, "The Translator's Playwright," 166.

11. To Lady Gregory, Synge notified "mission accomplished" like this: "I packed Mušek off last night" (CL1, 185). To his fiancée, Molly, he admitted his nonspontaneous efforts to entertain his translator: "I am fagged out with my efforts to amuse Mušek all day" (CL1, 184).

12. This is evident in particular in "A Landlord's Garden in County Wicklow."

13. Mary Burke, *"Tinkers": Synge and the Cultural History of the Irish Traveller* (Oxford: Oxford Univ. Press, 2009), 89.

14. Ibid., 91, 89.

15. The phrase "condition of psychic wholeness" comes from Clark, *Cambridge Introduction to Literature and the Environment*, 16.

16. Buell, *Writing for an Endangered World*, 8.

17. Buell, *The Future of Environmental Criticism*, 39.

18. Buell, *Writing for an Endangered World*, 18.

19. See note 6 in the introduction.

20. Finola O'Kane, *Ireland and the Picturesque: Design, Landscape Painting, and Tourism 1700–1840* (New Haven, CT: Yale Univ. Press, 2013), 110.

21. Patricia Butler and Mary Davies, *Wicklow through the Artist's Eye: An Exploration of County Wicklow's Historic Gardens, c. 1660–c. 1960* (Dublin: Wordwell, 2014), 3, 7.

22. Ibid.

23. Grene, introduction to Synge, *TI*, xviii.

24. On the nickname, see ibid., xviii.

25. Katharine Tynan, "Mr Parnell Not at Home: About and around Avondale. The House in the Wicklow Hills," *Providence Sunday Journal*, Nov. 21, 1890.

26. Ann Connerton Fallon, *Katharine Tynan* (Boston: Twayne, 1979), 46.

27. Marylin Gaddis Rose, *Katharine Tynan* (Lewisburg, PA: Bucknell Univ. Press, 1974), 52.

28. Donna Potts, "Irish Poetry and the Modernist Canon: A Reappraisal of Katharine Tynan," in *Border Crossings: Irish Women Writers and National Identities*, ed. Kathryn Kirkpatrick (Tuscaloosa: Univ. of Alabama Press, 2000), 81–82.

29. Tynan, "Mr Parnell Not at Home." According to Frank Callanan, Parnell's mother, Delia Tudor Stewart, was the daughter of an American commodore, Charles Stewart ("Parnell, Charles Stewart," in *Dictionary of Irish Biography*, ed. James McGuire and James Quinn [Cambridge: Cambridge Univ. Press, 2010], at http://dib.cambridge.org/viewReadPage .do?articleId=a7199).

30. Katharine Tynan, *Ireland*, Peeps at Many Lands (London: Adam and Charles Black, 1909), 2.

31. Ibid., 38–43.

32. Ibid., 87–88.

33. Banim, *Here and There through Ireland*, 2:2.

34. Ibid., 2:3.

35. On the traveler's quest, see Caren Kaplan, *Questions of Travel: Postmodern Discourses of Displacement* (Durham, NC: Duke Univ. Press, 1996), 60.

36. Banim, *Here and There through Ireland*, 2:4.

37. See Mathews, *Revival*, for further analysis of self-help and chapter 1 in this book for further discussion of Banim's narrative strategies.

38. William Bulfin, *Rambles in Éirinn* (Dublin: M. H. Gill, 1907), 205. For further discussion of Bulfin's patriotic landmarks, see Mathew Staunton, "Cycling between the Graves: The Pilgrimage of a Sinn Féiner in *Rambles in Éirinn* by William Bulfin," in "Imagining Ireland's Dead / La mort en Irlande le corps imaginé," special issue of *Interfaces: Image Text Language* 23, no.1 (2004): 55–66.

39. Bulfin, *Rambles in Éirinn*, 205.

40. Patrick Geraghty and Rebecca Geraghty, "An Exile Guidebook for the Inhabitants: The Reception of William Bulfin's *Rambles in Éirinn* in Ireland: 1901–1904," *Irish Migration Studies in Latin America* 7, no. 2 (July 2009): 220.

41. Bulfin, *Rambles in Éirinn*, 322–23. In *Journeys in Ireland: Literary Travellers, Rural Landscapes, Cultural Relations* (Aldershot, UK: Ashgate, 1999), Martin Ryle documents the

correspondences between the three young men and the three characters, drawing from Richard Ellman's biography of Joyce.

42. Ryle, *Journeys in Ireland*, 124–25.

43. Bulfin, *Rambles in Éirinn*, 327.

44. Ibid., 329.

45. Ibid., 334.

46. Flannery, "Ireland of the Welcomes," 86.

47. See Val Plumwood, *Feminism and the Mastery of Nature* (London: Routledge, 1993), as well as Maria Mies and Vandana Shiva, *Ecofeminism* (London: Zed Books, 1993).

48. Val Plumwood, "Androcentrism and Anthropocentrism: Parallels and Politics," in *Ecofeminism: Women, Culture, Nature*, ed. Karen J. Warren (Bloomington: Indiana Univ. Press, 1997), 338, 341.

49. For a discussion on the historical evolution of the trope of feminizing and othering the Irish landscape, see C. L. Innes, *Woman and Nation in Irish Literature and Society, 1880–1935* (New York: Harvester Wheatsheaf, 1993). See also Susan Cannon Harris, *Gender and Modern Irish Drama* (Bloomington: Indiana Univ. Press, 2002).

50. Sharae Deckard, *Paradise Discourse, Imperialism, and Globalization: Exploiting Eden* (London: Routledge, 2010), 12.

51. Mathews, "Re-thinking Synge," 9.

52. P. J. Mathews, "'In a Landlord's Garden': Synge and Parnell," in *Memory Ireland*, vol. 1: *History and Modernity*, ed. Oona Frawley (Syracuse, NY: Syracuse Univ. Press, 2011), 125, 126.

53. P. J. Mathews, "Travelling Home: J. M. Synge and the Politics of Place," in *Synge and Edwardian Ireland*, ed. Cliff and Grene, 173, 174. Mathews also examines other scientific influences on Synge: Charles Darwin and Herbert Spencer.

54. Grene, "Synge and Wicklow," 701, 703.

55. Mathews, "Travelling Home," 178.

56. Terence Reeves-Smyth, "The Natural History of Demesnes," in *Nature in Ireland: A Scientific and Cultural History*, ed. John Wilson Foster (Dublin: Lilliput Press, 1997), 550.

57. Ibid., 556.

58. Deckard, *Paradise Discourse*, 12.

59. Banim, *Here and There through Ireland*, 1:119.

60. See ibid., 1:141–42.

61. The phrase "as a process" comes from Buell, *Writing for an Endangered World*, 69.

62. Quoted in Grene, "On the Margins," 31.

63. The phrase "psychic wholeness" comes from Clark, *Cambridge Introduction to Literature and the Environment*, 16.

64. In a recent article, James Little looks at the impact of these institutions in Synge's play *The Shadow of the Glen*, focusing on the threat of institutionalization for Nora, the female protagonist, and using Synge's nonfiction only as a secondary source ("Home, the

Asylum, and the Workhouse in *The Shadow of the Glen*," *Irish University Review* 46, no. 2 [2016]: 260–74).

65. Grene, "On the Margins," 25.

66. Peter Bartlett and David Wright, "Community Care and Its Antecedents," introduction to *Outside the Walls of the Asylum*, ed. Bartlett and Wright, 5.

67. Foucault, *Madness and Civilization*, 259.

68. Walsh, "Lunatic and Criminal Alliances in Nineteenth-Century Ireland," 134–35.

69. Ibid., 142–43. Walsh presents as a case study the Connaught District Lunatic Asylum in Ballinasloe.

70. Ibid., 137.

71. Hilary Marland, "At Home with Puerperal Mania," in *Outside the Walls of the Asylum*, ed. Bartlett and Wright, 50.

72. In assessing the threat of institutionalization for the female protagonist in Synge's play *The Shadow of the Glen*, James Little draws on historical work by Maria Luddy and Aoife Breathnach to underline that women were "at particular risk of ending up in the workhouse" ("Home, the Asylum, and the Workhouse in *The Shadow of the Glen*," 266).

73. Grene, introduction to Synge, *TI*, xxxviii.

74. Fanon, *The Wretched of the Earth*, 200.

75. Walsh, "Lunatic and Criminal Alliances in Nineteenth-Century Ireland," 145.

76. Clifford, *Predicament of Culture*, 50.

77. J. M. Synge to Jack Yeats, July 22, 1907, in John Millington Synge, *The Collected Letters of John Millington Synge*, vol. 2: *1907–1909*, ed. Ann Saddlemyer (Oxford: Clarendon Press, 1984), 20; the term given in angle brackets is unclear in the original letter. A cakewalk was "a syncopated, strutting male dance of African-American origin," subsequently adopted in minstrel shows and vaudeville toward the end of the nineteenth century (Debra Craine and Judith Mackrell, "Cakewalk," in *The Oxford Dictionary of Dance* [Oxford: Oxford Univ. Press, 2010], http://www.oxfordreference.com.ucd.idm.oclc.org/view/10.1093/acref/978019 9563449.001.0001/acref-9780199563449-e-465).

78. Buell, *The Future of Environmental Criticism*, 142.

79. Buell, *Writing for an Endangered World*, 26, 24, 22.

80. Peter Foss and Catherine O'Connell, "Bogland: Study and Utilization," in *Nature in Ireland: A Scientific and Cultural History*, ed. Foster, 185.

81. Buell, *Writing for an Endangered World*, 22.

82. Mary Burke's book *"Tinkers"* amply covers this theme in Synge's oeuvre.

**Epilogue**

1. Robin Skelton, note in John Millington Synge, "(Abroad)," in *CW1*, 62.

2. Castle, "'Synge-on-Aran,'" 132.

3. Sisson, *"The Aran Islands* and the Travel Essays," 53.

4. Mathews, "Re-thinking Synge," 9.

5. Nelson Ó Ceallaigh Ritschel defines Synge's plays as more concerned with social realism than with romanticism ("*In the Shadow of the Glen*: Synge, Ostrovsky, and Marital Separation," *New Hibernia Review* 7, no. 4 [Winter 2003]: 85).

# Bibliography

**Primary Sources**

*John Millington Synge*

CORE TEXTS

Synge, John Millington. *The Aran Islands*. With original photographs by the author. Edited by Robin Skelton. London: Oxford Univ. Press, 1979.

———. *The Aran Islands*. Edited by Tim Robinson. London: Penguin, 1992.

———. *The Aran Islands: Collected Plays and Poems and the Aran Islands*. London: Everyman, 1997.

———. *The Autobiography of J. M. Synge, Constructed from the Manuscripts*. Edited by Alan Price. With fourteen photographs by J. M. Synge and an essay on Synge and the photography of his time by P. J. Pocock. Dublin: Dolmen Press; London: Oxford Univ. Press, 1965.

———. *Collected Works*. Vol. 1: *Poems*. Edited by Robin Skelton. Gerrards Cross, UK: Colin Smythe, 1982.

———. *Collected Works*. Vol. 2: *Prose*. Edited by Alan Price. Gerrards Cross, UK: Colin Smythe, 1982.

———. *Collected Works*. Vol. 3: *Plays, Book 1*. Edited by Ann Saddlemyer. Gerrards Cross, UK: Colin Smythe, 1982.

———. *Collected Works*. Vol. 4: *Plays, Book 2*. Edited by Ann Saddlemyer. Gerrards Cross, UK: Colin Smythe, 1982.

———. *In Wicklow, West Kerry, and Connemara*. With Essays by George Gmelch and Ann Saddlemyer. Photography by George Gmelch. Dublin: O'Brien Press, 1980.

———. *In Wicklow, West Kerry, and Connemara*. Dublin: Maunsel, 1911.

———. *J. M. Synge: Travelling Ireland, Essays 1898–1908*. Edited by Nicholas Grene. Dublin: Lilliput Press, 2009.

————. *Travels in Wicklow, West Kerry, and Connemara.* Illustrations by Jack B. Yeats. Foreword by Paddy Woodworth. London: Serif, 2005.

————. *My Wallet of Photographs: The Collected Photographs of J. M. Synge.* Arranged and introduced by Lilo Stephens. Dublin: Dolmen Editions, 1971.

————. *The Works of John M. Synge.* Dublin: Maunsel, 1910.

PUBLISHED LETTERS

Synge, John Millington. *The Collected Letters of John Millington Synge.* Vol. 1: *1871–1907.* Edited by Ann Saddlemyer. Oxford: Clarendon Press, 1983.

————. *The Collected Letters of John Millington Synge.* Vol. 2: *1907–1909.* Edited by Ann Saddlemyer. Oxford: Clarendon Press, 1984.

————. *Letters to Molly: John Millington Synge to Maire O'Neill, 1906–1909.* Edited by Ann Saddlemyer. Cambridge, MA: Belknap Press of Harvard Univ. Press, 1971.

JOURNALISM IN THE PERIODICAL PRESS
IN CHRONOLOGICAL ORDER

Synge, John Millington. "The Demonstrations in Rome, by an Eye Witness." *Irish Times,* Mar. 16, 1896.

————. "A Story from Inishmaan." *New Ireland Review,* Nov. 1898.

————. "Anatole Le Braz." *Daily Express* (Dublin), Jan. 28, 1899.

————. "A Celtic Theatre." *Freeman's Journal,* Mar. 22, 1900.

————. "The Poems of Geoffrey Keating" (review of Geoffrey Keating, *Danta Amhrain is Caointe: Sheathruin Ceitinn*). *The Speaker,* Dec. 8, 1900.

————. "The Last Fortress of the Celt." *The Gael/An Gaodhal,* Apr. 1901.

————. "La vieille littérature Irlandaise." *L'Européen,* Mar. 15, 1902.

————. "Le mouvement intellectuel Irlandais." *L'Européen,* May 31, 1902.

————. "An Epic of Ulster" (review of Lady Augusta Gregory, *Cuchulain of Muirthemne*). *The Speaker,* June 7, 1902.

————. "Irish Fairies Stories" (review of Seumas MacManus, *Donegal Fairy Stories*). *The Speaker,* June 21, 1902.

————. "An Irish Historian" (review of Geoffrey Keating, *Foras feasa ar Eirinn: The History of Ireland*). *The Speaker,* Sept. 6, 1902.

————. "The Old and New in Ireland." *The Academy and Literature,* Sept. 6, 1902.

————. "An Autumn Night in the Hills." *The Gael/An Gaodhal,* Apr. 1903.

————. "Loti and Huysmans." *The Speaker,* Apr. 18, 1903. [In the *Collected Works,* there is a mixed piece titled "Three French Writers" based also on another unpublished article, "A Tale of Comedians," on Anatole France.]

———. "A Dream on Inishmaan." *The Green Sheaf* 2 (1903): 6–10.

———. "A Dream on Inishmaan." *The Gael/An Gaodhal*, Mar. 1904.

———. "Celtic Mythology" (review of H. D'Arbois de Jubainville, *The Irish Mythological Cycle and Celtic Mythology*, translated by R. I. Best). *The Speaker*, Apr. 2, 1904.

———. "*The Winged Destiny*" (review of Fiona Macleod, *The Winged Destiny*). *The Academy and Literature*, Nov. 12, 1904.

———. "An Impression of Aran." *Manchester Guardian*, Jan. 24, 1905.

———. "The Oppression of the Hills." *Manchester Guardian*, Feb. 15, 1905.

———. "In the Congested Districts." Twelve-article series, *Manchester Guardian*, June 10 to July 26, 1905.

———. "A Translation of Irish Romance" (review of A. H. Leahy, *Heroic Romances of Ireland*, vol. 1). *Manchester Guardian*, Dec. 28, 1905.

———. "Irish Heroic Romances of Ireland" (review of A. H. Leahy, *Heroic Romances of Ireland*, vol. 2). *Manchester Guardian*, Mar. 6, 1906.

———. "The Vagrants of Wicklow." *The Shanachie*, vol. 1, nos. 1–2 (Autumn 1906): 93–98.

———. "The Fair Hills of Ireland" (review of Stephen Gwynn *The Fair Hills of Ireland*). *Manchester Guardian*, Nov. 16, 1906.

———. "The People of the Glens." *The Shanachie*, vol. 2, no. 3 (Spring 1907): 39–46.

———. "At a Wicklow Fair." *Manchester Guardian*, May 9, 1907.

———. "A Landlord's Garden in County Wicklow." *Manchester Guardian*, July 1, 1907.

———. "In West Kerry." Three installments in *The Shanachie*, vol. 2, nos. 4–6 (Summer, Autumn, and Winter 1907).

———. "Good Pictures in Dublin: The New Municipal Gallery." *Manchester Guardian*, Jan. 24, 1908.

———. "On the Road." *Manchester Guardian*, Dec. 10, 1908.

MANUSCRIPTS, ARCHIVAL MATERIAL, MULTIMEDIA
RESOURCES: SYNGE AND OTHER ARTISTS

Gregory, Augusta. "Lady Gregory Sketchbook 3033 TX." Prints and Drawings Department. National Library of Ireland, Dublin.

*Guardian* and *Observer* Digital Archive, 1791–2003. At https://pqasb.pqarchiver .com/guardian.

Kinmonth, Margy, dir. *To the Western World: J. M. Synge and Jack B. Yeats Journey.* Foxtrot Films, 1981. DVD, 2009.

*The Moderns.* Exhibition, Irish Museum of Modern Art, Dublin, 2011. At http://www.imma.ie/en/page_212249.htm.

*Providence Sunday Journal* Collection. Rockefeller Library. Brown Univ., Providence, RI.

Siamsa Tíre, curator. *John Millington Synge, Photographer.* Itinerant photographic exhibition. Inis Meáin, Tralee, Dún Chaoin, Paris, 2009.

Sligo, Leitrim, and Northern Counties Railways. *By-laws and Regulations.* Belfast: R. Carswell & Son, 1905. NLI EPH F6. Prints and Drawings Department. National Library of Ireland, Dublin.

Synge, John Millington. Aran photographs. Parcel 38. Jack B. Yeats Archive. National Gallery of Ireland, Dublin.

———. *The Synge Manuscripts in the Library of Trinity College Dublin.* A catalog prepared on the occasion of the Synge Centenary Exhibition. Dublin: Dolmen Press, 1971.

Synge, John Millington, Papers. Trinity College Library, Dublin.

Synge, John Millington, Photographs. Digital Collections. Trinity College Library, Dublin. At http://digitalcollections.tcd.ie/home/.

Yeats, Jack B., Archive. National Gallery of Ireland, Dublin.

———. Sketchbooks. Jack B. Yeats Archive. National Gallery of Ireland, Dublin.

———. Sketchbooks, looseleaf, 1900–1908. Jack B. Yeats Collection of Papers, 1899–1955. Henry W. and Albert A. Berg Collection of English and American Literature. New York Public Library, Aston, Lenox, and Tilden Foundations.

———. "Sketches of Life in London and Manchester." Unpublished Typescript Draft. Box 20-13 (Y1/JY/2/4/13). Jack B. Yeats Archive. National Gallery of Ireland, Dublin.

*Revival Travel Literature and Various Journalism*

Austin, Alfred. *Spring and Autumn in Ireland.* Excerpted in *The Tourist's Gaze: Travellers to Ireland, 1800–2000,* edited by Glenn Hooper, 156–60. Cork: Cork Univ. Press, 2001.

Banim, Mary. "The Catholic Charities of Dublin: The Children's Hospital." *The Catholic World: A Monthly Magazine of Literature and Science* 43, no. 53 (Apr. 1886): 48–59.

———. "The Claddagh of Galway." *The Catholic World: A Monthly Magazine of Literature and Science* 44, no. 264 (Mar. 1887): 798–809.

———. "Dublin Charities." *The Catholic World: A Monthly Magazine of Literature and Science* 45, no. 270 (Sept. 1887): 731–41.

———. *Here and There through Ireland*. Series 1. With Illustrations by Matilda E. Banim. Dublin: Freeman's Journal, 1891.

———. *Here and There through Ireland*. Series 2. With Illustrations by Matilda E. Banim. Dublin: Freeman's Journal, 1892.

———. "Miss Eliza and Miss Biddy." *The Catholic World: A Monthly Magazine of Literature and Science* 48, no. 285 (Dec. 1888): 327–41.

———. *Story of the Children's Hospital, Temple Street, Dublin. Under the Care of Sisters of Charity. A Sketch for Children at Home and Abroad*. Dublin: Dollard Printing-house, 1892.

Bigger, Francis J. "In Goldsmith's Country." *The Gael/An Gaodhal*, Nov. 1903.

Bulfin, William. *Rambles in Éirinn*. Dublin: M. H. Gill, 1907.

Campbell, Joseph. *Mearing Stones: Leaves from a Note-book on Tramp in Donegal*. Dublin: Maunsel, 1911.

Gregory, Augusta. "Ireland, Real and Ideal." *Nineteenth Century* 44 (Nov. 1898): 769–82.

———. *Lady Gregory's Diaries 1892–1902*. Edited by James Pethica. Oxford: Oxford Univ. Press, 1996.

———. *Visions and Beliefs in the West of Ireland*. In *An Aran Reader*, edited by Breandán Ó hEithir and Ruairí Ó hEithir, 68–70. Dublin: Lilliput Press, 1999.

Gwynn, Stephen. *The Fair Hills of Ireland*. Dublin: Maunsel, 1906.

———. *Highways and Byways in Donegal and Antrim*. London: Macmillan, 1899.

Haddon, Charles R., and Alfred Cort Browne. "Ethnography of the Aran Islands." In *An Aran Reader*, edited by Breandán Ó hEithir and Ruairí Ó hEithir, 50–62. Dublin: Lilliput Press, 1991.

Haverty, Martin. "The Aran Isles; or a Report of the Excursion of the Ethnological Section of the British Association from Dublin to the Western Islands in September 1857." In *An Aran Reader*, edited by Breandán Ó hEithir and Ruairí Ó hEithir, 43–46. Dublin: Lilliput Press, 1999.

Keogh, E. "In Gorumna Island." *New Ireland Review* 9, no. 4 (June 1898): 177–200.

Lawless, Emily. "An Addition to Mr Birchall's List of 'The Lepidoptera of Ireland.'" *Entomologist's Monthly Magazine* 3 (Jan. 1867): 187.

———. "A Biscayan Stroll." *Gentleman's Magazine* 28 (1882): 643–57.

———. "Florentine Gardens in March." *Nineteenth Century* 45 (1899): 327–35.

———. *A Garden Diary: September 1899–September 1900*. London: Methuen, 1901.

———. "Iar-Connaught: A Sketch." *Cornhill Magazine* 45 (Mar. 1882): 319–33.

———. "In the Kingdom of Kerry." *Gentleman's Magazine* 28 (1882): 540–53.

———. "Irish Captures in 1870 and 1871." *Entomologist* 6 (1872): 74–78, 97–100.

———. "North Clare—Leaves from a Diary." *Nineteenth Century* 46 (1899): 603–12.

———. *Traits and Confidences*. London: Methuen, 1898.

———. "Two Leaves from a Note-Book." *Alexandra College Magazine*, June 1895, 242–50.

———. "An Upland Bog." *Belgravia* 45 (1881): 417–30.

Long, James. "Cooperation in Agriculture." *Manchester Guardian*, Dec. 26 and 27, 1898; Jan. 3, 7, 16, and 20, 1899.

———. "The Solution of the Land Question in the West of Ireland." *Manchester Guardian*, Aug. 10, 1898.

Lynd, Robert. *Rambles in Ireland*. London: Mills and Boon, 1912.

Milligan, Seaton, and Alice Milligan. *Glimpses of Erin*. London: M. Ward, 1888.

O'Farrelly, Agnes. *Smaointe ar Árainn / Thoughts on Aran*. Translated and edited by Ríona Nic Congáil. Syracuse, NY: Syracuse Univ. Press for Arlen House, 2010.

Orwell, George. *Down and Out in Paris and London*. 1933. Reprint. London: Penguin, 1989.

———. *The Road to Wigan Pier*. 1937. Reprint. London: Penguin, 2007.

Russell, George W. *Letters from Æ*. Selected and edited by Alan Denson. With a foreword by Monk Gibbon. London: Abelard-Schuman, 1961.

———. *Selections from the Contributions to the Irish Homestead by G. W. Russell—Æ*. Vol. 1. Edited by Henry Summerfield. Gerrards Cross, UK: Colin Smythe, 1978.

Sinclair, W. J. *Irish Peasant Proprietors: Facts and Misrepresentations. A Reply to the Statements of Mr Tuke*. Edinburgh: Blackwood and Sons, 1880.

Somerville, Eith, and Martin Ross. "An Outpost of Ireland." In *Some Irish Yesterdays*, 1–32. London: Longman, Greens, 1906.

———. *Through Connemara in a Governess Cart*. London: Virago Press, 1990.

Stevenson, Charles. "West of Ireland Distress." *New Ireland Review* 10, no. 4 (Dec. 1898): 193–99.

Symons, Arthur. *Cities and Sea-coasts and Islands*. New York: Brentano, 1896.

Tuke, James Hack. *The Condition of Donegal: Letters with Further Suggestions for the Improvement and Development of the Congested Districts of Ireland and Promotion of Light, Railways, Fisheries etc.* London: Ridgway, 1889.

———. *Emigration from Ireland: Being the Third Report of the Committee of "Mr. Tuke's Fund"; Together with Reports by Mr. Tuke, Mr. Sydney Buxton, Mr. H. Hodgkin, Major Gaskell, Captain Ruttledge-Fair, and Mr. Harvey. July, 1884*. London: National Press Agency, 1884.

———. *Irish Distress and Its Remedies: The Land Question. A Visit to Donegal and Connaught in the Spring of 1880*. London: Hodges, Figgis, 1880.

———. *A Visit to Connaught in the Autumn of 1847* (1847). Excerpted in *The Tourist's Gaze: Travellers to Ireland, 1800–2000*, edited by Glenn Hooper, 85–90. Cork: Cork Univ. Press, 2001.

Tynan, Katharine. *Ireland*. Peeps at Many Lands. London: Adam and Charles Black, 1909.

———. "Mr Parnell Not at Home: About and around Avondale. The House in the Wicklow Hills." *Providence Sunday Journal*, Nov. 21, 1890.

———. *Twenty-Five Years: Reminiscences*. London: Smith Elder, 1913.

Yeats, Jack B. *The Selected Writings by Jack B. Yeats*. Edited by Robin Skelton. London: André Deutsch, 1991.

**Secondary Sources**

Alexander, Neal, and James Moran. "Introduction: Regional Modernisms." In *Regional Modernisms*, edited by Neal Alexander and James Moran, 1–21. Edinburgh: Edinburgh Univ. Press, 2013.

———, eds. *Regional Modernisms*. Edinburgh: Edinburgh Univ. Press, 2013.

Allen, Nicholas. *George Russell (Æ) and the New Ireland, 1905–1930*. Dublin: Four Courts Press, 2003.

———. "Synge, Reading, and Archipelago." In *Synge and Edwardian Ireland*, edited by Brian Cliff and Nicholas Grene, 159–71. Oxford: Oxford Univ. Press, 2012.

Althusser, Louis. "Ideology and Ideological State Apparatuses." In *Literary Theory: An Anthology*, 2nd ed., edited by Julie Rivkin and Michael Ryan, 693–702. Oxford: Blackwell, 2004.

Arnold, Bruce. "John M. Synge 1905–1909." In *Jack Yeats*, 133–51. New Haven, CT: Yale Univ. Press, 1998.

Ball, Stephen. "Crowd Activity during the Irish Land War, 1879–90." In *Crowds in Ireland c. 1720–1920*, edited by Peter Jupp and Eoin Magennis, 212–48. London: Macmillan, 2000.

Bartlett, Peter, and David Wright. "Community Care and Its Antecedents." Introduction to *Outside the Walls of the Asylum: The History of Care in the Community 1750–2000*, edited by Peter Bartlett and David Wright, 1–18. London: Athlone Press, 1999.

———, eds. *Outside the Walls of the Asylum: The History of Care in the Community 1750–2000*. London: Athlone Press, 1999.

Bassnett, Susan. "Travel Writing and Gender." In *The Cambridge Companion to Travel Writing*, edited by Peter Hulme and Tim Youngs, 225–41. Cambridge: Cambridge Univ. Press, 2002.

Beiner, Guy. *Remembering the Year of the French: Irish Folk History and Social Memory*. Madison: Univ. of Wisconsin Press, 2007.

Bertolini, John. "Shaw on Photography, Review." *English Literature in Transition, 1880–1920* 33, no. 4 (1990): 478—80.

Bourgeois, Maurice. *John Millington Synge and the Irish Theatre*. London: Constable, 1913.

Brannigan, John. *Archipelagic Modernism: Literature in the Irish and British Isles, 1890–1970*. Edinburgh: Edinburgh Univ. Press, 2015.

———. *Face Value: Race in Irish Literature and Culture*. Edinburgh: Edinburgh Univ. Press, 2009.

Breathnach, Ciara. *The Congested District Board of Ireland, 1891–1923: Poverty and Development in the West of Ireland*. Dublin: Four Courts, 2005.

———, ed. *Framing the West: Images of Rural Ireland 1891–1920*. Dublin: Irish Academic Press, 2007.

Bruna, Giulia. "'I Like Not Lifting the Rags from My Mother Country for to Tickle the Sentiments of Manchester': Synge's Subversive Practice in *In the Congested Districts*." In *The Politics of Irish Writings*, edited by Kateřina Jenčová, Michaela Marková, Radvan Markus, and Hana Pavelková, 46–56. Prague: Centre for Irish Studies, Charles Univ., 2010.

———. "'In the Heart of the Roman Metropolis': An Italian Prologue to Synge's Investigative Journalism." *Studi Irlandesi: A Journal of Irish Studies* 1, no. 1 (2011): 147–56.

———. "The Irish Revival en Route: The Travel Writing of William Bulfin and Robert Lynd." In "Irish Travel Writers," edited by Éadaoin Agnew, Michael Cronin, and Raphaël Ingelbien, special issue of *Studies in Travel Writing* 20, no. 2, (2016): 162–75. At http://dx.doi.org/10.1080/00220388.2016.1168544.

———. "On the Road in the Congested Districts with John Synge and Jack Yeats: Visual and Textual Shaping of Irishness." In *Founder to Shore: Cross-Currents in Irish and Scottish Studies*, edited by Shane Alcobia-Murphy, Lindsay Milligan, and Dan Wall, 43–54. Aberdeen: Arts and Humanities Research Council Centre for Irish and Scottish Studies, Univ. of Aberdeen, 2010.

Buell, Lawrence. *The Environmental Imagination: Thoreau, Nature Writing, and the Formation of American Culture*. Cambridge, MA: Belknap Press of Harvard Univ. Press, 1995.

———. *The Future of Environmental Criticism: Environmental Crisis and Literary Imagination*. Oxford: Blackwell, 2005.

———. *Writing for an Endangered World: Literature, Culture, and the Environment in the United States and Beyond*. Cambridge, MA: Belknap Press of Harvard Univ. Press, 2001.

Burke, John J. "A Stronghold of the Gael." *The Gael/An Gaodhal*, Dec. 1903.

Burke, Mary. "Synge, Evolutionary Theory, and the Irish Language." In *Synge and His Influences: Centenary Essays from the Synge Summer School*, edited by Patrick Lonergan, 55–72. Dublin: Carysfort Press, 2011.

———. *"Tinkers": Synge and the Cultural History of the Irish Traveller*. Oxford: Oxford Univ. Press, 2009.

Butler, Patricia, and Mary Davies. *Wicklow through the Artist's Eye: An Exploration of County Wicklow's Historic Gardens, c. 1660–c. 1960*. Dublin: Wordwell, 2014.

Buzard, James. *The Beaten Track: European Tourism, Literature, and the Ways to Culture 1800–1914*. Oxford: Clarendon, 1993.

Callanan, Frank. "Parnell, Charles Stewart." In *Dictionary of Irish Biography*, edited by James McGuire and James Quinn. Cambridge: Cambridge Univ. Press, 2010. At http://dib.cambridge.org/viewReadPage.do?articleId=a7199.

Cannon Harris, Susan. *Gender and Modern Irish Drama*. Bloomington: Indiana Univ. Press, 2002.

———. "Synge and Gender." In *The Cambridge Companion to J. M. Synge*, edited by P. J. Mathews, 104–16. Cambridge: Cambridge Univ. Press, 2009.

Carville, Justin. *"My Wallet of Photographs*: Photography, Ethnography, and Visual Hegemony in John Millington Synge's *The Aran Islands*." *Irish Journal of Anthropology* 10, no. 1 (2007): 5–11.

———. "Picturing Poverty: Colonial Photography and the Congested Districts Board." In *Framing the West: Images of Rural Ireland 1891–1920*, edited by Ciara Breathnach, 97–114. Dublin: Irish Academic Press, 2007.

———. "Resisting Vision: Photography, Anthropology, and the Production of Race in Ireland." In *Visual, Material, and Print Culture in Nineteenth Century Ireland*, edited by Ciara Breathnach and Catherine Lawless, 158–75. Dublin: Four Courts Press, 2000.

———. "Visible Others: Photography and Romantic Ethnography in Ireland." In *Irish Modernism and the Global Primitive*, edited by Maria McGarrity and Claire A. Culleton, 93–114. New York: Palgrave Macmillan, 2009.

———. "'With His Mind-Guided Camera': J. M. Synge, J. J. Clarke, and the Visual Politics of Edwardian Street Photography." In *Synge and Edwardian Ireland*, edited by Brian Cliff and Nicholas Grene, 186–207. Oxford: Oxford Univ. Press, 2012.

Castle, Gregory. "'Synge-on-Aran': *The Aran Islands* and the Subject of Revivalist Ethnography." In *Modernism and the Celtic Revival*, 98–133. Cambridge: Cambridge Univ. Press, 2001.

———. "Yeats, Revival, and the Temporalities of Modernism." *UCD Scholarcast*, series 12, "Modalities of Revival," podcast, edited by Giulia Bruna and Catherine Wilsdon, 2015. At http://www.ucd.ie/scholarcast/scholarcast55.html.

———. "Yeats, Revival, and the Temporalities of Modernism." *UCD Scholarcast*, series 12, "Modalities of Revival," podcast transcript, edited by Giulia Bruna and Catherine Wilsdon, 1–28, 2015. At http://www.ucd.ie/scholarcast/transcripts/Yeats_Revival_Modernism.pdf.

Chandler, Edward. *Photography in Ireland in the Nineteenth Century*. Dublin: Edmund Burke, 2001.

Clark, Timothy. *The Cambridge Introduction to Literature and the Environment*. Cambridge: Cambridge Univ. Press, 2011.

Clear, Caitríona. "Homelessness, Crime, Punishment, and Poor Relief in Galway 1850–1914: An Introduction." *Journal of the Galway Archaeological and Historical Society* 50, no. 1 (1998): 118–34.

Cliff, Brian, and Nicholas Grene, eds. *Synge and Edwardian Ireland*. Oxford: Oxford Univ. Press, 2012.

Clifford, James. *The Predicament of Culture: Twentieth-Century Ethnography, Literature, and Art*. Cambridge, MA: Harvard Univ. Press, 1988.

———. *Routes: Travel and Translation in the Late Twentieth Century*. Cambridge, MA: Harvard Univ. Press, 1997.

Colbert, Benjamin, ed. *Travel Writing and Tourism in Britain and Ireland*. Basingstoke, UK: Palgrave Macmillan, 2012.

Collins, Peter. "Railway." In *The Oxford Companion to Irish History*, ed. S. J. Connolly, 471–72. Oxford: Oxford Univ. Press, 1998.

Comerford, Richard Vincent. "Land Acts." In *The Oxford Companion to Irish History*, edited by S. J. Connolly, 295. Oxford: Oxford Univ. Press, 1998.

Connery, Thomas B. "A Third Way to Tell the Story: American Literary Journalism at the Turn of the Century." In *Literary Journalism in the Twentieth Century*, edited by Norman Sims, 3–20. New York: Oxford Univ. Press, 1990.

Connerton Fallon, Ann. *Katharine Tynan*. Boston: Twayne, 1979.

Connolly, S. J., ed. *The Oxford Companion to Irish History*. Oxford: Oxford Univ. Press, 1998.

Cosgrove, Patrick. "The Wyndham Land Act, 1903: The Final Solution to the Irish Land Question?" Thesis abstract. *Irish Economic and Social History* 36, no. 1 (Oct. 2009): 95–96.

Coulbert, Esme. "The Romance of the Road: 'Narratives of Motoring in England, 1896–1930.'" In *Travel Writing and Tourism in Britain and Ireland*, edited by Benjamin Colbert, 201–18. New York: Palgrave Macmillan, 2012.

Coulbert, Esme, and Tim Youngs. "Introduction." In "Travel Writing and the Automobile," edited by Esme Coulbert and Tim Youngs, special issue of *Studies in Travel Writing* 17, no. 2 (2013): 111–15.

Craine, Debra, and Judith Mackrell. "Cakewalk." In *The Oxford Dictionary of Dance*. Oxford: Oxford Univ. Press, 2010. At http://www.oxfordreference.com .ucd.idm.oclc.org/view/10.1093/acref/9780199563449.001.0001/acref-9780199 563449-e-465.

Cronin, Michael. *Across the Lines: Travel, Language, Translation*. Cork: Cork Univ. Press, 2000.

Dalsimer, Adele M. "'The Irish Peasant Had All His Heart': J. M. Synge in the Country Shop." In *Visualising Ireland: National Identity and the Pictorial Tradition*, edited by Adele M. Dalsimer, 201–30. London: Faber & Faber, 1993.

Daniels, William L. "Æ and Synge in the Congested Districts." *Éire-Ireland* 11, no. 4 (Winter 1976): 14–26.

Davis, Alex. "Learning to Be Brutal: Synge, Decadence, and the Modern Movement." *New Hibernia Review* 14, no. 3 (2010): 33–51.

Deckard, Sharae. *Paradise Discourse, Imperialism, and Globalization: Exploiting Eden*. London: Routledge, 2010.

Deppman, Jed, Daniel Ferrer, and Michael Groden. "A Genesis of French Genetic Criticism." Introduction to *Genetic Criticism: Texts and Avant-Textes*, edited by Jed Deppman, Daniel Ferrer, and Michael Groden, 1–16. Philadelphia: Univ. of Pennsylvania Press, 2004.

Dobbins, Gregory. "Synge and Irish Modernism." In *The Cambridge Companion to J. M. Synge*, edited by P. J. Mathews, 132–46. Cambridge: Cambridge Univ. Press, 2009.

Edwards, Elizabeth. *Raw Histories: Photography, Anthropology, and Museums*. Oxford: Berg, 2001.

"Emily Lawless." In *Field Day Anthology of Irish Writing*, vol. 5: *Irish Women's Writing and Traditions*, edited by Angela Bourke, Siobhán Kilfeather, Maria Luddy, Margaret Mac Curtain, Gerardine Meaney, Máirín Ní Dhonnchadha, Mary O'Dowd, and Clair Wills, 921. Cork: Cork Univ. Press, 2002.

Fanon, Frantz. *The Wretched of the Earth*. 1961. Reprint. London: Penguin, 1990.

Finlay, T. A. "The Economics of Carna." *New Ireland Review* 9, no. 2 (Apr. 1898): 65–77.

Fitzpatrick, David. "Synge and Modernity in *The Aran Islands*." In *Synge and Edwardian Ireland*, edited by Brian Cliff and Nicholas Grene, 121–58. Oxford: Oxford Univ. Press, 2012.

Flannery, Eóin. "Ireland of the Welcomes: Colonialism, Tourism, and the Irish Landscape." In *Out of the Earth: Ecocritical Readings of Irish Texts*, edited by Christine Cusick, 85–107. Cork: Cork Univ. Press, 2010.

Foss, Peter, and Catherine O'Connell. "Bogland: Study and Utilization." In *Nature in Ireland: A Scientific and Cultural History*, edited by John Wilson Foster, 184–98. Dublin: Lilliput Press, 1997.

Foster, John Wilson. "'Certain Set Apart': The Romantic Strategy—John Millington Synge." In *Fictions of the Irish Literary Revival: A Changeling Art*, 94–113. Syracuse, NY: Syracuse Univ. Press; Dublin: Gill and MacMillan, 1987.

———, ed. *Nature in Ireland: A Scientific and Cultural History*. Dublin: Lilliput Press, 1997.

Foucault, Michel. *Madness and Civilization: A History of Insanity in the Age of Reason*. London: Routledge, 1993.

Frawley, Oona. "Synge, *The Aran Islands*, and the Movement towards Realism." In *Irish Pastoral Nostalgia and Twentieth Century Irish Literature*, 81–103. Dublin: Irish Academic Press, 2005.

Gaddis Rose, Marylin. *Katharine Tynan*. Lewisburg, PA: Bucknell Univ. Press, 1974.

Gantz, Jeffrey, trans. *Early Irish Myths and Sagas*. London: Penguin, 1981.

Garavel, Andrew J. "*Beggars on Horse Back*: The Irish Cousins in Wales." *Studies in Travel Writing* 18, no. 2 (2014): 160–73. At http://dx.doi.org/10.1080/13645145.2014.896170.

Garnham, Neil. "Golf." In *The Oxford Companion to Irish History*, edited by S. J. Connolly, 222–23. Oxford: Oxford Univ. Press, 1998.

Garrard, Greg. *Ecocriticism*. London: Routledge, 2004.

Garrigan Mattar, Sinéad. "The Passing of the Shee: John Millington Synge." In *Primitivism, Science, and the Irish Revival*, 130–84. Oxford: Oxford Univ. Press, 2004.

Geraghty, Rebecca, and Patrick Geraghty. "An Exile Guidebook for the Inhabitants: The Reception of William Bulfin's *Rambles in Éirinn* in Ireland: 1901–1904." *Irish Migration Studies in Latin America* 7, no. 2 (July 2009): 213–21.

Gerstenberger, Donna. *John Millington Synge*. 1964. Reprint. Boston: Twayne, 1990.

Gibbons, Luke. "Mirrors of Memory: Ireland, Photography, and the Modern." In *The Moderns*, exhibition catalog, edited by Enrique Juncosa and Christina Kennedy, 331–39. Dublin: Irish Museum of Modern Art, 2011.

———. "Synge, Country and Western: The Myth of the West in Irish and American Culture." In *Transformations in Irish Culture*, 23–37. Notre Dame, IN: Univ. of Notre Dame Press in association with Field Day, 1996.

Gillen, Shawn. "Synge's *The Aran Islands* and Irish Creative Nonfiction." *New Hibernia Review* 11, no. 4 (Winter 2007): 129–35.

Gilmartin, Elizabeth. "'Magnificent Words and Gestures': Defining the Primitive in Synge's *The Aran Islands*." In *Modernism and the Global Primitive*, edited by Maria McGarrity and Claire A. Culleton, 63–76. New York: Palgrave Macmillan, 2009.

Goldman, Arnold. *Synge's "The Aran Islands": A "World of Grey," Joyce and Vico and Linguistic Theory*. Gerrards Cross, UK: Colin Smythe, 1991.

Gordon Bowe, Nicola. *Art and the National Dream: The Search for Vernacular Expression in Turn of the Century Design*. Dublin: Irish Academic Press, 1993.

Grene, Nicholas, ed. *Interpreting Synge: Essays from the Synge Summer School 1991–2000*. Dublin: Lilliput Press, 2000.

———. Introduction to John Millington Synge, *J. M. Synge: Travelling Ireland, Essays 1898–1908*, edited by Nicholas Grene, xiii–xlix. Dublin: Lilliput Press, 2009.

———. "On the Margins: Synge and Wicklow." In *Interpreting Synge: Essays from the Synge Summer School 1991–2000*, edited by Nicholas Grene, 20–40. Dublin: Lilliput Press, 2000.

———. "Synge and Wicklow." In *Wicklow History and Society: Interdisciplinary Essays on the History of an Irish County*, edited by Ken Hannigan and William Nolan, 693–722. Dublin: Geography Publications, 1994.

Griffin, Brian. "'As Happy as Seven Kings': Cycling in Nineteenth-Century Ireland." *History Ireland* 22, no. 1 (Jan.–Feb. 2014): 32–35.

———. *Cycling in Victoria Ireland*. Dublin: Nonsuch Press, 2006.

———. "The Tourist Gaze: Cycling Tourists' Impressions of Victorian and Edwardian Ireland." *Irish Studies Review* 25, no. 3 (2017): 238–315.

Hammond, J. L. *C. P. Scott of the* Manchester Guardian. London: Bell, 1934.

Hansson, Heidi. *Emily Lawless 1845–1913: Writing the Interspace*. Cork: Cork Univ. Press, 2007.

Harrington, John P., ed. *The English Traveller in Ireland: Accounts of Ireland and the Irish through Five Centuries*. Dublin: Wolfhound Press, 1991.

Henn, T. R. "The Prose of John Millington Synge." In *Synge, Centenary Papers*, edited by Maurice Harmon, 108–26. Dublin: Dolmen Press, 1972.

Henson, Louise. *Culture and Science in the Nineteenth-Century Media*. Aldershot, UK: Ashgate, 2004.

Hewitt, Seán. "'An Initiated Mystic:' Modernization and Occultism in Synge's *The Aran Islands*." *New Hibernia Review* 19, no. 4 (2015): 58–76.

Hobson, John A. *Problems of Poverty: An Inquiry into the Industrial Condition of the Poor*. London: Methuen, 1891.

Hodge, Anne. "Mary Jane Guinness, *Glena Cottages, Killarney, County Kerry*." In *Painting Ireland: Topographical Views from Glin Castle*, edited by Michael Laffan, 100–101. Tralee: Churchill House Press, 2006.

Hoggart, Richard. Introduction to George Orwell, *The Road to Wigan Pier*, i–xx. London: Penguin, 2007.

Holt, Eddie. "Yeats, Journalism, and the Revival." *UCD Scholarcast*, series 1, "The Art of Popular Culture: From 'The Meeting of the Waters' to Riverdance," podcast, edited by P. J. Mathews, Spring 2008. At http://www.ucd.ie/scholar cast/scholarcast3.html.

Hooper, Glenn. Introduction to *The Tourist's Gaze: Travellers to Ireland, 1800–2000*, edited by Glenn Hooper, xiii–xxx. Cork: Cork Univ. Press, 2001.

———, ed. *The Tourist's Gaze: Travellers to Ireland, 1800–2000*. Cork: Cork Univ. Press, 2001.

———. "Trekking to Downfall, 1820–1850." In *Travel Writing and Ireland, 1760–1860: Culture History, Politics*, 100–143. Basingstoke, UK: Palgrave Macmillan, 2005.

Hooper, Glenn, and Colin Graham, eds. *Irish and Postcolonial Writing*. Houndmills, UK: Palgrave Macmillan, 2002.

Hooper, Glenn, and Leon Litvack, eds. *Ireland in the Nineteenth Century: Regional Identity*. Dublin: Four Courts Press, 2000.

Hooper, Glenn, and Una Ni Bhroiméil, eds. *Land and Landscape in Nineteenth-Century Ireland*. Dublin: Four Courts Press, 2008.

Hulme, Peter, and Tim Youngs, eds. *The Cambridge Companion to Travel Writing*. Cambridge: Cambridge Univ. Press, 2002.

Hutton, Clare. "The Extraordinary History of the House of Maunsel." In *The Irish Book in English 1891–2000*, edited by Clare Hutton, 548–61. Oxford: Oxford Univ. Press, 2011.

Hyde, Douglas. "The Necessity of De-Anglicising Ireland." In *Poetry and Ireland since 1800: A Source Book*, edited by Mark Storey, 78–84. London: Routledge, 1988.

Ingelbien, Raphaël. *Irish Cultures of Travel: Writing on the Continent, 1929–1914*. Basingstoke, UK: Palgrave Macmillan, 2016.

Innes, C. L. "Postcolonial Synge." In *The Cambridge Companion to J. M. Synge*, edited by P. J. Mathews, 117–31. Cambridge: Cambridge Univ. Press 2009.

———. *Woman and Nation in Irish Literature and Society 1880–1935*. New York: Harvester Wheatsheaf, 1993.

James, Kevin J. *Tourism, Land, and Landscape in Ireland: The Commodification of Culture*. London: Routledge, 2014.

Joyce, James. *The Critical Writings of James Joyce*. Edited by Ellsworth Mason and Richard Ellmann. New York: Viking Press, 1964.

———. *Scritti Italiani*. Edited by Gianfranco Corsini and Giorgio Melchiori. Milan: Arnoldo Mondadori Editore, 1979.

———. *Ulysses*. London: Flamingo Modern Classic, 1994.

Kaplan, Caren. *Questions of Travel: Postmodern Discourses of Displacement*. Durham, NC: Duke Univ. Press, 1996.

Keeble, Richard. "On Journalism, Creativity, and the Imagination." Introduction to *The Journalistic Imagination: Literary Journalists from Defoe to Capote and Carter*, edited by Richard Keeble and Sharon Wheeler, 1–14. London: Routledge, 2007.

Kenna, Shane. *Thomas MacDonagh*. 16 Lives Series. Dublin: O'Brien Press, 2014.

Kennedy, Roísín. "Masquerade and Spectacle: An Introduction." In *Masquerade and Spectacle: The Circus and the Travelling Fair in the Work of Jack B. Yeats*, exhibition catalog, edited by Roísín Kennedy, 12–23. Dublin: National Gallery of Ireland, 2007.

Kennedy-O'Neill, Joy. "'Sympathy between Man and Nature': Landscape and Loss in Synge's *Riders to the Sea*." In *Out of the Earth: Ecocritical Readings of Irish Texts*, edited by Christine Cusick, 36–39. Cork: Cork Univ. Press, 2010.

Kerridge, Richard, and Neil Sammells, eds. *Writing the Environment: Eco-criticism and Literature*. London: Zed, 1998.

Kiberd, Declan. "The Blasket Autobiographies." In *Irish Classics*, 520–42. Dublin: Granta Books, 1996.

———. "'Dying Acts': Ó Rathaille and Others." In *Irish Classics*, 39–54. Dublin: Granta Books, 2000.

———. *Inventing Ireland: The Literature of a Modern Nation*. 1997. Reprint. Cambridge, MA: Harvard Univ. Press, 2002.

———. *Synge and the Irish Language*. London: Gill and Mac Millan, 1979.

———. "Synge's *Tristes Tropiques: The Aran Islands*." In *Interpreting Synge: Essays from the Synge Summer School 1991–2000*, edited by Nicholas Grene, 82–110. Dublin: Lilliput Press, 2000.

Kinsella, Thomas, trans. *The Táin*. Oxford: Oxford Univ. Press, 1969.

Knapp, James F. "Primitivism and Empire: John Synge and Paul Gauguin." *Comparative Literature* 41, no. 1 (Winter 1989): 53–68. At http://www.jstor.org /stable/1770679.

Kopper, Edward A., Jr., ed. *A J. M. Synge Literary Companion*. New York: Greenwood Press, 1988.

Kramer, Mark. "Breakable Rules for Literary Journalists." In *Literary Journalism: A New Collection of the Best American Nonfiction*, edited by Norman Sims and Mark Kramer, 23–34. New York: Ballantine Books, 1995.

Laffan, Michael. "Casement, Sir Roger David." In *Dictionary of Irish Biography*, edited by James McGuire and James Quinn. Cambridge: Cambridge Univ. Press, 2010. At http://dib.cambridge.org.ucd.idm.oclc.org/viewReadPage.do ?articleId=a1532.

Laffan, William, ed. *Painting Ireland: Topographical Views from Glin Castle*. Tralee, Ireland: Churchill House Press, 2006.

Laird, Heather. *Subversive Law in Ireland, 1879–1920*. Dublin: Four Courts Press, 2005.

Lele, Veerendra. "Reading Dialogic Correspondence: Synge's *The Aran Islands*." *New Hibernia Review* 11, no. 4 (Winter 2007): 124–29.

Letts, Winifred. "Synge's Grave" (1913). In *Poetry by Women in Ireland: A Critical Anthology 1870–1970*, edited by Lucy Collins, 181–82. Liverpool: Liverpool Univ. Press, 2012.

Levitas, Ben. "J. M. Synge: European Encounters." In *The Cambridge Companion to J. M. Synge*, edited by P. J. Mathews, 77–91. Cambridge: Cambridge Univ. Press, 2009.

Little, James. "Home, the Asylum, and the Workhouse in *The Shadow of the Glen*." *Irish University Review* 46, no. 2 (2016): 260–74.

Lloyd, David. *Ireland after History*. Cork: Cork Univ. Press in association with Field Day, 1999.

———. *Irish Times: Temporalities of Modernity*. Dublin: Field Day in association with the Keough-Naughton Institute for Irish Studies at the Univ. of Notre Dame, 2008.

———. "Taking the Long View: The Irish Revival." Lecture delivered at Irish Seminar 2010, Univ. of Notre Dame, Dublin, June 2010.

Lonergan, Patrick. "J. M. Synge, Authenticity, and the Regional." In *Regional Modernisms*, edited by Neal Alexander and James Moran, 65–82. Edinburgh: Edinburgh Univ. Press, 2013.

———, ed. *Synge and His Influences: Centenary Essays from the Synge Summer School.* Dublin: Carysfort Press, 2011.

Lyons, F. S. L. *Culture and Anarchy in Ireland, 1890–1939.* Oxford: Clarendon Press, 1979.

MacDonagh, Oliver, W. F. Mandle, and Pauric Travers, eds. *Irish Culture and Nationalism, 1750–1950.* London: Macmillan, 1983.

Malcolm, Elizabeth. "Popular Recreation in Nineteenth-Century Ireland." In *Irish Culture and Nationalism, 1750–1950,* edited by Oliver MacDonagh, W. F. Mandle, and Pauric Travers, 40–55. London: Macmillan, 1983.

Markey, Anne. "'The Price of Kelp in Connemara': Synge, Pearse, and the Idealization of Folk Culture." In *Synge and Edwardian Ireland,* edited by Brian Cliff and Nicholas Grene, 208–24. Oxford: Oxford Univ. Press, 2012.

Marland, Hilary. "At Home with Puerperal Mania." In *Outside the Walls of the Asylum: The History of Care in the Community 1750–2000,* edited by Peter Bartlett and David Wright, 45–65. London: Athlone Press, 1999.

Martineau, Harriet. *Letters from Ireland by Harriet Martineau.* Edited by Glenn Hooper. Dublin: Irish Academic Press, 2001.

"Mary Banim." In *The Oxford Companion to Irish Literature,* edited by Robert Welch, 30. Oxford: Clarendon Press, 1996.

Mathews, P. J., ed. *The Cambridge Companion to J. M. Synge.* Cambridge: Cambridge Univ. Press, 2009.

———. "'In a Landlord's Garden': Synge and Parnell." In *Memory Ireland,* vol. 1: *History and Modernity,* edited by Oona Frawley, 115–28. Syracuse, NY: Syracuse Univ. Press, 2011.

———. "Re-thinking Synge." In *The Cambridge Companion to J. M. Synge,* edited by P. J. Mathews, 3–14. Cambridge: Cambridge Univ. Press, 2009.

———. *Revival: The Abbey Theatre, Sinn Féin, the Gaelic League, and the Co-operative Movement.* Cork: Cork Univ. Press in association with Field Day, 2003.

———. "Travelling Home: J. M. Synge and the Politics of Place." In *Synge and Edwardian Ireland,* edited by Brian Cliff and Nicholas Grene, 172–85. Oxford: Oxford Univ. Press, 2012.

McCormack, W. J. *Fool of the Family: A Life of J. M. Synge.* London: Weidefeld and Nicolson, 2000.

McNeillie, Andrew. *An Aran Keening*. 2001. Reprint. Madison: Univ. of Wisconsin Press, 2002.

McQuillan, Deirdre. "Pictures of the Western World." *Irish Times*, May 16, 2009.

Mercier, Vivian. *The Irish Comic Tradition*. Oxford: Clarendon Press, 1962.

Micks, William L. *An Account of the Constitution, Administration, and Dissolution of the Congested District Board*. Dublin: Eason & Son, 1925.

Mies, Maria, and Vandana Shiva. *Ecofeminism*. London: Zed Books, 1993.

Mills, William Haslam. *The* Manchester Guardian: *A Century of History*. With a special introduction for the American edition by Charles Prestwich Scott. New York: Holt, 1922.

Morash, Chris. "Synge's Typewriter: The Technological Sublime in Edwardian Ireland." In *Synge and Edwardian Ireland*, edited by Brian Cliff and Nicholas Grene, 21–33. Oxford: Oxford Univ. Press, 2012.

Morris, Catherine. *Alice Milligan and the Irish Cultural Revival*. Dublin: Four Courts Press, 2012.

———, curator. *Alice Milligan and the Irish Cultural Revival*. Exhibition catalog, Nov. 2010–Mar. 2011. Dublin: National Library of Ireland, 2010.

———. "Republican *Tableaux* and the Revival." *Field Day Review*, Dec. 2010, 133–65.

Morrissey, Lee. "The Restoration and Eighteenth Century 1660–1780." In *English Literature in Context*, edited by Paul Poplawski, 211–305. Cambridge: Cambridge Univ. Press, 2008.

Morrissey, Thomas J. "Prose." In *A J. M. Synge Literary Companion*, edited by Edward Kopper Jr., 15–24. New York: Greenwood Press, 1988.

Murray, Peter. *George Petrie (1790–1866): The Rediscovery of Ireland's Past*. With an introduction by Joep Leerssen. Cork: Crawford Municipal Art Gallery, Gandon Editions, 2004.

Mušek, Karel. "Z irských glenů" (From an Irish Valley). *Zlatá Praha* 33, no. 43 (1916): 512–15, and 33, no. 44 (1916): 525–26.

Nash, Catherine. "'Embodying the Nation': The West of Ireland Landscape and Irish Identity." In *Tourism in Ireland: A Critical Analysis*, edited by Michael Cronin and Barbara O'Connor, 86–112. Cork: Cork Univ. Press, 1993.

Neeson, Eoin. "Woodland in History and Culture." In *Nature in Ireland*, edited by John Wilson Foster, 133–56. Dublin: Lilliput Press, 1997.

Ní Dhuibhne, Eilís. "The Best Field Worker: Synge and Irish Folklore." In *Synge and His Influences: Centenary Essays from the Synge Summer School*, edited by Patrick Lonergan, 93–110. Dublin: Carysfort Press, 2011.

———. "Synge's Use of Popular Material in 'The Shadow of the Glen.'" *Béaloides: The Journal of the Folklore of Ireland Society* 58 (1990): 141–67.

Nic Congáil, Ríona. "Editor's Introduction." In Agnes O'Farrelly, *Smaointe Ar Árainn / Thoughts on Aran*, translated and edited by Ríona Nic Congáil, 73–86. Dublin: Arlen House, 2010.

Nicholson, Asenath. *Annals of the Famine in Ireland*. Edited by Maureen Murphy. Dublin: Lilliput Press, 1998.

———. *Ireland's Welcome to the Stranger*. Edited by Maureen Murphy. Dublin: Lilliput Press, 2002.

———. *Ireland's Welcome to the Stranger: Or Excursions through Ireland in 1844–1845, for the Purpose of Personally Investigating the Condition of the Poor*. London: Gilpin, 1847.

Nixon, Rob. *Slow Violence and the Environmentalism of the Poor*. Cambridge, MA: Harvard Univ. Press, 2011.

Norstedt, Johann A. *Thomas MacDonagh: A Critical Biography*. Charlottesville: Univ. Press of Virginia, 1980.

O'C., S. "A Rambler's Notebook." Review. *Irish Review* 2, no. 24 (Feb. 1913): 670–71.

O'Ceallaigh Ritschel, Nelson. "*In the Shadow of the Glen*: Synge, Ostrovsky, and Marital Separation." *New Hibernia Review* 7, no. 4 (Winter 2003): 85–102.

———. *Shaw, Synge, Connolly, and Socialist Provocation*. Gainesville: Univ. Press of Florida, 2011.

O'Connor Barbara, and Michael Cronin, eds. *Tourism in Ireland: A Critical Analysis*. Cork: Cork Univ. Press, 1993.

Ó Giolláin, Diarmuid. "Folklore and Poverty." In *Locating Irish Folklore: Tradition, Modernity, Identity*, edited by Diarmuid Ó Giolláin, 142–64. Cork: Cork Univ. Press, 2000.

Ó hEithir, Breandán, and Ruairí Ó hEithir, eds. *An Aran Reader*. Dublin: Lilliput Press, 1991.

———. Introduction to *An Aran Reader*, edited by Breandán Ó hEithir and Ruairí Ó hEithir, 1–9. Dublin: Lilliput Press, 1991.

O'Kane, Finola. "Agostino Aglio, Abbey on Inisfallen Island, Killarney, County Kerry." In *Painting Ireland: Topographical Views from Glin Castle*, edited by William Laffan, 98–99. Tralee, Ireland: Churchill House Press, 2006.

———. *Ireland and the Picturesque: Design, Landscape Painting, and Tourism 1700–1840*. New Haven, CT: Yale Univ. Press, 2013.

O'Leary, Philip. *The Prose Literature of the Gaelic Revival, 1881–1921*. University Park: Pennsylvania State Univ. Press, 1994.

Pethica, James. "Editor's Introduction." In Augusta Gregory, *Lady Gregory's Diaries 1892–1902*, edited by James Pethica, i–xxxviii. Oxford: Oxford Univ. Press, 1996.

Pilný, Ondřej. "The Translator's Playwright: Karel Mušek and J. M. Synge." In *Synge and His Influences: Centenary Essays from the Synge Summer School*, edited by Patrick Lonergan, 153–80. Dublin: Carysfort Press, 2011.

Plumwood, Val. "Androcentrism and Anthropocentrism: Parallels and Politics." In *Ecofeminism: Women, Culture, Nature*, edited by Karen J. Warren, 327–55. Bloomington: Indiana Univ. Press, 1997.

———. *Feminism and the Mastery of Nature*. London: Routledge, 1993.

Pocock, P. J. "Synge and the Photography of His Time." In John Millington Synge, *The Autobiography of J. M. Synge, Constructed from the Manuscripts*, edited by Alan Price, with fourteen photographs by J. M. Synge and an essay on Synge and the photography of his time by P. J. Pocock, 41–46. Dublin: Dolmen Press; London: Oxford Univ. Press, 1965.

Porter, Denis. *Haunted Journeys: Desire and Transgression in European Travel Writing*. Princeton, NJ: Princeton Univ. Press, 1991.

Potter, George. *An Irish Pilgrimage*. Providence, RI: Providence Journal Company, 1950.

Potts, Donna L. "Irish Poetry and the Modernist Canon: A Reappraisal of Katharine Tynan." In *Border Crossings: Irish Women Writers and National Identities*, edited by Kathryn Kirkpatrick, 79–99. Tuscaloosa: Univ. of Alabama Press, 2000.

Pratt, Mary Louise. "Fieldwork in Common Places." In *Writing Culture: The Poetics and Politics of Ethnography*, edited by James Clifford and George E. Marcus, 27–50. Berkeley: Univ. of California Press, 1986.

———. *Imperial Eyes: Travel Writing and Transculturation*. London: Routledge, 1992.

Purdy, Anthony. "'Skilful in the Usury of Time': Michel Tournier and the Critique of Economism." In *Robinson Crusoe: Myths and Metamorphoses*, edited by Lieve Spaas and Brian Stimpson, 182–98. Basingstoke, UK: Macmillan, 1996.

Pyle, Hilary. "Illustrations for Synge and Masefield." In *The Different Worlds of Jack B. Yeats: His Cartoons and Illustrations*, 37–40. Dublin: Irish Academic Press, 1994.

Quinn, Anthony P. *Credit Unions in Ireland*. Dublin: Oak Tree Press, 1999.

Rafter, Kevin, ed. *Irish Journalism before Independence*. Manchester, UK: Manchester Univ. Press, 2011.

Reed, William. *Rambles in Ireland; or Observations Written during a Short Residence in That Country* (1815). Excerpted in *The Tourist's Gaze: Travellers to Ireland, 1800–2000*, edited by Glen Hooper, 18–19. Cork: Cork Univ. Press, 2001.

Reeves-Smyth, Terence. "The Natural History of Demesnes." In *Nature in Ireland: A Scientific and Cultural History*, edited by John Wilson Foster, 549–72. Dublin: Lilliput Press, 1997.

Řehák, Daniel. "Irsko jako téma a obraz v české literatuře 19. století" (Ireland as Topic or Image in the Czech Literature of the Nineteenth Century). In *Cizí, jiné, exotické v české kultuře 19 století* (The Foreign, the Different, and the Exotic in Nineteenth-Century Czech Culture), 156–67. Prague: Academia/ KLP, 2008.

Reynolds, Paige. "Synge's Things: Material Culture in the Writings of Synge." In *Synge and His Influences: Centenary Essays from the Synge Summer School*, edited by Patrick Lonergan, 73–92. Dublin: Carysfort Press, 2011.

Rivkin, Julie, and Michael Ryan, eds. *Literary Theory: An Anthology*. Oxford: Blackwell, 2004.

Robinson, Tim. "Place/Person/Book: Synge's *The Aran Islands*." Introduction to John Millington Synge, *The Aran Islands*, edited by Tim Robinson, vii–liii. London: Penguin Books, 1992.

Roche, Anthony. "J. M. Synge: Journeys Real and Imagined." *Journal of Irish Studies* 16 (Sept. 2001): 78–96.

Ryder, Seán. "The Politics of Landscape and Region in Nineteenth-Century Poetry." In *Ireland in the Nineteenth Century: Regional Identity*, edited by Leon Litvack and Glenn Hooper, 169–84. Dublin: Four Courts Press, 2000.

Ryle, Martin. *Journeys in Ireland: Literary Travellers, Rural Landscapes, Cultural Relations*. Aldershot, UK: Ashgate, 1999.

Saddlemyer, Ann. "Art, Nature, and 'the Prepared Personality': A Reading of *The Aran Islands* and Related Writings." In *Sunshine and the Moon's Delight: J. M. Synge 1871–1909*, edited by S. B. Bushrui, 107–20. Gerrards Cross, UK: Colin Smythe, 1972.

———. "The Essays as Literature and Literary Source." In John Millington Synge, *In Wicklow, West Kerry, and Connemara*, with essays by George Gmelch and Ann Saddlemyer, photography by George Gmelch, 20–26. Dublin: O'Brien Press, 1980.

———. Introduction to John Millington Synge, *The Collected Letters of John Millington Synge*, vol. 1: *1871–1907*, edited by Ann Saddlemyer, i–xxx. Oxford: Clarendon Press, 1983.

———. "'A Share in the Dignity of the World': J. M. Synge's Aesthetic Theory." In *The World of W. B. Yeats: Essays in Perspective*, edited by Robin Skelton and Ann Saddlemyer, 241–53. Dublin: Dolmen Press, 1965.

———. *Some Letters of J. M. Synge to Lady Gregory and W. B. Yeats.* Dublin: Cuala Press, 1971.

———. "Synge and the Doors of Perception." In *Place, Personality, and the Irish Writer,* edited by Andrew Carpenter, 97–120. Gerrards Cross, UK: Colin Smythe, 1977.

———. "Synge and Some Companions, with a Note Concerning a Walk through Connemara with Jack Yeats." *Yeats Studies* 2 (1972): 18–34.

———. "Synge's *The Aran Islands* (1907)." *New Hibernia Review* 11, no. 4 (2007): 120–23.

———. "Synge's Soundscape." In *Interpreting Synge: Essays from the Synge Summer School 1991–2000,* edited by Nicholas Grene, 177–91. Dublin: Lilliput Press, 2000.

———. "Synge to MacKenna: The Mature Years." In *Irish Renaissance: A Gathering of Essays, Memoirs, and Letters from the* Massachusetts Review, edited by Robin Skelton and David R. Clark, 65–79. Dublin: Dolmen Press, 1965.

Said, Edward W. *Orientalism: Western Conceptions of the Orient.* 1978. Reprint. London: Penguin, 1991.

Sexton, Sean. *Ireland: Photographs 1840–1930.* London: Laurence King, 1994.

Shoemaker, Michael Myers. *Wanderings in Ireland.* New York: Putnam's, 1908.

Shovlin, Frank. *Journey Westward: Joyce,* Dubliners, *and the Literary Revival.* Liverpool: Liverpool Univ. Press, 2012.

Sims, Norman. "The Art of Literary Journalism." In *Literary Journalism: A New Collection of the Best American Nonfiction,* edited by Norman Sims and Mark Kramer, 3–19. New York: Ballantine Books, 1995.

———. "The Literary Journalists." Introduction to *The Literary Journalists: The New Art of Personal Reportage,* 3–25. New York: Ballantine Books, 1984.

Sinfield, Alan. "Cultural Materialism, *Othello,* and the Politics of Plausibility." In *Literary Theory: An Anthology,* edited by Julie Rivkin and Michael Ryan, 743–62. Oxford: Blackwell, 2004.

Sisson, Elaine. "*The Aran Islands* and the Travel Essays." In *The Cambridge Companion to J. M. Synge,* edited by P. J. Mathews, 52–63. Cambridge: Cambridge Univ. Press, 2009.

Skelton, Robin. *Celtic Contraries.* Syracuse, NY: Syracuse Univ. Press, 1990.

———. "The Essays." In *The Writings of J. M. Synge,* 103–13. London: Thames & Hudson, 1971.

———. *J. M. Synge and His World.* London: Thames and Hudson, 1971.

Smith, Vanessa. "Beachcombers, Missionaries, and the Myth of the Castaway." In *Robinson Crusoe: Myths and Metamorphoses*, edited by Lieve Spaas and Brian Stimpson, 62–77. Basingstoke, UK: Macmillan, 1996.

Smyth, Sara. "Tuke's Connemara Album." In *Framing the West: Images of Rural Ireland 1891–1920*, edited by Ciara Breathnach, 29–60. Dublin: Irish Academic Press, 2007.

Spurr, David. *The Rhetoric of Empire: Colonial Discourse in Journalism, Travel Writing, and Imperial Administration*. Durham, NC: Duke Univ. Press, 1993.

Staunton, Mathew. "Cycling between the Graves: The Pilgrimage of a Sinn Féiner in *Rambles in Éirinn* by William Bulfin." In "Imagining Ireland's Dead / La mort en Irlande le corps imaginé," special issue of *Interfaces: Image Text Language* 23, no. 1 (2004): 55–66.

———. "Monumental Landscapes: Riding the Boundaries of an Independent Ireland with the Early Sinn Féin Movement." In *Irish Contemporary Landscapes in Literature and the Arts*, edited by Marie Mianowski, 131–41. Basingstoke, UK: Palgrave Macmillan, 2011.

Steele, Karen. *Women, Press, and Politics during the Irish Revival*. Syracuse, NY: Syracuse Univ. Press, 2007.

Steele, Karen, and Michael de Nie, eds. *Ireland and the New Journalism*. Basingstoke, UK: Palgrave Macmillan, 2014.

Stephens, Edward. *My Uncle John: Edward Stephen's Life of J. M. Synge by Rev. Samuel Synge*. Edited by Andrew Carpenter. London: Oxford Univ. Press, 1974.

Stephens, Lilo. Introduction to John Millington Synge, *My Wallet of Photographs: The Collected Photographs of J. M. Synge*, arranged by Lilo Stephens, ii–xvi. Dublin: Dolmen Editions, 1971.

Stevens, Julie Anne. *The Irish Scene in Somerville and Ross*. Dublin: Irish Academic Press, 2007.

Synge, Samuel. *Letters to My Daughter: Memories of J. M. Synge by Rev. Samuel Synge*. Dublin: Talbot Press, 1931.

Thompson, Carl. *Travel Writing*. London: Routledge, 2011.

Titley, Alan. "Synge and the Irish Language." In *The Cambridge Companion to J. M. Synge*, edited by P. J. Mathews, 92–103. Cambridge: Cambridge Univ. Press, 2009.

Uí Chollatáin, Regina. "Newspapers, Journals, and the Irish Revival." In *Irish Journalism before Independence*, edited by Kevin Rafter, 160–73. Manchester: Manchester Univ. Press, 2011.

Van Hulle, Dirk. *Textual Awareness: A Genetic Study of Late Manuscripts by Joyce, Proust, and Mann.* Ann Arbor: Univ. of Manchester Press, 2004.

Vizenor, Gerald. "Fugitive Poses." In *Fugitive Poses: Native American Scenes of Absence and Presence,* 145–65. Lincoln: Univ. of Nebraska Press, 1998.

Walsh, Oonagh. *Anglican Women in Dublin: Philanthropy, Politics, and Education in Early Twentieth Century.* Dublin: Univ. College Dublin Press, 2005.

———. "Lunatic and Criminal Alliances in Nineteenth-Century Ireland." In *Outside the Walls of the Asylum: The History of Care in the Community 1750–2000,* edited by Peter Bartlett and David Wright, 132–52. London: Athlone Press, 1999.

Welch, Robert, ed. *The Oxford Companion to Irish Literature.* Oxford: Clarendon Press, 1996.

Williams, Raymond. "Base and Superstructure in Marxist Cultural Theory." In *Problems in Materialism and Culture: Selected Essays,* 31–49. London: Verso, 1980.

———. "Observation and Imagination in Orwell." In *George Orwell: A Collection of Critical Essays,* edited by Raymond Williams, 52–61. Englewood Cliffs, NJ: Prentice-Hall, 1974.

Wilsdon, Catherine. "Daring to Be European: J. M. Synge Transformative Travels." PhD diss., Univ. College Dublin, 2015.

Woods, C. J. *Travellers' Accounts as Source-Material for Irish Historians.* Dublin: Four Courts Press, 2009.

"Wyndham Land Act." In *The Oxford Companion to Irish Literature.* Edited by Robert Welch 606–7. Oxford: Clarendon Press, 1996.

Yeats, Jack B. *Jack B. Yeats: His Watercolours, Drawings, & Pastels.* Edited by Hilary Pyle. Dublin: Irish Academic Press, 1993.

Yeats, William B. *Autobiographies.* London: Macmillan, 1956.

———. *The Collected Letters of W. B. Yeats.* Vol. 1: *1865–1895.* Edited by John Kelly. Oxford: Clarendon Press, 1986.

———. *Mythologies.* London: Macmillan, 1959.

———. *Uncollected Prose by W. B. Yeats.* Collected and edited by J. P. Frayne. Vols. 1 and 2. London: Macmillan, 1975.

Youngs, Tim. "Travelling Modernists." In *The Oxford Handbook of Modernisms,* edited by Peter Brooker, Andrzej Gąsiorek, Deborah Longworth, and Andrew Thacker, 267–82. Oxford: Oxford Univ. Press, 2010.

# Index

**Giulia Bruna** is a research associate of the University College Dublin (UCD) Humanities Institute in Ireland. She has written on J. M. Synge, the Irish Revival, and Irish travel writing in book collections and journals such as the *Irish Studies Review* and *Studies in Travel Writing*. She is the cofounder of the Irish Revival Network, an interdisciplinary network of researchers working on the Irish Revival. She has also coedited the podcast series "Modalities of Revival" with UCD Scholarcast and curated a physical and online exhibition on the Irish writer and revolutionary Thomas MacDonagh for UCD Library Special Collections.